CHURCH AND
CANADIAN CULTURE

CHURCH AND CANADIAN CULTURE

Robert E. VanderVennen, Editor

UNIVERSITY
PRESS OF
AMERICA

Lanham • New York • London

Copyright © 1991 by
University Press of America®, Inc.
4720 Boston Way
Lanham, Maryland 20706

3 Henrietta Street
London WC2E 8LU England

Co-published by arrangement with the
Institute for Christian Studies, Ontario, Canada

Library of Congress Cataloging-in-Publication Data

Church and Canadian Culture / Robert E. VanderVennen, editor.
p.   cm.
"Co-published by arrangement with the Institute for Christian
Studies, Ontario, Canada"—T.p. verso.
Contributions from a conference sponsored by the
Institute for Christian Studies in Oct., 1988.
Includes bibliographical references and index.
1. Christian sects—Canada—Congresses.
2. Christianity and culture—Congresses.
I. VanderVennen, Robert E.
II. Institute for Christian Studies.
BR570.C48   1991
277.1—dc20   91-26370 CIP

ISBN 0-8191-8420-9 (hardback, alk. paper)
ISBN 0-8191-8421-7 (paperback, alk. paper)

 The paper used in this publication meets the minimum requirements of
American National Standard for Information Sciences—Permanence
of Paper for Printed Library Materials, ANSI Z39.48–1984.

Contents

88325

Contributors

Lee Cormie is a member of the theology faculty of the University of St. Michael's College, Toronto School of Theology, Toronto, Ontario.

Wayne Dawes is pastor of Northview Pentecostal Church in Peterborough, Ontario, and former pastor of Evangel Community Church, Chatham, Ontario.

Brian J. Fraser is Dean and teaches history at St. Andrew's Hall of the Vancouver School of Theology, Vancouver, British Columbia.

Harry J. Groenewold is a member of the History Department at The King's College, Edmonton, Alberta.

Brian Hogan CSB is a member of the theology faculty of the University of St. Michael's College, Toronto School of Theology, Toronto, Ontario.

William Janzen is Director of The Mennonite Central Committee Canada, Ottawa, Ontario.

David Lochhead is a member of the faculty of Vancouver School of Theology, Vancouver, British Columbia.

Paul A. Marshall is Senior Member in Political Theory at the Institute for Christian Studies, Toronto, Ontario

David Pfrimmer is a member of the faculty of Waterloo Lutheran Seminary, Waterloo, Ontario, and director of its Institute of Christian Ethics.

Cyril Powles is a member of the faculty of Trinity College, University of Toronto, Toronto, Ontario.

George A. Rawlyk is a member of the History Department at Queen's University, Kingston, Ontario.

Daniel J. Sahas is a member of the Religious Studies Department at the University of Waterloo, Waterloo, Ontario.

Brian Stiller is Executive Director of the Evangelical Fellowship of Canada, Toronto, Ontario

Robert E. VanderVennen is Director of Educational Services at the Institute for Christian Studies, Toronto, Ontario, and Assistant Editor of *Calvinist Contact*, St. Catharines, Ontario.

Preface

Everyone knows, when they stop to think about it, that churches have impacted the Canadian culture and way of life enormously, and continue to do so. Not often do they ask how that is done, by whom, and how denominational impact arises from the theology and history of the church.

As a contribution to Canadian nation building, the Institute for Christian Studies, with the encouragement of Brian Stiller and the Evangelical Fellowship of Canada, decided to look squarely at this subject. It organized a three-day conference for October, 1988, where church leaders met to describe what their church has been doing to try to influence and bless Canada's culture.

Most contributors were selected by leaders in the churches themselves, people best qualified to give their church's story. Each was asked to tell what their church is doing, and how that relates to the theology and ethos of the church. The aim is to raise sensitivities to the often quiet social service of the churches, and to shape directions in the problematic days ahead. You will notice that contributors feel free to criticize what their church has contributed, and what it has failed to do. They also take quiet satisfaction in what has gone well.

Each contributor approaches the subject from a distinctive angle. The result is that the styles and approaches are very different. Each contribution is a succinct summary, and whole books should be written about the cultural public service of each church. Not much of that seems to have been written, and it is our hope that this modest volume will stimulate that.

To our knowledge this is the first time that the cultural and social service of the churches has been examined together. Certainly there are parts of the story not examined here, such as the massive service of the Salvation Army and the recent work of the ecumenical coalitions. There is also the enormous service of individual Christians not much recorded in this book on the service of the churches.

Special thanks are due to the Institute for Christian Studies, and to those who planned this consultation of churches. Kathryn Posthumus, Ross Mortimer and Clifford C. Pitt were all most helpful. We are grateful for permission to reprint George A. Rawlyk's contribution from *McMaster Journal of Theology*, where it first appeared.

Robert E. VanderVennen

1. Overview of Christ and Culture

Paul A. Marshall

The Categories of "Christ and Culture"

Much of the dominant framework for contemporary discussions of the cultural effects of Christianity has been provided by H. Richard Niebuhr in his book *Christ and Culture* (1951). Niebuhr described five basic ways that Christians can conceive of Christ, and themselves, relating to the culture in which we live. These ways are: Christ above culture, Christ against culture, Christ and culture in paradox, Christ of culture, and Christ transforms culture.

It is commonly accepted that these categories are insightful and useful. Most people who discuss our topic refer to Niebuhr's work. Clearly any framework this widely used has managed to identify what many people believe are the key issues. However, despite these virtues I want to mention some defects in Niebuhr's categories.

One problem in his scheme surfaces when we consider the disjunction between how people categorize others and how people categorize themselves. Each of us categorizes people of other theological traditions as Christ of culture, or Christ against culture, or the like. But we, almost no matter who "we" are, invariably classify *ourselves* as "Christ transforms culture" people. About the only people I have spoken to who do not do this are fundamentalists who don't like the categories anyway.

Since we proclaim ourselves as "transformers" we tend to be upset when somebody else describes (or labels or accuses) us of being "against culture," or "above culture." There is an epistemological gap: we do not see ourselves as others see us and we do not see others as they see themselves. While this is a common feature of life in general it does provoke some questions for us. One is whether the professed agreement on Niebuhr's categories is actually hiding a deeper disagreement about what these categories actually mean. Another is whether there are other deep differences upon which these categories do not touch. Let me give some examples.

The institution at which I teach, the Institute for Christian Studies, has grown up in a Reformed background. True to its lineage it wants to transform the world and, indeed, it sees its inherited Calvinism as virtually the ideal type of Niebuhr's "transformers." Most of its supporters regard more sacramental understandings of Christianity, for example, as necessarily manifestations of a "Christ above culture" mentality. However Niebuhr himself takes F.D. Maurice, a quite sacramental (and very active) nineteenth century Anglican, as his typical model of "Christ transforms culture" (Niebuhr 1951, 220ff.).

Calvinists also tend to put Anabaptists in a "Christ against culture" bracket, as does Niebuhr, and as do many other Christians. But the noted Mennonite theologian, John Howard Yoder, has complained strenuously about this. He points out that Mennonites consistently address fundamental problems in our society and that they work on solutions to them. Many Mennonites lobby about third world relations, about agricultural policies, about defense and about the criminal justice system. They suggest alternative patterns of farming or of mediation, and they try to make their own communities living models of a Christian pattern of society (Yoder 1985, 2-7). What they *don't* do, according to Yoder, is accept the principle of legitimate violence, despite the fact that this principle is accepted by society at large. He complains that it is only because of *this* that Mennonites, and other Anabaptists, are told that they are *against* culture *tout court*. Merely because they reject one practice they are categorized as (or accused of) rejecting the whole.

Yoder argues that, contrary to the common labels, Mennonites do believe that "Christ transforms culture" and that they are, in fact, far more consistent in this than anybody else. Their consistency is shown in that they are far more critical of the existing culture, in particular of its penchant for violence, and that they refuse to be conformed to it. Mennonites would criticize other Christians for accepting the present culture and its politics too uncritically. Many feel that other Christians accept the way things are and thus, usually unwittingly, slide into a "Christ of culture" position.

Another disjunction arises when Christians consider their *manner* of involvement with culture. Evangelicals traditionally have thought of social transformation as coming about largely by individual action. Anabaptists have seen transformation as coming about largely by the church as an alternative community. Reformed people have stressed that transformation will come about largely via Christian organizations, notably by Christian schools. Christians in "mainline" churches have emphasized action largely by the church itself. Unfortunately each of these groups has a regrettable tendency to see the others' form of action as a type of withdrawal. Evangelicals and mainline church people see Christian schools as a retreat from the world. Mennonites see evangelical individualism as a refusal to take a communal stand. Everybody else sees mainline churches working as if Christian activity were reducible to the activity of church officials.

There are many other possible and actual permutations of this mutual categorization but I will not attempt to list them all. I will merely note that we have a regrettable tendency to describe what others are doing as a retreat from society, rather than as an alternative attempt to change society, and that we often dress up our mutual representations and misrepresentations in Niebuhrian categories.

It could be argued that this confusion is the result of a *misuse* of Niebuhr and so does not demonstrate problems in his classification itself. However this misuse, if such it is, stems partly from the fact that there are many important features of the Christ/culture relation that these categories ignore but need highlighting. We have already touched on at least two of these features. One is the institutional *means* by which culture is to be transformed. The other is the way *different aspects* of culture (such as violence) should be treated. "Culture" is not a monolith. Perhaps some aspect of culture should be rejected, others adopted, others transformed. In short, Niebuhr's terms need to be disaggregated so that we can see the variety of different relations which they either cover or mask. I will try to make some suggestions about this disaggregation, beginning with the question of the institutional means of shaping culture.

Avenues of Transformation

Christians are usually connected with churches. This itself is not a problem, but it can become a problem when Christianity is identified with the organized church. When this happens the relation of Christ and culture is treated as the relation of the church and culture. This problem can be exacerbated by the fact that many, if not most, of the people who write and deal more or less intelligently with these questions are in church-related employment and are often clergy. This reinforces a type of clericalization wherein the role of clergy, bishops, synods, churches and inter-church coalitions is highlighted while the role of the 99 percent of the Christian community who are not involved in this way are downplayed, and sometimes ignored entirely. While the role of the church as an organized body is vitally important, we cannot forget that the greatest Christian impact, for good and ill, lies in what its ordinary members do each day of their lives outside of organized church activities.

Hence any study of Christ and culture in Canada needs to consider the effect of the organized church itself and also the effect of individual Christians. Besides these, we need to look at alternative Christian communities and Christian organizations. A study of the church could highlight doctrine, preaching, social teaching, synodical decisions, clergy activities, coalitions and so forth. Analysis of individual Christian responses requires a subtle sociological examination of how Christians respond differently, if they do, to the major currents of our culture, and how they are shaped by and in turn shape that culture. An assessment of communal Christian responses would cover examples such as the Hutterites and Old Order Mennonites, and consider politically active communes along the lines of the Sojourners community in Washington, to take an American example. A consideration of non-ecclesiastical Christian organizations leads us to the bewildering array of schools, universities, publishers, radio stations, charities, political groups, lobbies, hospitals, and so forth, spread throughout every aspect of human life.

While it is difficult to do justice to this range of interaction, it is important to be aware of this full range. And the way we deal with this range should be shaped by our own Christian commitment. In this respect it should be emphasized that, for example, an Anglican perspective should not be only a study of what Anglicans have done but also an Anglican perspective (that is, a perspective shaped by Anglican theological tenets) on what everybody has done, that is, on the nature of our means of cultural formation. Our theological traditions are not only demarcations of who has done what, but should also be particular means of understanding what has been, is, and can be done. We need to look not only at, for example, what Presbyterians have done but also for a Presbyterian perspective on what to do.

Aspects of Culture
I will consider only three aspects of culture: religion as the root of culture, secularization, and the relation of Canada and the United States.

Beyond Ethics
Another area in which Niebuhr's categories need to be re-shaped concerns the various aspects of culture with which we deal. The questions we face in dealing with military power are different from those of family life: the questions we face with political parties are different from those of universities; the questions we face in music are different from those of automobile manufacture. I will not try to cover all the ramifications of this diversity, but I will suggest that we need to expand our view of a Christian contribution beyond what is commonly covered.

There is a common Christian tendency to treat the relation of Christianity and culture largely as an "ethical" or "moral" one. In this tendency Christianity is pictured as a source of "ethical" or "moral" principles which are then "applied" to key social questions. The result verges on a kind of natural law view, wherein faith provides rules or guidelines. This approach can be applied by both the right and the left. Those on the right try to use principles of personal morality relating to personal responsibility, often with respect to work or sex. Those on the left try to use political principles of equality or compassion.

Both of these emphases have their merits, for there are certainly ethical consequences of our Christian faith. However we need to emphasize that being a Christian, or being a member of a Christian community, involves much more than believing in or following a particular set of principles, whether political or personal. Our faith shapes the whole of our life and involves more than the ethical dimension of life. It shapes not only particular questions of right and wrong but also basic questions about the nature of reality—what human nature is, what sin is and how it is manifested, what the nature and direction of history is, what law is, what idolatry is, and what the root of meaning of human life is.

These questions involve more than what is usually called ethics. They involve matters of epistemology, historical causality, jurisprudence, social structure, psychological variation—in short all the basic questions of social theory, philosophy, and human motivation. These are at the core of culture, and also at the core of faith. Particularly if we believe that "Christ transforms culture," as most of us—Niebuhr notwithstanding—seem to want to do, we must consider the full range of effects of our faith, and not be needlessly limited to versions of morality.

If religion is particularly concerned with the roots of our lives, then we need to give special attention to the roots of culture. Our words for the worship aspect of faith—cult—and for the interweavings of our lives—culture—stem from the same root. Both contain images of growth, development, nourishing and shaping. Indeed I think that the root of culture *is* religion, in the sense that the basic patterns of our lives are shaped by our basic commitment and belief in life which is our religion. Our "god" is that in which we place our faith and trust. Our culture expresses what lies in our heart. In a way culture is a type of incarnation—it reveals in flesh what we have within us.

Secularization

The relation of faith and culture requires that we pay special attention to the theme of secularization. By secularization I mean the increasing tendency to treat religion as a private matter which should not influence public life. In our desire to avoid Christian hegemony, and to repent of our previous triumphalism, we may sometimes take too accepting a view of secularization. Canada is certainly a pluralistic society, in the sense that it contains different and irreducible ways of life, but often we take what liberal individualists say about the consequences of this pluralism too much for granted.

One small example has arisen in the last few months. We received a letter at the Evangelical Fellowship of Canada from the Attorney General of Ontario asking about the use of oaths in Ontario law courts. Currently the oaths include the phrase "so help me God." The question the letter asked was whether, since there are people in Ontario who don't believe in God, or else believe in different gods, these words should now be removed in favour of a simple affirmation that one will speak the truth. This issue is not of major significance and I doubt if it will make much of a difference to our lives. But what *does* trouble me a great deal is the *rationale* offered for this proposed change. The argument for the removal of oaths and other aspects of Christianity from various areas of public life goes like this: "Some people like baseball, some people like basketball, some people like hockey, and some people don't like sports at all. There is a definite plurality of views about sport and there is no agreement about which is best. Given this situation, the only fair and impartial view, the only view that will remove tension, is not to have any sports at all."

The question of diversity is supposedly solved by eliminating many of the contending parties from the public realm. The eradication of any public religious expression is offered as a solution to the genuine problem of the diversity of religions. However, this approach does not accommodate or deal openly with diversity. It merely *excludes* religious diversity and establishes secularism in its place.

The problem is a type of multicultural one, but the solution advocated is not multicultural but *a*-cultural. The problems of religious pluralism are very real and very difficult, but they are not to be solved by pretending that a secular society is genuinely pluralistic when secularism is in fact only one part of our plurality.

The Survival of Canadian Culture

A consideration of what lies at the heart of Canadian culture is particularly appropriate at this time when the question of our relation with the United States has been brought to a focus by debate on the free trade treaty. Critics of the treaty have maintained that it will, among other things, undercut Canadian culture, which will, in turn, lead to our cultural, economic and, ultimately, political integration with the United States.

What are the differences between Canadian and American culture? A major part is captured by David Putter in his conclusion to a book-length survey of Canadian views of the United States. Putter sums up the contrast this way:

> What Canadians have sensed was that their culture and their system still largely accept the principle of authority while American society and the American system did not accept this principle in any comparable degree. . . . Canadians believed that the state through some authority should provide moral direction for the society it governed. Moral direction meant discipline, order, responsibility, obedience, even inhibition. America, too, has believed in discipline, order, responsibility and the rest, but it has believed in them as self-imposed, through the acceptance of a Protestant ethic, not imposed by public authority (Wise and Brown 1967, 128-29; see also Marshall 1987a).

George Grant expressed a similar view in his *Lament for a Nation*. Canadians had "an inchoate desire to build in these cold and forbidding regions, a society with a greater sense of order and restraint than freedom-loving republicans would allow. It was no better defined than a kind of suspicion that we in Canada could be less lawless and have a greater sense of propriety than the United States" (Grant 1965, 69-70).

If these depictions are correct, or rather, were correct, then we might ask what lies behind them: what basic view of life and what basic commitments in life have we had that are different from those in the United States? I believe that the difference lies in our Anglican and Catholic religious traditions as distinct from America's non-conformist traditions, but to defend this would take us too far afield and is, in any case, beyond my ability.

However, dealing with this question is ever more urgent precisely because of increased trade and other economic linkages. Will this interaction destroy whatever is unique in Canada or is there in fact nothing left in Canada that is unique and sustainable anyway? For many years the great Canadian political philosopher George Grant put aside discussion of Canada's relation with the United States because he believed that the basic assumptions about Canada's political life, what we understand to be the nature and meaning of human life, had already become the same as those of the United States. Hence he held that the integration of the two would be merely a matter of time. The core of whatever had been distinctive had already been destroyed, and what remains is just the rationalization of the process. I do not know whether he was right but I sense that he was. When I read books by Margaret Atwood, for example, I believe that she illustrates some ways in which Canadians *have been* different but that she can provide no foundation on which such differences can be maintained. In Canadian public life there is no longer anything really distinct from the forms of liberalism found in the republic to the south. (I am using "liberalism" in George Grant's sense of "a set of beliefs which proceed from the central assumption that man's essence is his freedom and therefore that what chiefly concerns man in this life is to shape the world as we want it" (Grant 1969, 141; see also Marshall 1989, 4-17).

As Christians we have not dealt well with this matter. Certainly there has been sporadic vocal opposition to free trade and to overt examples of undue American influence. There has been criticism of

American capitalism and individualism. Yet the Americanization of our political parties by leadership conventions and popularity contests, and the Americanization of our political theory by the adoption of the language of individual rights, equality and autonomy has continued with either little Christian comment or else with Christian support. The failure to challenge these trends stems in some part from our inability to consider the religious depths of culture, including such notions as individual rights. I agree with the sociologist Seymour Martin Lipset when he remarked, "Perhaps the most important step that Canada has taken to Americanize itself—far greater in its implications that the signing of the free trade treaty—has been the incorporation into its constitution of a bill of rights, the Charter of Rights and Freedoms, placing the power of the state under judicial restraint" (Lipset 1989; see also Marshall 1987b).

Closing Remarks
If the question of Canada's future is not already a large enough problem to think about we may also consider the future of Christianity itself. We live in a peculiar situation in the modern world. Despite many appearances to the contrary, we are living in the greatest age of missionary expansion in the history of the Christian church. The number of Christians worldwide increases by many millions each year. There has also been a shift—by now largely completed—of the weight, the centre of gravity, of Christianity from the North Atlantic region to the Third World. Hence we can be very hopeful about the future of our faith in the world, and we can be assured that the future of the West is not the future of Christianity.

Yet at the same time there is a continuing contraction in the influence of Christianity in the West. Our faith becomes ever less influential, at least in public life. There are many reasons for this, but a major part is our lack of understanding of what culture is, of what drives it, of what shapes it, and how it relates to our Christian faith. If this book can be even a small means of helping us understand and clarify some of these questions, it will have done the Christian church in this country a great service.

2. The Anglican Church
and Canadian Culture

Cyril Powles

When the central offices of the Anglican Church of Canada (at that time the Church of England in Canada) were first created, they consisted of three relatively autonomous departments: the Missionary Society of the Church of England in Canada (MSCC), the General Board of Religious Education (GBRE) and the Council for Social Service (CSS). Today, in a complete reorganization of the central structure, the last of these departments has been replaced by the Social Action cluster, made up of various units and task forces—public Social Responsibility, Violence Against Women, Native Affairs, Human Rights, and so forth—which relate the church as a whole to the many facets of Canadian society.

The change from Social Service to Social Action, from department to cluster, with the implied goal of relating the whole church to the whole of society, reflects the direction in which Anglican thinking about the church's mission to the world has developed. I will attempt to trace the way in which this change took place and go behind the symbolism to discover the characteristics of the Anglican approach.

But before we begin the investigation we need to get our signals straight on what we mean by the terms church and culture. The Toronto theologian Ray Whitehead in an important article has pointed out certain confusions that exist in H. R. Niebuhr's classic study, *Christ and Culture*. To summarize, he argues that Niebuhr, in setting up his Christ-culture typology, "neglects the question of power" (Whitehead 1985, 26). That is, Christ never comes to any culture without already being incarnate in the flesh of the culture from which he came. Moreover, this coming must take into account the power relations which form part of the structure of that culture. Writing from a western, pre-liberation standpoint, Niebuhr reflects the classical assumption that what is western is also universal. But for someone who has grown up in Asia, for example, that assumption cannot hold true. Historically, Christ came to China with opium and gunboats, under the aegis of a treaty structure which forced the Chinese to accept him.

Thus the relation of Christ to culture is never a simple one, regardless of how helpful it may be for a western Christian to review it in ideal terms. Even in the West, we can no longer accept the relation in a simplistic way, as feminist or black theologians continually remind us. Christ always comes incarnate in a particular cultural form—the Church—which, in turn exists in a dialectical relation of affirmation and denial to the society in which it exists.

For Canadian Anglicans it is particularly important to grasp the force of this argument. As John Porter has pointed out (1965), Anglicans in Canada are conscious that they do not represent a purely Canadian denomination but are members of a worldwide Anglican Communion. Whether theologically trained or lay, they possess, as Professor Peake has shown in a perceptive study of Anglicanism on the Prairies (1983), a strong sense of having received a heritage from the past. Although Anglicans claim continuity with the Church of the Apostles, our form has been moulded by the experience of the English Reformation, when the leaders of the church willingly submitted themselves to become an ideological branch of state power. When we examine the conditions under which Anglicanism came to Canada, this close tie with state power becomes exceedingly clear, as we shall see. So before we carry out our investigation of the Canadian Anglican approach to society, we must first look at the historical origins of Anglicanism as a whole, a history which colours our relations, both to society and to other Christian denominations.

Characteristics of Anglicanism

Probably the first characteristic to remember about Anglicanism, after its Englishness, is its theological pluralism. It is possible to identify most churches coming out of the continental Reformation by their characteristic theological stance, whether Lutheran, Reformed (Calvinist), or Anabaptist. But the English Reformation started, not as a theological but as a political reform, the Tudor declaration of independence from European (Roman) domination. Thus it considered theology to be secondary, as serving rather than causing the change. National unity was the overarching and urgent need. Consequently, a wide variety of theological positions came to be accepted, just as long as obedience to the Crown was clear. Cranmer, Henry VIII's reforming Archbishop of Canterbury, saw himself first as Lutheran and later as Reformed, but the argument still goes on around what type of Reformed theology he espoused: Bucerian, Zwinglian, or what. Later, under Elizabeth I, some sort of Calvinism probably predominated. But both Henry and Elizabeth were theological conservatives who prized the old liturgical practices and insisted on maintaining the Catholic structure of bishops, priests and deacons. Cranmer knew the early Church Fathers well, and later leaders stressed Catholicity over against the agitation of aggressive Puritanism. Finally, the humanistic studies of the Renaissance exercised a strong attraction for scholars who had been formed in the old university centres of Oxford and Cambridge.

As time went on, three main streams coalesced—Catholic, Protestant and Humanist—bound together by a common bond of loyalty to the nation, if not to the Crown. But later movements, while deepening one or another stream, resulted in a weakening of the tie with the state. The Evangelical Revival of the eighteenth century stressed personal conversion and Christian asceticism over against a corrupt society. The Oxford Movement, fifty years later, rebelled against government tinkering with church polity and exalted the bishop (who had become a kind of ecclesiastical bureaucrat) as a spiritual leader, a successor of the Apostles who would guard the church from the depredations of a secular state. Thus in the nineteenth century we see the emergence of High (Anglo-catholic), Low (Evangelical) and Broad (Humanist) parties. But in typical Anglican fashion, much intermingling took place, so that an Anglo-catholic could show humanist sympathies (Dean Church) and the Evangelical could move toward the High end of the spectrum (Edward Bickersteth). Nevertheless, theological pluralism, not to say conflict, persisted for over a century as we can see clearly by the existence of our two colleges in Toronto, Wycliffe and Trinity, facing each other across Hoskin Avenue.

What, then, tied this diversity together when the state ceased to bind? Probably the commonest answer in the past would have been: a mutual respect for the Book of Common Prayer (the Prayer Book). Thomas Cranmer combined with his reforming zeal a deep love of the ancient liturgical formularies of the church. He also possessed the ability to express them in beautiful and rhythmic English. Against the criticism of his Continental advisors, who considered his compositions dangerously close to the papistic forms they had rejected, he and those around him insisted on preserving many of the old practices in worship. These were passed on through successive revisions and became part of the heritage of Anglican faith and practice. Evangelicals, with their propensity for long, extemporary prayers, and Anglo-catholics attracted by the Roman Catholic customs of their day, weakened this tradition somewhat. Today, the liturgical diversity that has resulted from the acceptance of cultural plurality in the new revisions has made it almost impossible to speak of a common prayer book. Yet the love of liturgical worship persists, an important contribution of Anglicans to the wider ecumenical movement.

Perhaps an even more important tie between Anglicans of different hue was a common experience of, and esteem for, parish ministry. John Wesley got into trouble with the bishops because he left the parish for the life of an itinerant preacher ("The world is my parish"). The Evangelicals whom he influenced, though, on the whole never deserted the parish. Indeed the best of them worked for a raising of standards in pastoral care. The same might be said of the Anglo-catholics. Their strong emphasis on the sacramental life led them to concentrate on what went on in church. Many of them went into the slums of Birmingham or London to found new parishes where they led dedicated lives as slum priests, fighting absentee landlords as advocates of their poverty-stricken parishioners. Even the academics all spent some time as curates in parish life so that their academic utterances usually included some measure of pastoral concern, a characteristic which distinguished them from colleagues in Germany, who tended to despise English scholarship for yielding to such non-academic pursuits.

It is important to remember that this emphasis on pastoral care was not limited to care for the active members of the congregation but extended (at least in theory) to all who lived within the geographical area whose boundaries had, in many cases been set by law from early medieval times. These territories, which before the Industrial

Revolution had usually been coterminous with a rural village, were bound together into larger units—rural deaneries and dioceses—with a bishop at the head. Even after the great urbanization that occurred in the eighteenth and nineteenth centuries this concept of the parish and diocese persisted, together with the idea that priest and bishop were responsible for everyone in their respective territories (the cure, or care, of souls). Thus when a long and bitter strike broke out in the coal mines around Durham in 1892, the distinguished New Testament scholar B. F. Westcott, who was then bishop of Durham, took it on himself to mediate between miners and owners, helping to bring the dispute to a quicker and more humane conclusion than might otherwise have happened.

The blurring of the bounds between the sacred community (the church) and the secular society (the parish) reflected the classical Anglican view of the relation between church and state. Developed under the centralized rule of Tudor and Stuart monarchies, it continued one stream of the medieval European tradition, albeit considerably modified under the stresses of Puritan and liberal criticism. In its earliest form it was defined by the sixteenth century Anglican divine, Richard Hooker, in Book VIII of his *Laws of Ecclesiastical Polity*. Church and state were seen as two sides of a coin ("the realm turned Christian"). During the Middle Ages the Catholic Church had tended to develop a theory of tension between two principles of authority, the Emperor and the Pope. But because the "spiritual" authority of the church was always considered superior to the "secular" authority of the state, the rise of a strong secular ruler was always viewed with concern. When the Tudors broke away from the papacy under just such a strong ruler, they appealed to an older tradition dating from Constantine the Great and now mostly associated with Eastern Orthodoxy. According to this idea the church was no longer considered to be a kind of spiritual state, set over against a secular state. Rather it was thought to infuse the whole of society, acting as the soul, or conscience, of the state.

Thomas Hughes, one of the early Anglican socialists and author of *Tom Brown's School Days*, reflected this idea when he wrote in 1878,

> The connection between State and Church as it exists in England ... forces ... on all men engaged in public affairs—and so upon

the national conscience—the fact that the nation in its corporate capacity has a spiritual as well as a material life.

This view has been restated in modern times by C. F. Garbett, a former Archbishop of York, in his book *Church and State in England* (1950).

Anglicans usually justified such a view theologically by a strong emphasis on the Incarnation of Christ, with its corresponding practice of a full sacramental life (often viewed as the way through which the Incarnation extends itself into history). It would be wrong to deny that the pluralistic nature of Anglicanism means that there is a spectrum of emphasis on this belief, with Evangelicals stressing the atonement and personal conversion, while Anglo-catholics stress Incarnation and spiritual growth. But the care for parish and diocese, as well as the view of church-state relations, reflects a pervading sense of concern for the material world as God's creation, closely related to Incarnational belief and sacramental practice.

One final characteristic of Anglicanism, the emphasis on voluntary activity, deserves consideration. Unlike other Protestant churches, which tended to develop official departments to deal with areas of mission, the English church customarily relied on dedicated individuals, clerical and lay, to initiate new actions in its name. The oldest British missionary society, for example, the Society for the Propagation of the Gospel in Foreign Parts (SPG), was founded in 1701 as one of a number of societies for the improvement of the moral life of the nation. When the Evangelical Revival of the eighteenth century raised the level of consciousness among Anglicans about overseas missions, several prominent laymen, in cooperation with their parish priest John Venn, founded the Church Missionary Society in 1799, which was one among a number of voluntary societies being founded at the time for prison reform, abolition of slavery, and so forth.

Thus the name "society" stood for a voluntary association, roughly parallel in function to a religious order in Roman Catholicism, which was able to initiate action in a certain area, even before the whole membership of the church was ready to support such action. In Canada, when Anglicans began missionary work on the frontier and overseas, they first organized the Domestic and Foreign Missionary Society, and later the Missionary Society of the Church of England in

Canada, in both of which this concept of the voluntary society was retained.

Perhaps more important for our purposes are the many societies which emerged in Britain during the height of the Industrial Revolution to express concern for the plight of labourers in factories. The early Christian Socialists like F. D. Maurice and J. M. Ludlow formed one such society, while later such movements as the Guild of St. Matthew and the Christian Social Union worked and wrote to make the church more conscious of its obligation to workers and poor in its day. The Anglican Fellowship for Social Action, which began in Montreal in 1943, represents a similar emergence in Canadian Anglicanism.

Practices in the Canadian Context
What, then, were the contextual factors which formed Canadian Anglicanism, distinguishing it from both parent body in England and sister in the United States? Briefly, and at the risk of oversimplification, they might be summed up as (1) the influx of Loyalists from the United States during and after the War of Independence; (2) the dominance of agriculture in a country of few cities; (3) regionalism, arising from a scattered population whose centres were distant from one another, and (4) the basic influence of merchant capital on both economic and cultural development.

The influence of the Loyalists is an ambivalent one. Anglican Loyalists stressed the British establishment, while Methodists opposed it. The Anglican emphasis on geographical parishes proved unwieldy in comparison with the far-ranging and flexible work of the Methodist circuit-riders. Thus began what S. D. Clark has called the elite nature of Anglicanism. In Nova Scotia, for instance, its "top down" approach kept it a minority in the face of the predominance of New England Congregationalism and German Lutheranism. In Upper Canada the fact that Loyalist Anglicans were also Tories meant that city merchants and colonial officials predominated, while Methodists could claim a majority in the countryside and among the rising bourgeoisie (those "in trade"). Yet Anglican influence among Native people had already begun with the association of men like John Stuart with the Mohawks, and Anglican influence in the country, while trailing the Methodists, made steady progress.

As with politics in general, the Loyalist influence brought certain democratic practices with it. For instance, it pushed the Tory John

Strachan to establish synodical government (including lay repre-
sentation), as early as 1811. This same Synod in 1857 elected a bishop
for the newly sub-divided diocese of Huron (London), an action
hitherto reserved to the British Crown. This led to a final step in
self-government when Francis Fulford, Bishop of Montreal, was appointed Metropolitan (presiding bishop) for the Canadas. The
Provincial Synod over which he presided became the basis of an
independent "Church of England in Canada." This name remained
until it was changed to "The Anglican Church of Canada" in 1955.

Such "democratic" changes were, however, limited. Unlike the
Episcopal Church in the USA, where episcopal decisions were made
within a collegial framework of the Standing Committee made up of
clergy and laity, Anglican bishops followed the British pattern and
occupied an absolute position in relation to their dioceses. They were
more absolute, in fact, than in England, where centuries of tradition
had built up certain checks and balances, like Parson's Freehold, to
limit episcopal authority.

The nineteenth century party structure of the English church was
also imported into Canada. In general, the Loyalists produced Low
churchmen like the Baldwins, while the Crown appointed English
bishops in Nova Scotia and New Brunswick who had been influenced
by the Tractarian (Anglo-catholic) Movement. As in England, though,
it was hard to generalize about party allegiance. The High Churchman
John Strachan, for instance, had received a Scottish education which
made him a bit of a humanist. This showed up in his enthusiasm for
education, as seen in his role as founder of institutions as diverse as
McGill, King's College (forerunner of the University of Toronto), and
Upper Canada College.

Anglicanism is traditionally a faith of the countryside. In Canada
this side of its nature was strengthened by the fact that until World
War II Canada's primary economic product was agriculture, so that
even in the city economic activity was geared to that end. This explains
to a certain degree why Anglicans lagged behind Methodists and
Presbyterians in their response to industrial problems in the
nineteenth and early twentieth centuries. The latter included among
them representatives of the rising bourgeoisie, the Eatons and the
Masseys, who were beginning to employ city workers long before
World War I. Anglicans had their Molsons and Galts, but these were
more often related to the older merchant tribe who had become part
of the ruling class of the country. Only a handful of imports from the

slum-priest movement in Great Britain were sensitive to industrial problems. An interesting exception to the rule was Canon F. G. Scott (father of F. R. Scott, the Canadian poet and socialist), who took what was then a quite radical stand in favour of the workers during the Winnipeg General Strike of 1919 and again later during a strike of steelworkers in Sidney, Nova Scotia.

We have already referred to the point which sociologists like Clark (1948) and Porter (1965) have emphasized, the predominance in the Anglican Church of members of the Canadian corporate and social elite. Porter mentions the names of Augustus Nanton, E. B. Osler, the Molsons and Herbert Holt, and estimates that the Anglicans could boast among their membership 25 percent of the economic elite, though the entire church membership represented only 14 percent of the general population (Porter 1965, 288-90). As Naylor has shown (1972), the particular nature of Canadian capitalism, overwhelmingly mercantile rather than industrial, gave to Canadian society a cautious and legalistic tone which was reproduced among Anglicans. Although many of the early bishops such as Strachan and Mountain, Bompas and Machray were colourful pioneer types, their successors tended to be safe, bureaucratic managers. The method of choosing bishops, by election at a Synod, meant that individuals with character were usually passed over because they alienated one segment of the electorate. In their cautiousness they shared with other Canadian churches, as the American historian Handy has remarked, a much greater conservatism than in American religion, "less experimentation, less willingness to take fresh starts and make new departures. . . ." (1976, 259).

In its closeness to the Mother Church in Britain, Canadian Anglicanism contributed to the regionalism which became characteristic of the nation as a whole. By the latter half of the nineteenth century, Anglicanism was on its way to becoming more indigenous. But in the West a more direct tie with the English missionary societies persisted, and this meant that the division between High and Low became features of various regions. Thus most of the work among Indians and Inuit, "more than any other Protestant body" (Handy 1976, 349), was sponsored by the Low Church CMS, as was other work in the Northwest Territories, the Yukon, and the northern parts of Alberta, Saskatchewan, Manitoba, and Northwest Ontario. The High Church SPG was active among British settlers in the southern regions of Manitoba, Saskatchewan and Alberta. This dependence on British support, which continued until World War II, made the transfer of finances impossible, helped to make Anglicanism in the West more "British" than in the East.

In common with other Protestant bodies, Anglicans saw part of their mission in Canada as involving the "Canadianizing" (read "Anglicizing") of the non-British minorities who were increasingly populating the west. The first Primate of All Canada, the redoubtable Archbishop Machray, "sought to mobilize the resources of church and state for the formation of a new society that would be an outpost at the same time of Britain and of Christendom" (Grant 1972, 51). Under the same policy the national church, not without criticism from its field workers, worked to assimilate the Japanese and Chinese immigrants who began coming into British Columbia at the turn of this century. When the policy proved difficult because of the visible nature of this particular minority, the church, again with the exception of the local workers and a few politically progressive individuals, sided with those who agitated to have all Orientals expelled from the country (Bamford 1988).

Consequently, it seems natural that Anglicans, when faced with social problems, should adopt the same stance of paternalistic humanitarianism that had been passed on to it from its forebears. In 1911 the church established the Council for Social Service and appointed as its first General Secretary the Rev. C. W. Vernon, a Nova Scotian. In the heat of postwar reconstruction, some views were expressed by this body about the benefits of socialism and the need for the church to side with labour, but the opposition of the elite laity soon dampened this ardour. Thus the main concern of the CSS during the interwar period proved to centre around prohibition (to which Anglicans gave only limited support) and immigration, where efforts were made "to keep the proportion of British immigrants as high as possible" (Pulker 1986, 69).

The advent of the Great Depression forced CSS to return to the problems of capitalism and unemployment. A motion of sympathy, proposed at the General Synod of 1931, "with all who suffer as the result of an 'imperfect social and industrial order,'" was passed by the Synod but vetoed by the bishops. This action spurred CSS to delve deeper into the question of capitalism's failure, with the net result that its Bulletin began increasingly to advocate fiscal reform and the establishment of such social security measures as unemployment insurance and old age pensions. But any attempt to imply that capitalism itself was a failure continued to be met with opposition from both conservative bishops and representatives of the business world.

Under Vernon's successor, Canon W. W. Judd, the CSS continued to pursue much the same kind of policy. But the coming of World War II stimulated Canada's industrialization so that it became increasingly difficult for some Anglicans at least to disregard the questions being raised by the increase in factory labour and urbanization. During the Depression, Christians—mainly United Church, but also Anglicans and Presbyterians and even a few Roman Catholics, many of whom had shared a common experience in the Student Christian Movement (SCM)—had formed the Fellowship for a Christian Social Order (FCSO). When that organization ran down in the 1940s, Anglicans grouped together to form the Anglican Fellowship for Social Action (AFSA). This organization, whose charter members numbered a mere dozen clergy and laity from Montreal, grew apace, with branches in Nova Scotia and Newark, New Jersey, and sympathetic individuals in Toronto, Winnipeg and other parts of Canada. Its purpose was twofold: to show the support of church people for labour and to proclaim within the church the need, not only for social service, but also for social action to effect basic change in a social system under which so many were suffering.

Action to support workers at Valleyfield and Lachute textile strikes, and agitation for a more just salary scale for clergy, represented two projects based on these purposes. In common with like organizations in England, it saw the two areas of church and society coming together in corporate worship. So it pushed the Parish Communion Movement, an offshoot of the wider Liturgical Movement, and taught a sacramental theology which linked the Eucharistic Offertory closely with social action.

As far as the church as a whole was concerned, AFSA attempted with some success to infiltrate the boards of both diocesan and General Synod Councils for Social Service, pushing these bodies— and through them, the delegates to diocesan and national synods—to face up to the need for fundamental change in the economic order. In this they appealed characteristically to the example of the English Church, whose great Primate, William Temple, had given such outstanding leadership over many years, climaxed by a short period as Archbishop of Canterbury (1942-44). Temple was a middle-of-the-roader whose classic booklet, *Christianity and Social Order*, could be read approvingly by a Conservative prime minister like Edward Heath.

But he represented the triumph of a process that had been going on for over a century whereby the idea that the church should be involved in social action (rather than concentrating only on individual conversion) had come to be accepted by a sizeable minority, influential enough to send one of its leaders to the pinnacle of the church's hierarchy.

The most effective organ for disseminating AFSA's ideas throughout the Canadian church proved to be its journal, *Anglican Outlook*. This journal had been founded in 1945 by an Ottawa cleric, Gregory Lee, as a critical foil to the *Canadian Churchman*, the semi-official organ which had become conservative and uninteresting. But when General Synod decided to throw its support behind the *Churchman*, Lee turned to AFSA, which took over editorial responsibility in 1949 and ran it in cooperation with its founder until the growing conservatism of the 1950s forced it to turn to ecumenical sources for support. For a short time it appeared as the *Christian Outlook*, then ceased publication entirely in 1963. During its comparatively brief life, it succeeded in producing a wide variety of lively articles and editorials on church and society, supporting an overtly socialist position. At the height of its popularity, its circulation reached five or six thousand copies, according to its business manager (Pulker 1986, 171). The present writer sat on the editorial committee and contributed frequently to its columns.

Contemporary Developments

To sum up, with all this activity somewhat the same process has gone on (though over a much shorter time span) in the Anglican Church of Canada as happened earlier in England. When E. W. (Ted) Scott was elected Primate of All Canada in 1971, he represented the end of a process which had begun with the setting up of CSS and continued with the organization of AFSA and the circulation of the *Anglican Outlook*. Paralleling this process was the increasing urbanization of Canada and a growing concern with such questions as native affairs. In 1945 Ted Scott had been SCM secretary at the University of Manitoba and director of social service for the Diocese of Rupertsland (Winnipeg). He was instrumental in starting a centre for native people there before going to work with CSS in Toronto and thence to be bishop of the British Columbia diocese of Kootenay. By the time of his election as Primate, a sizeable minority in the church could see the need for a church which would be involved in action not just to ameliorate but to change the structure of society.

Even before Scott's election other significant changes in the Anglican Church's stance had begun to take place. In 1967, on the recommendation of a study by the accounting firm of Price Water-house, Church House was restructured in the manner to which I referred in the introduction. In 1969 General Synod commissioned Charles Hendry, retired dean of Social Work at the University of Toronto, to carry out a study of the church's role in work among native people. The Hendry Report, *Beyond Traplines*, resulted in some fundamental changes in a policy that had been followed for a century, from the paternalism of the residential schools to solidarity with the native struggle for liberation. At the same General Synod that elected Scott Primate, the recommendations of the report were accepted and the new relationship instituted. By 1974, this policy gave birth to ecumenical cooperation between Anglicans, Roman Catholics and United Church members in the founding of the interchurch coalition Project North, under the leadership of two Anglicans, Karmel and Hugh McCullum.

Project North (now called Aboriginal Rights Coalition) was only one of many inter-church coalitions born at this time in which Anglicans played an active part. Tom Anthony, at the time Director of World Mission, took a prominent part in the organization of the Task Force on the Churches and Corporate Responsibility (TCCR) from 1972 until his resignation. My wife and I also participated in the founding of the Canada-China Programme of the Canadian Council of Churches. My wife is just finishing a two-year term as chair of the Programme. These names represent just a few examples of Anglicans in leading positions in the inter-church coalitions, a phenomenon that reflects the broadened understanding of the church's mission to the world that has characterized all denominations in the latter half of the twentieth century. But for a church which represented at one time, in Disraeli's words, the Conservative Party at prayer, this switch appears particularly notable, leading the *Toronto Globe and Mail* to parody these words when it wrote, "The Anglican Church is now the NDP at prayer!"

One final example of this changed attitude, in which Anglicans have made a contribution to the church's mission to society, remains to be identified. One feature of the Ted Scott era at Church House was the formation of a team of key people brought in to head clusters and units, often regardless of whether they were Anglicans or not. One of these has been Jeanne Rowles, first coordinator of women's concerns and now of the entire Social Action Cluster. She has changed the face of women's work in the Anglican Church of Canada. A member of the United Church who worked in Tanzania and Pakistan with the YWCA and in social work in Toronto, she has translated the latent feminism that had lain suppressed by Anglicanism's traditional paternalistic nature into forms of activity hitherto unimaginable. One of the more recent examples of this activity has been the Task Force on Violence Against Women which met for three years and produced a report (Anglican Church 1987) which has been acclaimed throughout the Anglican Communion and beyond. One aspect of its research has been working with a growing concern with exclusive language in worship as something which reinforces masculine oppression of women. The work of this Task Force, which still meets, has led to many other results whose influence is yet to be felt.

In conclusion, to summarize the way in which the Anglican Church has related to Canadian society, we can still perceive the ambivalence in the relationship which was noted at the beginning. On the one hand, Anglicanism remains the church of the elite. It can still generate a Confederation of Church and Business with a Dean as its chaplain. Yet it also continues to generate energy for the reform of Canadian society through such projects as support for native people, the liberation of women, solidarity with liberation movements in the Third World, and so forth. In spite of well-publicized opposition from the conservative wing, support for such programmes continues from General Synod to General Synod, so that it becomes difficult not to conclude that they are supported by those at the grass roots who take their faith seriously.

This stance of mission to Canadian society and to the world has come as the result of a long struggle, beginning with a small minority of people who were regarded as belonging to a marginal group of extremists, what Pulker has termed the "Unofficial Church" or "the activists" (161). Although he seems to have felt that the polarization which they produced was unhealthy, it is the conclusion of this paper that, had they not existed, the church would not now be where it is.

As in all ages of church history, it has been those who were willing to risk marginalization who were able to push the church toward reform. Their action in turn has led to a fresh impact of the church on the society within which it exercises its mission.

3. The United Church of Canada and the Conscience of the Nation

David Lochhead

The 1988 election of the Rev. Sang Chul Lee as Moderator of the 32nd General Council is symbolic of a profound shift in the way that the United Church of Canada perceives itself, in the way it perceives the reality of Canadian culture, and in the way it perceives its own relation to Canadian culture.

On the surface, the election of Dr. Lee might seem simply one more step in the church's attempts to be inclusive and to symbolize that inclusiveness in its highest office. Prior to 1968, the occupants of the office of moderator of the General Council had been drawn exclusively from the ranks of ordained males. Furthermore, they were drawn from people whose ancestors originated in the British Isles. They were not only exclusively white, they were exclusively of Anglo-Saxon or Scottish stock. In 1968 a layman, Robert McClure, was elected to the office of Moderator. In 1974 a black, Wilbur Howard, was elected. Lois Wilson, an ordained woman, was elected in 1980 and Anne Squires, a laywoman, was elected in 1986. The election of Sang Chul Lee might be viewed, then, as simply an extension of the apparent desire of the United Church to include groups that previously had been excluded from consideration for high office in the Church.

I want to argue that Lee's election is more than just a symbolic gesture toward non-Anglo-Saxons. The election goes to the very root of our topic: the relation of the church to culture. The election of Lee underlies a fundamental shift in the self-perception of the United Church.

The United Church of Canada came into being as a self-declared "national" church. The union movement, bringing into one church Methodists, Presbyterians and Congregationalists was perceived by the advocates of union as more than just an organizational merger. It was the fruit of the movement of the Holy Spirit in our national life. The United Church of Canada was to be a "uniting church." It was to be a church that was distinctively Canadian and, as a corollary, it was to be the church that would be in some sense "normative" for Canadian Christianity. The idea of an established church was, of course, anathema to the traditions which came together in the United Church of Canada. To think of the United Church as a "national church" had no trace of the suggestion that there should be any union between church and state. The independence of the church from the state was prized in the churches which came into union. That independence was not understood to be in doubt when the new church described itself as a "national church."

The new church, however, did not have any clear doctrine of the separation of church and state. Still less did it have any clear doctrine of the separation of church and culture. It regarded itself as a normative Canadian church. In its sense of its own normativeness, some of the prejudices of the United Church can be seen.

First, to be a national church meant, for the United Church, not to be a foreign church or an ethnic church. Obviously, simply in terms of numbers, the Roman Catholic Church represented more Canadians than the United Church could ever claim. Nevertheless, in the eyes of United Church people, to claim the Roman Church as a "national" church would have been a contradiction in terms. The Roman Church was, in the first place, Roman. In Protestant eyes, it took its orders from the Pope. Its loyalties, its ethos, as the United Church perceived it, could never qualify it as a genuinely Canadian Church. Should the Roman Church ever claim to be a "national" church, that claim would have been heard by United Church people as an imperialistic grab by Rome for power in and over the Canadian state. (If this seems an excessively intolerant view of the Roman Church from our post-Vatican II perspective, we should remember that, for Protestants, the political aims of the Roman Church constituted an issue as late as the American presidential campaign of 1960 when for the first time a Roman Catholic, John Kennedy, was elected

President of the United States.) The United Church was an indigenous church in a way that the Roman Catholic Church could never claim.

The United Church of Canada was national in the sense that it was not an ethnic church. The Presbyterian Church prior to church union had been, in a sense, a Scottish church. To many, the union movement was a coming of age. The Canadian Presbyterians were "leaving home." The new church would be distinctively Canadian in a way similar to the way the Presbyterian Church had been distinctively Scottish. This apparent separation of the new church from its Scottish roots was in the background of the bitter division that the union movement created among Canadian Presbyterians. After union, the Scottish accent was much more discernable in the continuing Presbyterian church than it was in the new United Church of Canada.

The other major denomination in Canada, at the time of union, was the Anglican church. That church, in United Church eyes, was clearly identifiable as an English church. It was, indeed, the Church of England in Canada. The United Church, then, considered itself the only major Christian denomination free to be the authentic voice of indigenous Canadian Christianity. It perceived the other Protestant churches, by and large, as branches of British and European denominations.

In the first place, then, the idea of a national church was the idea of a church that was indigenous, independent of cultural, racial, national or religious loyalties outside of Canada. Secondly, the idea of a national church involved the vision of a church which functioned as the conscience of the nation.

The United Church of Canada came into being at a time when what we call the "Social Gospel" was at its zenith. Much of the rhetoric of the Social Gospel is echoed in the rhetoric of the unionists in the early decades of this century. The idea of the public life of the nation as the arena for the coming of the kingdom of God, whether established by the ideal of neighbourly love or by the activity of God in the ministry of the Church, appears and reappears in the thinking of the new United Church. From the beginning, the United Church has been an activist church. It has seen the reform of society and the christianizing of Canadian national life as central to its mission. Over the years the rhetoric and the strategies by which this mission was engaged have changed. But the idea that the church has a responsibility to speak to the nation, being an advocate for the claims of the gospel on Canadian national life, has been constant. Whether it was a J. R. Mutchmore thundering against liquor and lotteries, or a Ray Hord tweaking the conscience of the Pearson government about Viet Nam, or a John Foster lobbying against free trade, the United Church has entrusted its leaders with the responsibility for telling the state what, from our reading of the gospel, is required in our national policy decisions. We speak to the government constantly. We speak, in our eyes, not out of self interest but out of concern for the gospel, for righteousness, for justice.

It may be that at one time the United Church saw its role as conscience to the nation as its own peculiar calling. I do not think that was the case. It certainly is not the case today. More and more, the United Church exercises its ministry in an ecumenical way. The ecumenical coalitions, in themselves an ecclesiastical form peculiar to the Canadian way of relating Christ and culture, have become the major vehicles for United Church social activism at the national level. The role of conscience to the nation, which lies very close to the heart of the sense of identity of the United Church of Canada, is increasingly shared with other churches. In this sense, the United Church has abandoned its claim to be "the national church" and has actively supported and cooperated with other churches, even the previously suspect Roman Catholic Church, as they have been willing to join in the responsibility to speak to the nation of the social calling of the gospel.

If one looks at the record of the United Church through the lens of its social activism, one can trace the shifts in the social priorities of the church. One will not, however, detect much of a change in basic attitudes to the question of the relation of church and state. The church does not seek political establishment. The church does not seek to be the religious voice of the state. Rather, the church seeks to be the means through which the claims of the gospel are put before the state.

However, if one uses other lenses, one gets a different picture of the relationship of Christ and culture in the United Church of Canada. The lens we have been using is the one that informed the work of the Board of Evangelism and Social Service and its successors. But the work of that agency has only been one of the ways that the United Church has institutionalized its relation with the surrounding culture.

Another agency that was also charged with specific responsibility in this area was the Board of Home Missions and its successors.

A word of explanation is required about what the words "home missions" suggested in the United Church. It meant, in essence, two things that were not always clearly separated. First, and this is its "ideal" meaning, home missions were those activities of the church which sought to bring the presence of the church to "unchurched" parts of our society. Home missions were the outreach activities of the church at home. Home missions were to be understood in a parallel sense to "foreign missions" which attempted to bring the gospel to nations outside of Christendom.

But the second meaning of home missions, and perhaps the operative definition, was that home missions were the ways the church supported church communities and activities in Canada that were not financially self-supporting. Thus, many small rural churches were designated as "home missions" simply because they required a home mission grant to meet their basic expenses. The only difference, in these cases, between home mission churches and regular churches was financial. Mission churches were aid-receiving churches.

When we look at the relationship of Christ and culture through the "Home Missions" lens, the relationship seems more complex, more difficult to put into a simple description. If we bracket the work of the Board of Home Missions in supporting poor congregations, we can begin to see the assumptions about the church and culture that were operative in the United Church. Through this lens, we get a picture of a church and a society that were (a) white, (b) of British stock and (c) of middle or upper class. The sense that these characteristics are normative both for Canadian identity and for the United Church understanding of itself underlies much of the home mission literature. It is white, British, middle class people who provide the money and personnel for the home missions of the church. The recipients of home missions, typically, are immigrants—European and Asian, native Indians, transient workers and their families in frontier situations, the French in Quebec and elsewhere, and the inhabitants of the inner cities, of "skid row." There is a clear distinction assumed between those who provide missions and those who receive them. The aim of home missions is to integrate these groups in Canadian life, which means to integrate them into a society that is dominated by a white, "Anglo-Saxon," middle class ethos.

Now I would not want to argue that those who administered the home missions programs of the United Church were blind to the ways in which the dominant Canadian culture was hurting those who did not fit its standards of normality. Many of the home missionaries functioned as advocates for the marginalized groups against the oppression of the dominant culture. Nevertheless, the aim of "home missions" was to integrate these people into Canadian society by helping them to reach financial independence (that is, to become middle class), to "fit in" to Anglo-Saxon communities and to become United Church members and adherents.

The missions to native Indian communities reflects this strategy. John Webster Grant in *Moon of Wintertime* shows that the missionary stance to native Indians taken by the church in the mid-twentieth century was, in some important respects, a departure from traditional missionary practice. In particular, the place of residential schools in that strategy embodies those differences. While earlier missionaries had made some attempt to adapt the practice of the faith to the reality of native communities, the church of the mid-twentieth century attempted to replace native culture by integrating Indians into the dominant culture. The residential school was necessary to take young native people out of their home communities so that they might be taught to function in the dominant culture. That strategy, we know now, did not work. From the perspective of the late twentieth century we are inclined to believe that it was misconceived from the very beginning, that it would have been a tragedy if it had worked. Nevertheless, the strategy came out of conviction that the normative way of being Christian was very close to the normative way of being Canadian. In "Christianizing" the marginal groups of our culture, we were often also "Canadianizing" them. Using this lens, the relation between Christ and culture is very close indeed.

A prominent spokesman for Home Missions in the United Church of Canada during the middle years of this century was the Rev. Malcolm C. Macdonald. Macdonald was a senior administrative officer of the national Board of Home Missions for many years. Macdonald articulated the goals of Home Missions in words that make his attitude to the relation of Christ and culture quite clear:

Objectives in Home Missions:
(a) To share in giving every citizen the privilege of public worship and Christian fellowship;

(b) To minister to the least and lost on every frontier—geographic and social;

(c) To keep up the morale and faith of people in days of stress and strain, of readjustment and expansion;

(d) To unite the cosmopolitan population of our land into one real brotherhood;

(e) To make Canada Christian and to help her share in the evangelization of the whole world (Macdonald 1961a, 12; Macdonald 1961b).

Changes were made in the second printing of this text to make the language less pretentious. Where the earlier text had read "to unite the cosmopolitan population ..." and "to make the nation Christian ..." Macdonald qualifies the goals with the insertion of the verb "to help."

Macdonald pays particular attention to the church's responsibility to immigrants and to non-Anglo-Saxon communities that are the by-product of immigration. The Board of Home Missions had established in many urban areas a series of churches—or rather Home Missions institutions—that went by the name of "All People's Churches" or the "Church of All Nations." These institutions would provide a place for ethnic, or what Macdonald calls "language" churches to form. Macdonald comments:

> "Language" churches exist primarily for those who cannot understand English and for those who have just come out as immigrants. The constituency has therefore a changing and transient character. Another part of the "language" churches' function is to help non-Anglo-Saxon people become merged or assimilated into the community and the church life of the district in which they live. The second or third generations speaking English readily are encouraged to join and share in the life of the regular churches in their own areas (Macdonald 1961a, 53-54; Macdonald 1961b, 11).

This attitude, widely shared in the mid-century United Church makes it clear why ethnic congregations have always been marginalized in the United Church. They are transitional, half way houses of the spirit. They exist for the purpose of integrating the non-Anglo-

Saxon into an Anglo-Saxon church in an Anglo-Saxon culture. They are not, in Macdonald's words, "regular churches."

The role of ministers in ethnic congregations has not been easy. Generally, ethnic congregations live apart from the mainstream of United Church life. They live at the edges, in the shadows where they are rarely visible. Not feeling fully accepted in United Churches, ethnic congregations may not even attempt to maintain a visible presence in their local presbytery. The "regular church," the church that participates in decision making and for whom decisions are made, is "Anglo Saxon." Ministers in ethnic churches have little sense of support from fellow clergy. The ethnic congregation and minister are isolated, surrounded by an "Anglo-Saxon" sea.

The vision of the United Church as the salt which savors a peculiarly Canadian version of Christendom is not one that continues to inform the ministers and membership of the United Church. The attitude is not quite dead, but it no longer drives the United Church as it understands its relation to Canadian culture. The election of Sang Chul Lee is the decisive symbol of that fact. The United Church of Canada always makes a statement in its election of its Moderator. It picks a person for that office on the basis of its perception of what the church is and of how it relates to the wider culture. It was now appropriate in 1988 that the minister of an ethnic church should occupy its highest office. The election of Sang Chul Lee was a powerful acknowledgement of the pluralism of the culture in which we live. The idea of an Anglo-Saxon Canada no longer corresponds to our experience. The church is now able to see it as appropriate that a Korean with a pronounced accent should represent the church to the world. This is not something that would have been deemed appropriate in the United Church of a few years ago.

What, then, is the vision of the relation of Christ and culture that informs the United Church of Sang Chul Lee? That is not easy to say, but a few general remarks are possible.

1. The United Church today attempts to understand its relationship to Canadian culture without the assumptions of Christendom. That is, the United Church does not generally assume that Canada is, or can be, a Christian nation. The culture is understood to be secular and pluralistic. Consequently it is more inclined to accept, as a given of Canadian culture, the existence of communities that are neither Anglo-Saxon nor Christian. In the situation of pluralism, then, the United Church acts, in part, as a voice for equal treatment under the

law, for justice, for communities which in the past it regarded as foreign and as competitors for the religious allegiance of Canadian society.

2. The United Church increasingly views itself as a permanent minority in the Canadian mosaic. That is, while the United Church still includes elements that can be clearly identified a part of the Canadian establishment, the church itself has ceased to think of itself as the voice of a distinctive and normative Canadian religious identity. While the church in the past may well have viewed itself, in a not quite unconscious way, as the appropriate religious expression of Canadianism, it no longer views itself that way. The church views the "principalities and powers" which control Canadian society as "out there." Since the mid 1960s, at least, the church has seen itself not as a part of the Canadian establishment, but as part of that establishment's sometimes loyal opposition.

3. The church has tended to see its mission less as a voice for abstract moral principles and more as a voice for the marginalized in society. Thus, in relation to native peoples, the church has less sought to "Christianize" native communities and has more attempted to speak with native communities in their demands for justice. That does not mean that the church has succeeded in giving marginalized communities its consistent support, nor that the support of the church has always been welcomed by marginalized communities. Nevertheless, the Church understands its relations to those communities in a different way. Where previously it sought to integrate marginalized communities into the majority culture, now it seeks more to ally itself with those communities against the majority culture. And insofar as the majority culture still exists within the United Church of Canada, it finds itself in continual trouble with maintaining the confidence of that part of its constituency that is still committed to that culture.

This point is illustrated, of course, by the acute crisis which the question of the ordination of gays and lesbians has precipitated in the United Church. The question involves many dimensions, and it ought not to be reduced to its cultural or sociological dimension. However, this cultural or sociological dimension is of crucial importance. In recent years, an identifiable gay and lesbian community has emerged in major Canadian urban areas. Where previously gay and lesbian people have either been isolated as individuals or they have been part of an underground community, the community is beginning to emerge, particularly in the urban area. The gay and lesbian community is not

visibly and self-consciously present in many smaller Canadian communities. That community, where it has visibly emerged, has characterized itself as oppressed by the dominant culture in Canada. When
the church, then, attempts to speak with and for the oppressed
community against the majority culture, it finds itself in conflict with
its own constituency who, on this issue at least, still identify themselves
with the majority culture.

The crisis is not new. In the mid 1970s, for example, United
Church fruit growers were incensed by the support of the California
grape boycott by the United Church. They felt personally attacked by
the church's stand. In the same way, much of the constituency of the
denomination feel personally attacked by the apparent support given
by the church to the gay and lesbian community. The issue has tended
to divide those in the church who want to continue to speak the
language of moral principle from those who want to speak the language of justice for the marginalized. Put another way, the current
crisis separates those who see the gay and lesbian community as a
legitimate piece of the Canadian mosaic from those whose view of
culture is less pluralistic.

Any discussion about Christ and culture usually relates itself to
the categories developed by H. Richard Niebuhr in his book, *Christ
and Culture*. If the United Church could choose which category it
would prefer, it would undoubtedly choose Niebuhr's own favourite:
Christ the transformer of culture. That choice would, in fact, fit much
of the practice of the United Church. In attempting to provide a voice
of conscience in the nation's business, in attempting to be identify
itself as best it can with the suffering of marginalized communities, the
United Church operates in the faith that through a faithful witness,
the Holy Spirit will work to make our corporate life more humane,
more like the Kingdom of God.

In practice, however, the theological models that we act upon are
not always identical to the models that we say we believe. During the
first fifty years of the life of the United Church, many of the operative
models of the church were those of Christendom. Canada was, or
ought to be, a "Christian" nation. The boundary between Christ and
culture was often difficult to draw. The Christ we imagined was made
in the image of a white Anglo-Saxon middle class community. This was
a Christ of culture. Since the mid-1960s, the danger has been the
opposite. In our practice we have often turned Christ against culture.
We have been less inclined to see our national life as guided by

servants of God and have spoken, in a more sectarian way, of "principalities and powers."

One can, then, only speculate on how the United Church will respond to Canadian culture in its new pluralistic form. In some respects, the United Church of Canada is well prepared to celebrate pluralism with the new non-Anglo-Saxon, non-Christian communities in our midst. The work of the Division of World Outreach in addressing the question of global religious pluralism has made resources available to the United Church that other denominations may not yet have developed. The shape of the church's ultimate response to pluralism may be impossible to predict. What one can predict is that the pain involved in responding to pluralism has only begun. The trauma that is evident today in the United Church of Canada is only a foretaste of what every denomination that attempts to engage the contemporary Christian reality must eventually face.

4. "See, Judge and Act":

Social Catholicism and Canadian Society prior to Vatican II

Brian Hogan, CSB

The dimensions of the question "How churches and theological traditions have related with, and influenced Canadian society" are as broad
as they are significant. The question arises from the injunction to "go
forth and teach all nations," and invites critical reflection as to
whether and how that task has been accomplished so that a nation's
cultural values and institutional structures reflect gospel teaching. In
his letter on evangelization in 1975 Pope Paul VI observed that "The
split between the Gospel and culture is without a doubt *the* drama of
our time, just as it was of other times" (Pope Paul VI 1975, 17). To
track this drama through Canadian history is a demanding task. A
recent copy of *The Economist* speaks of Canada as having an
"egalitarian, progressive" character, meaning a care for justice, for
some roughly balanced share in the distribution of goods and services
(*Economist* 1988, 4). If true, then surely some of this egalitarian
concern has been influenced by Christian churches with their various
emphases on social ethics and social gospel traditions.

A proper study of the Catholic Church in Canada in terms of this
topic would include a presentation of the impact of the Catholic
school systems in Canada. The historical concern for education,
broadly considered, includes a belief in the benefits of education for
the stability, maturity and general welfare of a population. A study of

Catholic influence would have to take into account the enormous investment in education at every level since the commencement of colonization and the establishment of the Collège de Québec in 1635. Such a study would have to reflect on the failures and limitations associated with these enterprises. Romeo Maione, for one, has commented that the Catholic Church in Canada has succeeded in providing immigrant populations with the tools to ensure social and economic advancement, but has failed to provide a social conscience to accompany and direct this upward mobility (Maione 1980).

Staying with institutions, a proper appreciation of the impact of the church on Canadian society would have to take account of the range of social services provided by organizations. These would include such foundations as orphanages, hospitals, and homes for the elderly, and the cadres of religious men and women, as well as laity, who have staffed these institutions and provided them with an animation flowing from vocational commitment to human care. Again, conclusions would have to be tempered by an awareness of limitations and a query as to why a country with such a large proportion of Roman Catholics has not done rather better on handling such questions as divorce, abuse, abortion, or other bio-ethical and environmental issues. Here our "egalitarian" tradition has either escaped or betrayed us.

Finally, this appreciation should look to the influence of mission work abroad and the prism which such exposure has provided for missionaries to apply more critical gospel perspectives on domestic questions and church work. It is clear that the experience of Canadian Catholic missionaries in Central and South America in the 1950s and 1960s has had a strong influence on the development of church social teaching and practice at home.

Here, however, an apologia. Much, if not most of the research has yet to be done to provide a clear understanding of the dimensions of these questions. Canadian Catholics, apart from Quebec, have not been well served by systematic, critical, historical reflection. There is no single or multi-volume history of the church in Canada. There are few serious monographs on either health care or educational institutions. Marta Danylewycx's recent work, *Taking the Veil: An Alternative to Marriage, Motherhood and Spinsterhood in Quebec, 1840-1920*, represents a change in the direction of more sensitive and sophisticated studies of the interrelation of religious and social questions in Canada (Danylewycx 1987). These questions are beginning to be addressed, and a recent brace of theses dealing with the Catholic population of the Archdiocese of Toronto gives promise of much that is yet to come. Such work provides a sound basis for assessment and reflection, but much remains to be done before a clear picture, or rather, a picture reflecting the complexity and nuances of the reality, emerges.

With this caveat established, we may proceed to a consideration of three examples of Canadian social Catholicism, in the seventeenth and twentieth centuries, for the purpose of establishing some of the difficulties associated with the transmission of religious social thought. This is followed by a section presenting three levels of structures by which to track and analyze the interactions of the various planes of religious social activity. The major emphasis of this paper is directed towards the third and fourth sections. The third introduces three persons influential in the expression of social Catholicism in Canada in this century. The succeeding section reviews a number of constitutive elements of such activity in the decades prior to Vatican II.

Social Catholicism: The 1630s and the 1980s

To begin then, three examples of Christian-cultural interaction in Canadian society from today and yesterday. The release of the statement "Ethical Reflections on the Economic Crisis" by the Episcopal Commission for Social Affairs of the Canadian Catholic Conference of Bishops, at the New Year in 1983, drew unprecedented media and public attention to Catholic social teaching in Canada. There followed months of intense debate and dialogue, some of it contentious, but overwhelmingly favourable to the idea of a church role in socio-economic questions. Toronto's Archbishop, Emmett Cardinal Carter, registered considerable dissatisfaction, initially, with the manner of the document's compilation and communication. Subsequently, the archbishop sponsored seminars and reflections throughout the archdiocese leading to the publication of a book including responses to the document and the economic crisis by individuals and groups throughout the archdiocese (Archdiocese of Toronto 1983, 220). This event was the most dramatic with regard to capturing the attention of the Canadian media and public concerning a Catholic Church statement (Canadian Conference of Catholic Bishops 1983).

At some distance in time, in seventeenth century New France, it is interesting to examine a pair of legislative efforts devised to influence social customs and economic activity. The first of these addressed the continuing Canadian dilemma of demography: how to develop and retain a population in a land which Voltaire dismissed as "acres of ice and snow." One device was the importation of *Les filles du roi*, young French women with few prospects for marriage at home, who were provided with passage to Canada and some of the necessaries to begin married life in a new land. It was hoped that the presence of these eligible French women would encourage some of the *coureurs du bois* to marry, settle into farming and raise the families needed to secure the colony and to expand French prospects beyond the small settlements huddled along the St. Lawrence.

In the event, many of these *coureurs du bois* were willing to look, but few to marry—so few that it became necessary to pass an ordinance prohibiting young unattached males from leaving the colony to engage in the interior fur trade until all the young women had been claimed as brides. That effort at legislation was a total failure, the twin facts of forest and distance combining with the imperatives of the fur trade to expedite marital avoidance for the men. For the fur traders this meant a continuance of the less confining sexual alliances according to "the custom of the country." This custom of casual combination without benefit of either religious or civil recognition persisted into the nineteenth century in the far west and north. The first missionaries at Red River frequently reflected on this area of pastoral and social concern: "In 1819 Dumoulin had noted that the missionaries were having difficulty persuading Canadians to regularize their country marriages with Indian or Métis women, because they 'liked this liberty of being able to get rid of their wives.' That year Provencher in a letter to Lady Selkirk had noted that 'concubinage' was 'rife,' especially in the distant posts" (Lemieux, 720). It finally yielded, only after some considerable resistance, to the persistence of missionaries and the increasing, and even less tolerant, presence of European women (Pannekoek 1976, 72-90).

A matter of even graver concern by reason of its extended, continuing and devastating effect on the Amerindian population involved the role of alcohol as a key element in the fur trade. Reasons of economic advantage and geo-political imperial strategy suggested that if the English and Dutch south of the Great Lakes employed rum as a medium in the fur trade, then the French must match their effort with brandy. Otherwise, furs and even native allegiances, might slowly slip south. The effects on the host population were immediate and wholly destructive. They were also carefully catalogued, as were ecclesiastical attempts in Canada and France to terminate this trade.

In 1636 Père Le Jeune writing in the *Relations,* referred to the physical disciplining of some Catholics who had sold alcohol to Amerindians, noting that "The best laws in the world are of no value if they are not observed. As to Ecclesiastical Jurisdiction, it is only exercised as yet in the hearts and consciences" (Le Jeune 1636, 145; Moir 1967, 3-4). Evidently the Jesuit was pleased that the law was being enforced, but lamented the limitations on ecclesiastical jurisdiction. By 1660 the devastating effects of the brandy trade were even clearer, and Bishop Laval prohibited the exchange of brandy on pain of excommunication. This censure was upheld by the civil Council, but it had little effect on curbing the trade. "Even the public execution in 1661 of two traders for this crime did not stop the trade" (Moir 1967, 16). Although the twin pressures of Gallicanism in religious affairs and mercantilism in commercial matters caused the removal of the prohibition in the so-called "Brandy Parliament" of 1668, Laval continued the pressure, and absolution was refused to anyone involved in selling brandy to Indians. The matter continued to rankle, and if the ecclesiastics could not have their way completely, it was obvious that the religious strictures had some effect. In 1773, with Laval visiting France, Frontenac wrote to Minister Colbert in an attempt to terminate the bishop's imposition of ecclesiastical censures with regard to the trade. In his letter he complained that penalties such as the withholding of absolution, imposed even against pregnant women, "bothered consciences extremely" (Moir 1967, 16). The point of conscience is, of course, the key consideration. Just how successful is the church at informing, influencing or directing conscience in such matters?

These instances from 1635 to 1983 provide us with some points for reflection as we consider social Catholicism more closely in twentieth century circumstances. In the first place, social questions usually involve the body politic and require some interaction with a state or society which is not always compliant, and which in fact, frequently opposes moral considerations with its own agenda of matters economic, political or military. The blatant, and rather successful efforts by the state to direct the church's energies to its own purposes after the mid-seventeenth century serves as a judicious reminder of historical difficulties in church-state relations in many countries over many centuries. As well, as can be seen in the case of the 1983

Canadian Bishops' statement on economics, these questions are often rather immediate, highly complex, and given to many nuances of understanding and interpretation. The processes involved in the church coming to know its own mind, and being reluctant to speak forcefully in the face of shifting evidence or even cultural practices, frequently forestalls forceful responses in respect to many matters. Finally, and most importantly, we have the question of personal response and responsibility. For reasons of ignorance, individual advantage, and conscience, many members of a church may not follow its teaching in respect to many particulars. Closer to our own time, we might refer to the clear recognition of the right of workers to their own representative organizations provided in Pope Leo XIII's encyclical *Rerum novarum*, 1891. This teaching met with active opposition by Catholics at the time of its release, in Canada and elsewhere. It continues to face massive passive (and increasingly active) opposition in many jurisdictions to the present. In considering the impact of churches and their theologies on particular societies at any given time such difficulties and oppositions, internal as well as external, must be remembered.

Generative Structures

To assist in uncovering and examining the various dimensions of social action initiatives it is helpful to look at the three levels which combine to create or to encourage action and change. These levels are identified as "structures," since they provide the underpinning and skeletal form for stimulating and sustaining social thought and action. They may be identified as: structures for application, structures of implementation, and structures of actualization.

"Structures for Application" include the generative ideas and principles associated with any institution or undertaking. At this level any consideration of twentieth century social Catholicism must include papal teachings, particularly encyclical letters, beginning with *Rerum novarum* in 1891, and continuing beyond the documents of the Second Vatican Council. The principles and teachings found in this body of material offer a coherent and systematic development in response to experiences of urbanization, industrialization, decolonization and globalization. Such consideration must also include the variety of philosophical movements, including solidarism, personalism, Christian existentialism, and a renewed Thomism, with a special concern for the writings of Jacques Maritain. Maritain's work in Thomism and his tenure in Canada have left a significant mark on social reflection by Canadian Catholics since the 1930s.Developments in theological method and thought are also crucial to such an investigation. Here it is particularly important to consider the implications of the significant shift towards an emphasis on the incarnational dimensions of Christianity, with all that implies for anthropology. Hierarchical, philosophical and theological thought have been strongly influenced at key points by developments in the social sciences through the century. It is no surprise therefore that church teaching frequently reflects a response to (and sometimes against) schools of thought and developments in political, economic and social theory. At this level, what church teachings and teachers have said, for example, about such ideologies as socialism, Naziism and communism has had a definite influence on the way in which the majority of Canadian Catholics have received and responded to these phenom - ena. This level is termed "structures for application" because it deals with realities which find their existence at the reflective, intellectual level. While such are of crucial significance and pregnant with potential, they demand something more by way of communication, transformation and implementation.

The second level for this review deals with structures of implementation. These can be identified as the second-level of response to social questions, the points at which general principles and ideas are shaped to particular contexts and find expression in national and regional reflections and communiques, as well as in organizations and institutions founded for the purpose of handling dimensions of such questions. At this level of reflection concern is for the full range of topographical response from the parish to national hierarchical organization. Alternatively, it is this range of experience which feeds back into the intellectual structures, informing and directing this plane of analysis to direct it to new considerations and developments. In the church generally, and in this country in particular, the variety of associations collectively identified as "Catholic Action" offer the first and foremost range of twentieth century implementation of social principles. These groups range from the more immediately evangelical Legion of Mary to the much more political Young Christian Worker movement. These associations, along with Young Christian Students, Young Christian Farmers, the Christian Family Movement and others, played a very significant role in the social and political life of Quebec up through the Quiet Revolution. Such organizations likewise played a part in the development of lay leadership in English-speaking Canada.

The watchwords of Catholic Action groups were "See, Judge and Act," and the watchwords provided the basic methodology for such organizations and their members: analyze a situation, come to some conclusion as to what should and could be done, and then do it. Only when each of the three steps was followed would the response be considered integral or complete. Such associations were multi-tiered, from the immediate neighbourhood to the parish, diocese and province, and were connected with other national structures abroad. This methodology, especially because of its insistence on inculcating patterns of life which presumed both critical reflection and concrete action, has had very important consequences for Canadian Catholicism, especially in relation to social justice questions.

If these Catholic Action organizations were the most obvious and pervasive, they were complemented by a number of other structures of implementation. Here a number of pastoral letters from Canadian bishops, both collectively and individually, are of considerable importance. During the Second World War the Canadian Bishops formed a permanent secretariat and began patterns of more regular meetings which accelerated with the years leading into and through Vatican II. By the end of the Council the Canadian Conference of Catholic Bishops had an established life with full organizational structure to handle significant questions at the national level. This structure has been buttressed by regional organizations of the bishops which meet on a regular basis and often address particular questions of immediate concern to their region.

Earlier, in response to the wave of immigration following the conclusion of the war, the Social Action Department (SAD) of the CCCB was founded. This department came to be responsible for initiating and sustaining a wide variety of national and local social initiatives, including support for cooperative, credit union and labour union activities. To complement the *Semaine sociales* which had been active in Quebec since 1919, similar Catholic Social Study Weeks were organized in the early 1950s for English-speaking Catholics. Among other activities the CCCB began the process of an annual Labour Day Statement, a practice which was interrupted by Vatican Council II and then taken up again with telling effect in the 1970s. It was such a statement which generated the national response at New Year's of 1983.

The third and final level of review is that of structures of actualization. These are identified as the immediate organizations and persons responsible for concrete events and accomplishments. There are, of course, many crossovers between this third level and the second, and many ways in which the third level feeds into, animates and directs the more distant and intellectual activities of the first level. In spite of these crossovers it is best to establish and maintain the distinctiveness of the third level, because this is the level where the verification of ideas and possibilities is established. The finest ideas and the simplest or most sophisticated structures of implementation are effectively of little use if they are never adopted by persons and organizations who apply, adapt and sustain them on a regular basis.

An illustration of the three levels in action is helpful here. The concept of the credit union was developed in North America by House of Commons Recorder Alphonse Desjardins, of Lévis, Québec, in about 1906, built on examples from European experiences. This idea was clearly seen by many Catholics to correspond closely to serving, in Pauline terminology, the "Body of Christ." The relationship between the mundane activity of savings and loans and the observable, concrete improvement of human circumstances which such planning represented, was dramatic. The intention of the organization was proved out many times and was clearly recognized as an excellent application of gospel principles of justice and charity working to advance the wellbeing of thousands of Canadian families. This was just one area where church support was significant for religious-social interaction. A review of the work of some English-speaking Catholics will touch on other areas of endeavour.

Generative Persons
An introduction to the lives and labours of three twentieth century Canadian Catholics will advance the task of illustrating the relationship between religious belief and social activity, and will serve further to expose some of the dimensions of interaction among these three structural levels.

Moses M. Coady
Moses M. Coady (1882-1959) was a teacher, priest, social activist and something of a prophet (Coady 1939; Baum 1980, 189-211; Lotz 1975, 99-116; Sacouman 1979, 37-58 and 107-26). He was born and raised in Cape Breton, studied in Nova Scotia and Europe, and spent his life

as a priest of the diocese of Antigonish promoting social action activities, initially in the Maritimes, and increasingly in Canada and North America. In the year of his death a special institute was opened to facilitate the expansion of the "Antigonish Movement" to the Third World. His base was St. Francis Xavier University and his whole approach towards socio-economic problems developed from his belief that education was basic to any development undertaking. In his work *Masters of Their Own Destiny* Coady insisted that real democracy would be accomplished only when full economic participation on the part of the whole population completed the political democracy which was achieved with universal suffrage. With Dr. "Jimmy" Tompkins, Coady secured the confidence of the people, and through the depression decade and afterward he taught his people to develop their own skills through collaborative efforts.

One of the first results of these efforts led Atlantic fishermen to press for a Royal Commission investigation into conditions attending the fishing industry in Atlantic Canada. Out of this Commission emerged the United Maritime Fishermen in 1930. Later activities saw the Extension work of St. Francis Xavier reach out to assist farmers and miners. Fieldworkers were hired to carry programmes and the methods of cooperative activity to people throughout Cape Breton and other areas of the province. The "People's School" brought farmers and workers to the campus for short courses. Radio was employed for outreach efforts, and at the local level study groups were organized to examine larger and smaller regional problems and to initiate response to them.

The range of these activities was extensive and they resulted in successful initiatives in the areas of producer and marketing cooperatives, credit unions, labour unions, and housing cooperatives. St. Francis Xavier University and the Coady International school have served as training centres for thousands of men and women, Catholics and others, from North America and around the world.

The Antigonish Movement has won worldwide recognition and the labours of Coady, Tompkins and other initiators have had an impact at both national and international levels far in excess of what might be expected of this small eastern university. The double emphasis on instruction and action has led to a creative and productive balance among the three levels of structures for application, implementation and actualization, as thousands of ventures around the world will attest.

Henry Somerville

Henry Somerville (1889-1953) was born and raised in England (Somerville 1933; Beck 1975, 91-108; Beck 1977). He came from a worker background, managed to secure a sound education in England and emigrated to Canada just before the First World War. An initial period spent in Antigonish was followed by an experience in Catholic journalism in Toronto before returning to England after the war. He remained in England until his return to Toronto in 1933. From that date until his death he served as editor of the *Catholic Register* which, following amalgamations, became the *Canadian Register*. In England he was thoroughly involved in Catholic social initiatives generally, and during the 1920s he served as *Toronto Star* European correspondent. That portfolio permitted a tour of Russia, still in the first decade of growth following the revolutionary wars. These experiences provided him with an excellent awareness of the international scene and a horizon against which to measure local undertakings and achievements.

Somerville's writings in the *Register* were in support of a wide range of endeavours and interests, from international concerns to unions and affordable housing. He ran several extended series examining such questions in some considerable depth and urging public response and political action. His activities were very much at the level of clarifying structures for application. He was a frequent lecturer, panelist and participant in ecclesial, university and public forums investigating and commenting on social affairs. He had a well-deserved national reputation, within and without the church, and by the late 1940s it is probably fair to say that he was the leading Catholic layman in English-speaking Canada. He carried a keen mind, buttressed with wide experience and steady conviction to the task of journalistic commentary. In Somerville church and community found a critical and compassionate Christian conscience, motivated, active and directive.

Catherine de Hueck

The third of these generative persons for Canadian social Catholicism is Catherine de Hueck (1900-1985). Born in Russia and raised in Europe and Asia, Catherine fitted no one's pattern or expectation. As a young nurse caught up in the maelstrom of the First World War and the Russian Revolution, she fled to England and then Canada with her husband, Baron Boris de Hueck. Here the responsibility of raising a young son, estrangement from her husband (their marriage was later declared to be annulled) and the demands of adjustment to entirely new cultural and social patterns, all but broke her. From these certain depths she reached rather incredible heights as star lecturer and performer on the North American Chautauqua circuit. With the deepening of the depression she discovered new depths of spiritual life and strength. In the poorest area of Toronto she founded a "Friendship House" and began a life of social service which has provided structures of implementation and actualization in Canada, the United States and several other countries for well over half a century (de Hueck 1975, 1977, 1978; Sharum 1977; Hogan 1986, chap. 3).

Her initial period of vocational activity in Toronto ended in a rude and unfortunate manner in the mid-1930s when de Hueck was required to withdraw from the work and to witness its dismemberment. There followed journalistic work in Europe and the founding of a settlement-type house in Harlem, devoted to interracial works. This led to a number of such houses from the east to the west coast. In the mid-1940s, now married to an American newspaperman, Eddie Doherty, she returned to Canada and established the basis of the Madonna House Apostolate.

There are several characteristics of this unique woman and apostolate which demand attention. From the beginning she wished to live among the poor, and like the poor, to live simply. She believed this was essential if she was really to engage the task of serving the poor. In order to accomplish such service, she rapidly recognized the necessity of having a group of persons working with her. From this has developed the lay association of Madonna House, single and celibate men and women who dedicate themselves to lives of serving the poor in simple and fundamental fashion. Wherever de Hueck established herself books, journals and libraries were regarded as precious attendants, and from the founding of *Social Forum* in the early 1930s through the decades-long printing of *Restoration*, the newspaper was regarded as a key feature for information and formation of Christian minds.

Animating the service and intellectual components of this apostolic work has been a keen concentration on a life of prayer and spiritual works, focused on the liturgy, and building on a variety of spiritual disciplines recovered from her heritage in the Eastern Church. Catherine wrote many books, founded a dozen centres and developed a novel structure to provide for the continuance of the work after her death. Madonna House has served as a place of rest and refreshment, of contemplation and of formation and re-formation for a host of Christians in search of vocational discernment and activity. The intense faith and prayer dimension of the work, joined with an uncommon concern for the immediate relief of the corporal needs of persons has fostered a unique and sustained response, particularly at levels of implementation and actualization.

In the lives of these three persons we see attempts to vivify gospel principles and values in Canadian society over several decades. The fourth section of this article identifies a number of elements common to these persons and activities.

Constitutive Elements of Canadian Social Catholicism
The following eight components are identified as constitutive elements of Canadian social Catholicism. Dimensions of them are present to undertakings and programmes at every level, where they provide generative, integrative and substantive assistance.

In the first place, any investigation of these persons or efforts must take account of the faith perspective which is basic to them. In every case there has been conscious effort to respond to perceived need and in so doing to enflesh gospel values such as charity, justice, peace, and the principles of human care best summarized in the beatitudes. For some persons and undertakings there would be little direct advertence to the faith perspective, much less to its incarnation in a specific ecclesial body. For others the connection would be immediately evident and constant. Labour union activities, outside of Québec, were hardly ever of a confessional nature in Canada, and Catholics worked alongside others in promoting such activities in many areas. While it would be clear that some clerics were actively supporting such efforts in some places, the faith dimension would not often be adverted to in any conscious way. It is equally clear that these persons and their activities found nourishment and support in their ecclesial communities, and sometimes conflict also!

A second significant factor which is evident as we consider the manner in which the Catholic church has influenced Canadian society is the place of education. The watchwords of Catholic Action organizations, "See, Judge and Act," from the 1930s through the 1960s, provided the methodology for a pedagogy aimed at the integration of theory and praxis. One of Fr. Coady's first principles for cooperative homebuilding was: "Education before Excavation." From the very beginning the Antigonish movement was based on a variety of innovative educational techniques. Women's groups were very well represented in these activities and frequently led the way in many cooperative ventures. There was a recognition and respect for the complexity of undertakings and a willingness to take the time to learn what must be learned in order to carry the enterprise through to completion. The educational component continues to be paramount for this work. There were correspondence courses from the *Centre sociale* at the University of Ottawa during the 1940s and 1950s, and similar courses sponsored by the Institute of Social Action at St. Patrick's College in the 1950s and 1960s. These provided a variety of helps from domestic organization, marriage preparation programmes, personal budgeting, the development of credit unions, cooperatives, and trade unions. There were also numerous "Study Clubs" throughout the country, some lasting for many years, which provided a "base-community" type support system for individuals to continually monitor and critique living and working environments. Together this range of activities suggests the emphasis and dependence placed on educational activities as essential for fuelling and abetting social Catholicism.

The Catholic Church is a hierarchical church in which the role of the teaching magisterium has historically carried some considerable weight. Beginning with the papal encyclical *Rerum novarum* in 1891, church teaching began a more systematic response to urban/industrial conditions. Here a concern, tone and direction was established. The encyclical was hesitant in part, but altogether quite progressive. Principles were set forth which were gradually employed and expanded during subsequent decades. These included the principle of the right to a living wage, and the right to representative associations for workers.

There was a reinforcement of these principles and attitudes at the national, regional and diocesan levels through the twentieth century. Encyclicals, pastoral letters, and urgings from the CCCB enabled those who were active in social questions to offer appeal to authority in support of their initiatives. This proved to be an important recourse time and again, in the face of resistance to implementation of church teachings.

Kenneth Latourette, in his multi-volumed history of Christianity, termed the twentieth century the "century of the laity" for the Roman

Catholic Church. The rapid spread of the variety of Catholic Action organizations, and the encouragement of laity thus to "participate in the apostolic work of the hierarchy," led to the involvement of tens of thousands of Catholics in non-traditional activities—and even in the re-direction of traditional activities. For example, in a small company-owned town outside of Sudbury, the local Sodality group, traditionally dedicated to works of piety and evangelization, came to challenge the company dominance of municipal elections, and to instruct workers and immigrants how to participate in the electoral process. Within a short time the people were electing their own candidates.

This very initial introduction into church work was at a different level than that understood or experienced by Catholic laity during recent centuries. It led to encouragement and training for more participation in the social and political order, and a recognition of such participation as constituting Christian service. The constant employment of the critical methodology inherent in the "See, Judge and Act" catchwords of Catholic Action groups represented the beginnings of a new preparation of laity who would be responsible for accepting and actualizing the teachings of Vatican II. An understanding of the dramatic shift in attitude, with regard to lay initiative, which has taken place since Vatican II can be seen in the Revised Code of Canon Law, Canon 215: "Christ's faithful may freely establish and direct associations which serve charitable or pious purposes or foster the Christian vocation in the world, and they may hold meetings to pursue these purposes by common effort" (Canadian Catholic Conference of Bishops 1983, 35-36). Apostolic work is no longer exclusively "participation in the work of the hierarchy," then, but it may well be begun and pursued by Catholics at their own initiative. The movement is from the grassroots, rather than from the "top down."

Involvement in social justice concerns provided many Catholics with their first, or only, ecumenical experience in the decades prior to Vatican II. By the 1940s and 1950s, earlier in some areas, cooperative undertakings were common. Fr. Coady insisted that there was "No Catholic way to catch fish or protestant way to mine coal," and he hired protestant as well as Catholic field-workers (some of them ministers—certainly a unique experience by Canadian Catholics at the time!).

Overcoming generations of mistrust and hostility was not an easy task, and any consideration of the impact of churches on Canadian culture must take account of the serious and enduring tendency to social divisiveness which has accompanied the transfer of Christian religious traditions to this land. Tens of thousands of people from different denominations, however, contributed to the development of credit unions, frequently stimulated by Catholic pastors, and many participated in cooperative ventures of different types, regardless of religious affiliation. Different in kind from the ecumenical groups which would emerge later, these developments were still a step beyond Catholic Action, narrowly conceived, towards action by Catholics in the social order along with other members of the civic community. This principle was strongly advanced in Canada by Jacques Maritain as a result of the renewed interest in Thomistic philosophy and the scholastic method, acknowledging the integrity of the natural order (Maritain 1936; 1938).

A sixth constitutive factor in this review of church influence on society concerns the use of communications media. Newspapers had played an essential role in promoting and defending church interests since after the middle of the nineteenth century in English-speaking Catholic circles. Of course, the French Catholic press was well established by then. Many activities founded their own organ or looked to established newspaper/journal/publishing houses to publicize their positions. With the depression decade there was considerable concern to interpret economic questions from scriptural-theological perspectives. In the United States the former Canadian priest Fr. Charles Coughlin successfully exploited radio to reach millions of American and Canadian listeners with his brand of socio-economic advice, increasingly and disturbingly moving to the far right as the depression deepened.

Catherine de Hueck played a key role in the founding of the *Social Forum* (1935-1945), a *Catholic Worker* type of paper published in Ottawa and then Toronto. Later the Madonna House Apostolate which she initiated promoted *Restoration*, a publication now in its forty-first year. Henry Somerville was a regular columnist in the paper he edited, developing extended series on civics, economics and a wide variety of social questions. Under his editorship the *Register* exhibited a consistent and balanced concern for social questions.

Through all of this there was a clear understanding of the importance of communication, and attempts were made to exploit media in the most effective ways to best influence society. In Quebec the *Institut social populaire* turned out books, journals, pamphlets and brochures addressing every type of social issue over a half century. Neither there nor in English-speaking Canada, however, could it be said that a successful transition was made from print to electronic media in this area of ecclesial activity. Although the foremost western theoretician of communications, Marshall McLuhan, was longtime professor at St. Michael's, there has been an incredible lag in moving from structures for application towards structures for actualization in the church's exploitation of electronic media.

A seventh area of consideration involves theological activity and new categories and approaches which developed with the century. It would be difficult to exaggerate the linkages of social action with the liturgical renewal movement which gained impetus as the century progressed. This movement enjoyed close relations with biblical scholarship and exhibited a determination to link liturgy and life activities more consciously and concretely in the minds of worshippers. As well, there was an increasing interest and emphasis on the anthropological implications of the humanity of Christ. This presaged a growing concern with and commitment to the temporal order, and discouraged spiritual initiatives which were seen as too heavily favouring the divine/transcendent at the expense of the human/temporal.

The return to scholastic method and the shift away from "scholasticism" as the memorization of learned responses, meant a greater concentration in theology on contemporary investigation. Continental church historians encouraged a greater openness to the insights and implications of existentialist/phenomenological philosophical categories and investigations as they developed through the early twentieth century. Again, these trends tended towards a closer scrutiny of and sympathy for human needs. Altogether, these theological directions suggested a more dynamic, participatory thrust, rooted in historical and contemporary experiences.

An eighth and final category for this consideration treats of twentieth century developments in missiology. Going forth to teach all nations means one's own as well as others and, historically, Christians have understood their commitment as implying mission responsibility near and far. The involvement of Canadian Catholic mission-aries in other countries, particularly in Central and South America, assisted in the development of a more critical perspective from which to view domestic events. By the late 1940s missionaries to these countries were carrying not only Bibles, but structures and institutions such as the Young Christian Workers, leading to "See, Judge and Act" initiatives which were of immense pedagogical significance during the following decades. A credit union, a producing or marketing cooperative, a trade union—all of these are highly political activities, with their own inevitably pedagogical methodologies, drawing people together, providing them with context and content for critique of their societies. In turn missionary journals, letters, and visits to Canadian parishes all contributed to a deeper sympathy for the plight of marginalized peoples abroad, and in later decades, awareness of connections, frequently exploitative, between home and foreign economies.

Conclusions

The very number of churches and church-related institutions across the country suggests some considerable influence on Canadian society. The reflections in this paper point to the existence of a broad variety of undertakings intended to engage particular problems and the inertia or complicity of society in the face of these problems. Rather than attempt to deal with one or two persons or organizations in great detail this paper has provided a topographical review of social Catholicism as an introduction to the topic. To facilitate this effort the essay reviewed the realities of society, then and now, noting the difficulties and limitations involved in identifying and addressing social issues, from state or social opposition to the resistance of the church membership itself. Keeping these realities in mind the paper then proceeded to a presentation of three levels of structures by which to interpret and locate efforts in these areas: structures for application, structures of implementation and structures of actualization. The third section of the paper illustrated the interrelations of these structures in the lives of three Canadian Catholics in this century. The final section then offered a review of eight constitutive components operative in the application and actualization of the gospel in Canadian society through this century. These examples provide some understanding of how the Catholic Church has attempted to influence structures and values in Canadian society.

In the seventeenth century the church failed to stop absolutely the exploitation of Amerindians through the use of alcohol. The Canadian Bishops' statement of 1983 has not been fully accepted or employed. In fact, the task is never fully accomplished, and the terms of reference are constantly shifting, calling for adaptation and innovation. Still, each effort has its purpose. While the fullness of the

Kingdom yet awaits, the transformation of persons, and the inclination of social structures, is addressed and, at times, advanced.

5. Revolutions in Canadian Catholic Social Teaching

Lee Cormie

As we approach the twenty-first century, the world, indeed all of creation as we know it, is being transformed in unprecedented ways. The forms of social order are being rapidly transformed by international free trade agreements, the shifting international division of labour, largely unregulated global financial markets, the eruption of democracy in the Soviet Union and Eastern Europe, and the decline of major features of the cold war. And the very nature of nature is being transformed under the impact of pollution, ecological devastation and genetic engineering.

In the midst of these great changes, there are many signs of hope, in the growing awareness about these issues and in the commitment to shape a different future.

But there are also many signs of great and growing suffering, among the Third World poor suffering under the impossible burden of pollution, and in ecological devastation. In Canada regional inequalities are deepening, and crisis on the farms and in rural communities is pervasive, unemployment is rising (due in part to plant shutdowns under the Free Trade Agreement, and thus permanent), violence against women and children especially is widespread and apparently growing, and racial divisions are deepening.

Strangely, though, there is remarkably little disciplined concern for analyzing the actual impact of church teachings or programs, or the impact of the churches themselves. This lack of interest is in sharp contrast to the intense interest in the effectiveness of their evangelization of other powerful preachers of visions and values, of corporate public relations officers, industry-sponsored think-tanks, lobbies and political action campaigns, and the advertising industry. Generally, though, we Christians avoid looking very closely at the concrete effects of what we preach and of our policies and organizations.

If we are not to rest content with "blind" faith, we must take our own past experience more seriously. In this paper, I offer a small contribution to that by addressing the Roman Catholic Church in Canada in the post-World War II period. In the hope of contributing to further discussion of the lessons of this rich experience, I propose a tentative hypothesis concerning the nature of the shift in Canadian Catholic social teaching between the documents of the 1940s and 1950s on the one hand, and those of the 1970s and 1980s on the other. This shift represents, I suggest, a shift in the content of specific ethical teachings, in the theological-ethical framework for articulating these concerns, in the method for articulating such teachings, and in the character of church authority projected in these documents concerning economic and political matters. It is more than a shift in details. I suggest that it represents a shift in the kind of social teaching, a different experience of God, a different understanding of the world, and a different conception of the mission of the church in this world, a different starting point and method, and a different kind of authority.

In following sections I will briefly sketch the general frameworks and main points of the teaching of these two periods, illustrated with reference to particular documents. I will then briefly compare them, and conclude by raising the possibility that if these insights prove helpful in understanding the past, they suggest that in the 1990s we ought to confront again the fundamental choices concerning the mission of the church in the world. We may, in fact, be on the verge of another revolution in Canadian Catholic social teaching.

Class Collaboration and Progress In a World Menaced by the Communist Threat

There is one major feature of the analytic horizon of the documents between 1945 and 1960: a perception of a worldwide communist threat against all that was good: belief in God, democracy and free enterprise. For example, in a document that was released in 1945, even before the end of World War II, the bishops said:

We warn once more against materialistic and atheistic communism, which now personifies in the world all the unleashed forces against the Church and against the moral values of which she has the care, namely human dignity and Christian liberty. [On the one hand we need to recognize] the courageous part that the Russian people have played in turning away from the world the frightful Nazi domination, but this must not blind us regarding the world revolution which the leaders of international communism always seek. Governments and simple citizens alike have the very grave obligation of checking amongst us communistic infiltrations under whatever external appearance they present themselves. Otherwise they are preparing for our dear country, for which so many of our sons offer each day their life and their future, the worst disorders and calamities (National Board 1987; Sheridan 1987, 54).

While this doctrine did not so completely dominate politics and official Catholic thinking in Canada as it did in the United States, this analytic horizon on the world's problems was reaffirmed in a Canadian document from 1958:

What has been called "the crisis of our times" has been precip - itated by the rulers of the USSR in a clear declaration of economic warfare, the stated objective of which is the final destruction of all forms of society not based on atheistic materialism. This economic warfare, which has already begun, will be waged with calculated ferocity and may well be more menacing to us than the hydrogen bomb and intercontinental ballistic missiles (Social Action Department 1958; Sheridan 1987, 76).

In fact, in this view communists are responsible for the basic problems confronting the world, and Canada, too. Not only the threat of warfare, even nuclear warfare, but also economic problems—all are due to the communists.

The strategy of this warfare is to bring about civil chaos; the tactics include provoking class hatred, unemployment, and all forms of disorder where they do not already exist. The struggle is between total control by a godless state, on the one hand, and various combinations of free enterprise and democracy on the other (Social Action Department 1958; Sheridan 1987, 76).

In this framework, then, military, economic and political issues are all linked. And there are only two alternatives: Christian faith, freedom, private property and capitalism on the one hand and atheism, repression and state domination of the market in communism on the other.

Apart from the fear of the communist threat, though, these documents express a modest confidence in the functioning of Canadian society and the economy. Indeed, they equate economic progress with God's plan for the universe.

In 1956 for example, quoting an Italian Cardinal Dell'Acqua speaking on behalf of the Pope, they wrote that "the Church asks the faithful to see in the astounding progress of science the realization of the plan of God, who has entrusted to man the discovery and exploitation of the wealth of the universe: Fill the earth and subdue it" (Gen. 1:28) (Social Action Department 1956; Sheridan 1987, 62). They referred here to a rising living standard and increased leisure time activity.

Yet, progress can be ambiguous, too. The bishops continued: "Is it necessary to abandon oneself with blind confidence to those perspectives of technical progress and economic expansion?'Productivity is not an end in itself,' the Holy Father said recently'" (Social Action Department 1956; Sheridan 1987, 62). In this and other documents they listed a number of problems. Automation, for example, was raising a host of new problems, they said, problems that must be solved if technological progress is not to degenerate into another instrument of corruption. They also expressed concern over the increased geographical mobility required of workers in the postwar Canadian economy; they stressed that moving from place to place in search of jobs puts a stress on family life.

The bishops also insisted that "nowadays when powerful economic and financial combinations are pushing the little man into obscurity, the Holy Father [and they are clearly identifying with his position here] champions man's natural rights" (Social Action Department 1956; Sheridan 1987, 60-61). Moreover, in a statement that could well have been issued in the late 1980s when housing prices had soared out of sight, they pointed to the widespread scarcity of reasonably priced housing as a basic problem. They also raised the issue of consumerism:

An increasingly serious modern disease is the desire to consume beyond the limits of reasonable need. Modern advertising, stimulated by ever-increasing production, strives ceaselessly and by every means to create a climate of opinion in which men and women are never satisfied but must, to be 'normal,' buy more and more (Social Action Department 1956; Sheridan 1987, 63-64).

We see that in the perspective of this period there is progress but also ambiguity about some of its features, and the powerful external threat of world communism.

What is the vision of society reflected in these documents? The bishops insisted that in the first place the vicars of Christ, the popes, have given us a program for the reconstruction of the social order. This ideal is of an organic society, organized to meet the common societal interests of diverse groups. The image is a body with different parts or organs each quite different from one another. Ideally the parts function together in the interests both of the whole and of each of the parts, which could not survive apart from the whole, just as the heart and lungs could not survive apart from the body of which they are quite different parts. "Even in the simplest forms of society, concerted, cooperative effort for the common good is necessary. It is immeasurably more necessary now, even vital, when our society is composed of large and highly complex groups" (Social Action Department 1958; Sheridan 1987, 77).

How should this harmonious cooperation be promoted? It cannot be achieved, they insisted, "by state control. It must arise from the educated social consciousness of groups themselves if it is to conform to the social nature of man" (Social Action Department 1958; Sheridan 1987, 77). So the key to the improvement of society is moral conversion, which happens to be the speciality of the church.

As a detailed social ethical approach to specific concrete issues, though, this teaching was full of ambiguities. Indeed, the Canadian economy was defined as basically good, and the causes of whatever problems that were perceived at that time or in the future were defined as external to Canada, the fault of "communists." But this claim did not help much in addressing concrete problems and tensions within Canada.

For example, the bishops acknowledged in the same message that "class distinctions do in fact exist." In this view, class consciousness "that derives from solidarity in the pursuit of common interests is in itself a natural, even a praiseworthy thing." But somehow in this view these common interests, defined in terms of the interests of employers on the one hand and of workers on the other, are not fundamentally opposed, cannot be opposed: "According to the social documents of the church there are no insuperable barriers between classes" (Social Action Department 1959; Sheridan 1987, 80).

These different interests do not, indeed can not, lead to class divisions and conflict: "To confuse class consciousness with class warfare, which is its abuse and distortion, would be as unjust as to equate enlightened patriotism with aggressive nationalism" (Social Action Department 1959; Sheridan 1987, 80). This bald assertion, which seems to contradict their own admissions about the reality of different classes, is not supported by data or by any kind of appeal to experience or argumentation; it is simply asserted.

Asserting this allows church officials to project the image of a harmonious society in which there are no basic differences in power (while differences in income and wealth are largely overlooked), in which radical critics are condemned as if they *created* the differences and divisions rather than called attention to them. There seems, then, to be ample reason for hope that modest reforms will be undertaken through the harmonious collaboration of workers and capitalists, so that church leaders can present the agenda of the church as being equally concerned about all segments of society.

Accordingly, they urged, "Management organizations and those of workers thus have the duty of avoiding all class antagonism. . . . Any doctrine which states that such [class] warfare is inevitable is directly opposed to Christian doctrine and aspirations" (Social Action Department 1959; Sheridan 1987, 80).

In this connection, the right of workers to form unions is prominent, as it has been in Roman Catholic social teaching since *Rerum Novarum* (1891) of Leo XIII. But carefully avoiding any signs of partiality, the Canadian bishops cautioned in 1956 that as unions grow bigger—and they were growing in Canada in the 1950s—growth brings new strength and should reflect an increased sense of responsibility for the common good. So they urged, for example, that labour use its strength and authority for the betterment of the existing social and economic order by promoting a program of social change that will bring reality more nearly into conformity with the ideal. They looked for labour to show initiative in labour-management relations, economic cooperation, housing, finance, credit, insurance, taxation. In short, they insisted that "organized labour must move into the area where morality, economics and social behaviour are inextricably meshed" (Social Action Department 1956; Sheridan 1987, 62).

Another staple of Catholic social teaching at this time concerned private property. "Governments must not use their political strength," the Canadian bishops insisted, "to usurp the functions of private enterprise; nor should they attempt to do the work of those organizations which act as intermediaries between the citizen and the state" (Canadian Catholic Hierarchy 1956; Sheridan 1987, 69). In Catholic social teaching since the 1930s subsidiarity has meant that, in principle, higher levels of social order should not usurp functions that can be appropriately performed at lower levels. And here, as elsewhere in Catholic social teaching, this principle is wedded to the defense of private property.

But as with the teachings on the different social classes, this position on private property is presented with no regard at all to the evolution of the ownership of private property, as if a carpenter and his or her tools were in more or less the same category as the huge transnational corporations whose shares are publicly traded on the stock exchanges around the world and which are managed by corporate executives and boards of directors with little accountability to workers, local communities, the nation or the environment (cf. Herman 1981).

"The role of government is to support [the efforts of all these different groups including property owners, owners of the means of production, and labour], to coordinate them, to arbitrate when necessary between groups whose interests conflict" (Canadian Catholic Hierarchy 1956; Sheridan 1987, 69). So the duty of government, then, is not to interfere with private ownership of the means of production, beyond certain limits, nor to usurp the power of intermediary groups of entrepreneurs who own and control this property. Its role is to promote the general conditions in which they can all flourish and do what they are ordained to do.

In the matter of material prosperity, for instance, the state should not be expected continually to increase the allowances or grants paid directly to individuals, but rather should seek to develop and sustain general economic conditions which permit every citizen to provide adequately for his needs and for those of his family. . . . Yet in some cases preference may legitimately be given to citizens in poorer circumstances, as a means of modifying social injustice which can not be entirely eradicated (Canadian Catholic Hierarchy 1956; Sheridan 1987, 68-69).

Note again that in these teachings "communism" is opposed, not as a "political" but as a "religious" ideology, "private" property is blessed as a "religious" principle, and participation in the worldwide crusade against godless communism is, by implication, endorsed (Canadian Catholic Hierarchy 1956; Sheridan 1987, 70). Clearly, as suggested above, church officials are endorsing the limited welfare state in the context of the capitalism structured primarily in terms of the private ownership of the means of production and of the free market.

And yet, in their teachings regarding politics, they specifically rejected religiously sanctioned partisanship: "Religion must not be used to bolster any specific political ideology" (Canadian Catholic Hierarchy 1956; Sheridan 1987, 69). Thus, they continued, "the Catholic church leaves her members free to belong to the party of your choice . . . ." Of course, there was one major exception: "those parties that are opposed to their religious faith, as in the case of the communist party."

Specifically in terms of Canada, in 1959 the bishops celebrated the situation in Canada; it is "privileged . . . , since it permits us to avoid two excesses which have caused great damage in other countries, that is: war between management and labour [on the one hand,] and [on the other an] exaggerated intervention of the state" (Social Action Department 1959; Sheridan 1987, 81). The ideal is open discussion and sincere collaboration. "In our country," they claimed, "we have no experience of open and systematic warfare between management and labour" (Social Action Department 1959; Sheridan 1987, 80). This quite sweeping analytical judgment is made categorically, with no reference to the actual course of labour-management struggles in workplaces and local communities.

Nevertheless, in their view, the situation in Canada still fell short of the Christian social ideal. They continued, "If there is no bitter struggle between the leaders of management and labour, neither is there any effective, constructive collaboration, except during times of armed conflict." And thus "It is not sufficient for Christians to reject class warfare in theory. They must will and create class collaboration, in fact and in spirit."

So, while Canada has been preserved from the social struggles plaguing other societies, caused in their view not by class divisions and the conflicts of interests inherent in them but by "class hatred" fomented by communists, there was still room for improvement. "We earnestly wish that the leaders of management and labour in Canada would come together to exchange ideas."

In addition, the bishops advocated promoting worker enterprises, developing agriculture along family lines, and fostering cooperatives in both medium and large enterprises "where the workers' desire to take an active part in the life of the enterprises where they are employed, is a legitimate aspiration" (Social Action Department 1961; Sheridan 1987, 89). There is no indication, though, of how these ideas fit in a society organized around the sacred principle of "private property," or even that the bishops perceived any tension between these notions.

Other topics are mentioned in these documents. The bishops indicated their support for immigration policies that do not discriminate against people on any basis that would be contrary to the principles of justice and peace. And they affirmed that any policy governing the flow of immigration should be democratic.

"In regard to housing," they insisted, "as in other matters, public authorities should favour and not oppose private enterprise, and in the case of low cost housing especially, they should favour cooperatives" (Social Action Department 1956; Sheridan 1987, 63). From the perspective of the housing crisis in cities like Toronto by the end of the 1980s, it seems clear that the functioning of these two quite different principles—private enterprise and cooperatives (presumably supported by the government in some form)—have been very inadequate. But, again, these documents reflect no awareness of tension or conflict between them.

Finally, concerning the role of the church reflected in the documents of this period, I mentioned above the standard claim in Catholic social teaching between the end of the nineteenth century and Vatican II that the popes have presented a program of social reconstruction. The image is clear: the answers already exist, or at least the general principles already exist; the Roman Catholic Church has them. There is no need, then, for theories and analyses, and for political debates about the foundations of the system. Nor is there need for political struggle for power to decide the shape of society, nor a struggle over how to define—and who has a voice in defining—the ordering principles of society; only moral teaching is necessary. And the church especially posses this moral wisdom.

In this framework, history is at best secondary; the enduring principles underlying social order remain the same, and historical change concerns more the superficial aspects of society than its essence. "The solution of social problems," they said, "demands the application of moral principles by all segments of society and the willingness of all to adopt programs of action in conformity with these principles" (Social Action Department 1956; Sheridan 1987, 64).

Accordingly, beyond some very broad generalizations, economic, political and social analysis are not necessary either, for in this perspective there is little to debate. And similarly in politics; apart from the choice between "communism" and Christianity, political choices concern only the details of the organization of life in society and not its fundamentals.

The ideals, in this perspective, clearly exist. It is just a question of learning about how to apply them.

> Grave dangers threaten the world today which have their roots in profoundly different ideologies. Catastrophe will only be averted by a close collaboration based on justice and charity between all who control our social and economic life. If Christian social doctrine is ignored by the world, our fate will be either slavery or destruction. Only by action inspired by Christian unity [as defined in this Catholic version of it] can we find our way out of today's agonizing dilemma (Social Action Department 1959; Sheridan 1987, 79).

Charting the Course of the Church in Treacherous Seas Following World War II

Close examination of the history of these and other social teaching documents makes it clear that they can not be understood primarily as texts in "social ethics." Every social ethics, I propose, involves a more or less developed "analysis" of the causes of some significant social issue; a statement of relevant sensibilities, concerns, commitments, values and principles which inform a vision of what should be;

a specification of the appropriate or "realistic" hope concerning the possibilities of change; and a grounding in an articulation of faith of this response in the face of often great obstacles to this hope.

Of course, there are many discourses for addressing these issues, including both those of other religions and secular discourses. Not every social ethics includes explicit reference to each of these dimensions. And there are many different logics, methods, for relating them, which together express different forms of authority. Nevertheless, I suggest, sooner or later every ethic must come to terms with the issues pertaining to these various dimensions.

My hypothesis concerning Catholic social teaching in the period before Vatican II is that it did not represent a social ethics in this sense. Rather, I propose, official documents like those reviewed above can be read as navigators' charts of the officers at the helm of the barque of St. Peter going through often stormy and hazardous seas. In other words, these documents reflect above all church officials' general sensibilities about what is happening in the world as those developments inpinge on the life of the church. The centre of gravity of these documents is the church and its passsage to a safe harbour much more than it is particular social ethical issues in their own terms.

Part of the problem in recognizing the character of these teachings is that the elements of this perspective on the world, on social problems in Canadian society, and on the appropriate Christian response—centering around opposition to communism, the right to private property, and cross-class collaboration in promoting certain reforms—are still widely accepted as obvious, as virtually common sense in many discussions in Catholic circles. For in its main outlines, this teaching has deep roots going back to the famous encyclical of Pope Leo XIII in 1891, *Rerum Novarum* (Cormie 1990a, 255-67). And, in continuity with this teaching, the Canadian bishops in their documents of the cold war world of the 1940s and 1950s were aligning the Canadian church with a vision of society and of the global economy in sharp opposition to socialism and communism. This put them on the side of the defenders of freedom and Christian values led by U.S. elites, with their Canadian and European allies, in opposition to all the critics of this version of order, who were quickly labelled "communists" (Cormie 1990b).

Undoubtedly, the tendency to see the world in these bipolar terms has in some respects been reinforced by the apparent "collapse" of socialism in Central and Eastern Europe and the Soviet Union, and in Nicaragua. This attitude, however, blocks recognition of the historically contingent character of this framework, the nature of the choices that were made, and their significance. There are many reasons for questioning this perspective on the world and on the church's mission within it.

There is no space here to examine all the relevant issues in detail. It is important, though, at least to note that there are many grounds for rejecting the historical adequacy of this highly polarized view of the world in the years following World War II. Since these claims turned on the view of the Soviet Union as a powerful military threat to the whole world, it is important to demythologize this claim in particular.

Basically, this claim was wrong. For at the end of World War II the Soviet Union, in the wake of all the enormous destruction of World War II, did not really have the capacity to dominate the world, or even Western Europe. It certainly posed no military threat to the U.S. or Canada (Cormie 1990b).

Moreover, the territorial ambitions of Soviet leaders were very traditional, concerning defense of the Soviet Union from attacks from the West, which had already occurred twice in this century with devastating results. In other words, even if the protestations of Soviet leaders concerning their desires for world peace were not believed, "there was no Soviet'blueprint' for expansion in the postwar period," and no capacity to carry it out if there had been one (Paterson 1988, 15).

Of course, with the development of a Soviet nuclear capability by the 1970s and of an increasingly powerful economy able to aid allies, Soviet leaders did pose a threat. But U.S. leaders consistently maintained superiority in a number of key areas of war-fighting capacity and in the extent of U.S. economic, political and covert (CIA) "influence" in nations around the world, and in the major institutions for managing international relations, like the International Monetary Fund and World Bank, and the General Agreement on Tariffs and Trade.

These critical insights expose the extent to which the cold war view of the world, which came to be so widely accepted as common sense, was in fact false. They raise a host of questions concerning how this framework for interpreting and organizing the world came to be so dominant, and who benefitted from it. Without addressing all these questions, it is clear that, following the lead of the Vatican and in agreement with Catholic officials around the world, in the years following World War II the Canadian bishops were aligning the church in Canada with the political, economic and military agenda of Canadian elites and their allies in the U.S. and Europe in support of the capitalist world system created at the end of World War II. In this perspective, these were *religious* matters. Nothing could be more serious. And everything—literally heaven and earth—was at stake in this struggle.

Recognizing the concerns that informed these documents from the bishops helps to explain their vagueness and ambiguity on certain concrete issues. Indeed, from the point of view of church interests as defined by church officials, vagueness and ambiguity on particular issues seemed to have been, we might say in retrospect, a requirement of official teaching.

Denying, in a world of classes, that there was, that there *could be*, any class conflict was a condition of tolerance and support for the church by the wealthy and by ruling elites especially. And it was central to the claim of church officials to be addressing all in society equally, thus identifying the agenda of the church with the interests of all, and hopefully avoiding antagonizing and driving away from the churh significant numbers in either group.

Thus, rather than seeing these documents in the image of the theologian or philosopher, or more recently of a social scientist systematically analyzing a problem and proposing solutions, I suggest the image of the captain and the navigator at the helm of a ship in stormy and dangerous seas, trying to determine which way the wind is blowing and how the waves are moving, and trying to detect the not so visible hazards just under the surface of the water. Sometimes the documents project a horizon of calm seas and smooth sailing, and at other moments they obviously are informed by an image of a quite rocky and terror-filled passage which threatens the very existence of the barque.

Concretely, then, these documents reflected the Canadian hierarchy's identifying with the status quo through sanctifying private ownership of the means of production, religiously condemning all who questioned it as communists and sanctioning the worldwide crusade against them, and urging cross-class collaboration as the only path toward progress. Clearly, in this perspective, there was room for progress, but it did not seem urgent and the magnitude of change required not very large. The authority of these teachings depended heavily on their echoing the perspective of papal social teaching which expressed the timeless truths concerning the proper principles for organizing society revealed by God, entrusted to the church, and properly interpreted by its officials.

The Option for the Poor and Oppressed and the Prophetic Voice of the Church

I wish to show that there has been a fundamental shift in Canadian Catholic social teaching since the 1950s toward a much more critical view of Canadian society and the existing world order, and toward a more prophetic stance for the church within the society. My hypothesis is that what occurred has involved not just changes in various aspects of this teaching but a shift to another kind of social teaching, and that this shift, evident above all in the documents of the famous Medellin conference of 1968 which marked the official baptism of Latin American liberation theology, was also especially evident in the documents of the Canadian bishops.

Of course, this shift took place in the context of a whole variety of developments in the church and the world. Vatican II symbolized a revolution within global Catholicism. Third World liberation movements, along with black, feminist, peace, ecology and Third World solidarity movements within the First World, all contributed to the profound transformation of the cultural and political landscape. And the irruption of historically marginalized voices in the churches—of the poor and working people in the Third World, of women and people of colour, of indigenous peoples, and of all those speaking on behalf of the earth itself—all these voices transformed discussion of every aspect of theology and ethics in the churches. In Canada in particular, these developments lead to the creation, beginning in the late 1960s and early 1970s, of the ecumenical interchurch social justice coalitions which have played significant roles over the last twenty years in shaping both political debates in Canada on important issues and debates within the churches over their mission in this unjust and divided world.

It would be interesting to look more closely at the documents of the late 1960s and 1970s concerning the shape and pace of these changes in the official teaching of the Canadian church. For my purposes here, though, I will focus on two documents from the 1980s. My hypothesis is that these documents represent radical shifts in every dimension of Catholic social teaching. The first is the pastoral letter

"Ethical Reflections on the Economic Crisis" (EREC) from 1982. The second is the brief to the Macdonald Commission in the name of the Canadian Conference of Catholic Bishops submitted in December, 1983, about twelve months after "Ethical Reflections." Entitled "Ethical Reflections on Canada's Socio-Economic Order" (ERSO), it is a fuller expression of the same basic thrust that is found in the pastoral letter, and therefore serves to amplify and fill out its basic orientation. References to these documents are identified by page numbers in Sheridan 1987.

The bishops began "Ethical Reflections on the Economic Crisis" by noting that there are many symptoms that our economy in Canada is in serious trouble. Then they testified to their own experience and perceptions.

> In our own regions we have seen the economic realities of plant shutdowns, massive layoffs of workers, wage restraint programs, and suspension of collective bargaining rights for public sector workers. At the same time we have seen the social realities of the abandoned one-industry towns, depleting unemployment benefits, cut-backs in health and social services, and line ups at local soup kitchens. [As Christians we are called to respond because of the immense suffering this crisis causes in the lives of poor and working people, evident in the emotional strain,] the loss of human dignity, family breakdown and even suicide (EREC, 400).

It is this experience and their belief in the gospel that forms the basis of the bishops' response. "As pastors our concerns about the economy are not based on any specific political options. Instead, they are inspired by the gospel message of Jesus Christ" (EREC, 402).

Actually this is the first reference to Jesus Christ in all the quotations I have taken from the social teaching documents. One of the important shifts in Catholic social teaching in the post-Vatican II years is that it is theological in a more obvious and straightforward way than the pre-Vatican II teaching. In particular the bishops referred to two fundamental motivating principles. The preferential option for the poor, the afflicted and the oppressed is the first. "As Christians we are called to follow Jesus by identifying with the victims of injustice, by analyzing the dominant attitudes and structures that cause human suffering, and by actively supporting the poor and oppressed in their struggles to transform society."

And "the second principle concerns the value and dignity of human work in God's plan for Creation" (EREC, 400). Here they are referring to Pope John Paul II's encyclical on human work where he referred to the significance of work in the development of people's sense of self-worth and identity, and in the development of society. In other words, in this view, work is the avenue for the development both of the individual person's sense of identity, capacities, and abilities, but also the way in which each contributes to the development of society. Thus, the bishops provide a Christological grounding for their concern with work: "The importance of human labour is illustrated in the life of Jesus who was himself a worker" (EREC, 400).

These gospel principles stimulate the bishops' reflection on major features of recent development in Canada and in the world economy. "The present recession," they note, "appears to be symptomatic of a much larger structural crisis in the international system of capitalism" (EREC, 402). Many observers have pointed to the profound changes in both capital and technology with inevitably serious impacts on labour. "Transnational corporations and banks can move capital from one country to another in order to take advantage of cheaper labour conditions, lower taxes and reduced environmental restrictions" (EREC, 402). Automation and computers are increasingly replacing workers on assembly lines and in administrative centres. "In effect, capital has become increasingly capital-intensive" (EREC, 402). "And both have become increasingly concentrated in fewer centres of power" (ERSO, 420). These developments are resulting in a new global economic environment, restoring "'laissez-faire' competition on a global basis as nation states compete with one another for investment," promoting a new international division of labour, and inevitably increasing global tensions which fuel "the escalating nuclear arms race and the increasing militarization of national economies (especially in the Third World)" (ERSO, 421).

The Economic Crisis Is a Moral Crisis
The economic crisis in Canada, then, can be seen in this context, as a manifestation of these shifts in the world economy: "Nation states like Canada (and its provinces) are being compelled to restructure their economies for the'tough new world of competition'" (ERSO, 421).

Economic strategies of government and business elites are to be understood in this context.

In other words, "an industrial future is already planned by governments and corporations" (EREC, 406). "As recent economic policy statements reveal, the primary objective is to restore profitability and competitiveness in certain Canadian industries and provide more favourable conditions for private investment in the country. The private sector is to be the'engine' for economic recovery" (EREC, 404; cf. ERSO, 421). But the policies associated with such strategies are problematic, because stimulating a more favourable climate for private investments requires "reduced labour costs and lower taxes . . . if countries are to remain competitive. And as a result, most governments are introducing austerity measures, such as wage restraint programs, cutbacks in social services and other reductions in social spending in order to attract more private investment" (EREC, 403).

This means, the bishops point out, that "working people, the unemployed, young people and those on fixed incomes are increasingly called upon to make the most sacrifice for economic recovery" (EREC, 404). And "yet there are no clear reasons to believe that working people will ever really benefit from these and other sacrifices they are called to make" (EREC, 405). For these strategies, energy—megaprojects for example—"generally end up producing few permanent jobs while adding to a large national debt" (EREC, 405).

In general what these strategies promise is the adoption of monetarist policies reflected in major cut-backs in government social spending, literally the dismantling of the social welfare apparatus that gradually was put in place following World War II; increasing concentration of job producing industries in the major metropolitan centres, aggravating regional disparities; growing disparities between classes, due in part to increases in personal income taxes and reductions in corporate taxes; the increasing marginalization of many people from the new high technology workplace, resulting in downward social mobility for significant numbers even in the middle class; intensified concentration of power in the hands of a small number of large corporations, and the forcing out of the market of many small businesses and producers, reflected in farm bankruptcies, plant shutdowns, and small business closures; the increasing export orientation of the Canadian economy, with the resulting reduction of capacity to produce for the basic needs of Canadians; lowered environmental standards or decreased monitoring of the environment; increasing social breakdown manifested in alcoholism, suicides, family breakdown, vandalism, crime, racism, and street violence (ERSO, 422-26).

In addition, the bishops see in these strategies advocated by government and business leaders a growing integration of Canada into the international arms economy, a retooling of Canadian industries for military production, and shifts in military policy, like involvement in Cruise missile testing, toward a more militaristic foreign policy (ERSO, 425).

These patterns mean that "there is a deepening moral disorder in our society" (ERSO, 426). Specifically, the bishops insisted that the economic crisis is a moral crisis because the strategies for recovery reveal values and sensibilities fundamentally at odds with core Christian values. For through the structural changes in the Canadian and the world economy "'capital' is being reasserted as the dominant organizing principle of economic life . . . . [T]here is a tendency for people to be treated as an impersonal force having little or no significance beyond their purpose in the system" (EREC, 403). In the bishops' judgment "this orientation directly contradicts the ethical principle that labour, not capital, must be given priority in the development of an economy based on justice." And in their view this inversion of values is manifested in the results of these policies: in this changing economic environment, "the renewed emphasis on the'survival of the fittest' as the supreme law of economics is likely to increase the domination of the weak by the strong, both at home and abroad" (EREC, 403).

In the bishops' view, "the fundamental challenge involves a combination of moral vision and political will" (ERSO, 426-27). It is not simply a question for them of managing the economy better in a new high-tech age, or of simply helping people to adjust. Rather, in their view the central problem of our times ". . . is a moral or ethical problem in the structural order of our economy and society . . . . [T]he basic social contradiction of our times is the structural domination of capital and technology over people, over labour, over communities. What is required is a radical inversion of these structural relationships. In other words, ways must be found for people to exercise more effective control over both capital and technology so that they may become more constructive instruments of creation by serving the basic needs of people and communities. This requires in turn that efforts be made to stimulate social imagination concerning alternative economic visions and models" (ERSO, 426-27).

A Christian Approach to Economic Issues

The bishops hope to contribute to the development of such an alternative vision, and to the political will to carry it forward. And so they articulate the sensibilities and commitments that have informed their critical analysis of Canadian economic development in a changing and conflictual world, a world which they hope will inform the articulation of an alternative development agenda in Canada.

First, they refer to the scriptural perspective on persons as made in the image of God, and thus having certain inalienable rights to life and to all that makes for a more fully human life, and having responsibility for being "co-creators of the Earth and stewards for the sake of present and future generations" (ERSO, 415). Second, they emphasize that the Earth is understood to be God's gift for present and future generations, and thus that the resources of the Earth are destined to serve equitably the needs of all people (ERSO, 416).

Third, following Pope Paul VI, they insist that models of development cannot be limited to mere economic growth, that we must see development as "integral, involving encompassing social, economic, cultural and spiritual needs of the whole person," and the community (ERSO, 416). Fourth, they refer to the priority of labour: "the basic rights of working people take priority over the maximization of profits and the accumulation of machines in an economic order" (ERSO, 416-17).

Fifth, the insist on the priority of the poor: "Jesus repeatedly identified with the plight of the poor and the outcasts of society, . . . [and] took a critical attitude towards the accumulation of wealth and power that comes through the exploitation of others." Accordingly, for them "the needs of the poor take priority over the wants of the rich" (ERSO, 417). Sixth, in their view, following Pope John Paul II, "the means of production should not be owned in opposition to human labour or owned for the sake of owning them . . . . The only title to their ownership is that they serve the basic needs of all people, especially human labour and the needs of the poor" (ERSO, 417).

Seventh, for the bishops "all peoples have rights to self-determination, to define their own future and to participate effectively in decisions affecting their lives." This means that they should have "an effective and meaningful role to play in social and economic planning regarding the use of capital and technology." Indeed, for them, "this kind of effective participation in these kinds of decision-making processes is a basic part of being human, . . . and essential for an integral model of development" (ERSO, 417-18).

Eighth, this principle points to the priority which must be given to development strategies which promote self-reliance. In other words, directing our energies toward developing local resources to serve basic human needs requires "that local communities identify their basic needs, assess their human and material resources and acquire communal control over the necessary means of production" (ERSO, 418).

Ninth, their emphasis on reasonable stewardship for all of creation points toward "sustainable models of development based on renewable as well as non-renewable resources" (ERSO, 418).

Tenth, they emphasize global solidarity. Because they are convinced that "the structural causes of poverty and oppression in the Third World for example are linked to the international economic order dominated by affluent and powerful nations states of the First World," they call us to "new forms of global solidarity—with and among working and non-working peoples—with and among the poor and oppressed peoples of the world—in the building of a new international economic order" (ERSO, 419).

Elements of an Alternative Economic Agenda
On the basis of these orienting sensibilities and commitments the bishops suggest elements of an alternative agenda. Clearly, what is required first of all, they insist, is a basic shift in values: "The goal of serving the human needs of all people in our society must take precedence over the maximization of profits and growth, and priority must be given to the dignity of human labour, not machines" (EREC, 405). They insist that the shift in values they call for requires a fundamentally different economic model that would place emphasis on socially useful forms of production; labour-intensive industries; the use of appropriate forms of technology; self-reliant models of economic development; community ownership and control of industries; new forms of worker management and ownership; and

greater use of renewable energy sources in industrial production (EREC, 406).

They call for a revision of the economic order as a whole, and for comprehensive planning, for renewed commitment to full employment with an emphasis on permanent and meaningful jobs, new patterns of work, and adequate personal or family income, more meaningful and effective ways of providing for basic social services, and more effective ways of redistributing wealth and power among both people and regions in this country (ERSO, 428-29).

Above all, they call for new efforts to empower the poor and the marginalized so that they play a more meaningful and effective role in shaping future development. In general they call for "more participatory and effective forms of economic planning," involving "a new approach to both centralized and decentralized planning…" (ERSO, 429).

In other words, the bishops' criticism of current corporate and government development strategies goes to the roots of the system; they call for fundamental changes in our economic life, a "radical inversion" of the structural principles that currently dominate our lives nationally and internationally (ERSO, 427).

A Pastoral Method
Finally, the Canadian bishops affirm that the Church has an important role to play in this process of economic and social renewal. They specifically identify the pastoral methodology which has informed the development of these documents and which they urge for local parishes and Christian communities. It involves five steps: (a) being present with and listening to the experiences of the poor, the marginalized, the oppressed in our society; (b) developing a critical analysis of the economic, political and social structures that cause human suffering; (c) making judgments in the light of gospel principles and the social teachings of the church concerning social values and priorities; (d) stimulating creative thought and action regarding alternative visions and models for social and economic development; and (e) acting in solidarity with popular groups in their struggles to transform economic, political and social structures that cause social and economic injustices (ERSO, 412-13).

The Revolution in Canadian Catholic Social Teaching
It is clear, I hope, that these two documents from the early 1980s represent shifts not only in the content of Canadian Catholic social teaching, but in every element of it—in the image of God which informs it, in the vision of the mission of the church teaching, in the overall logic and method which unites the various elements, in the authority they express, and in the ethical conclusions it points to. In this sense, they represent a different kind of social teaching.

The perspective presented in these two documents is much more comprehensive than anything presented earlier. It touches on a greater number of developments, and does so in conventional terms widely used in the social sciences and in public discussions of these issues. There is no space here to go into the adequacy of this perspective, though in my judgment this offered a more adequate analysis of some of the major forces and tendencies operating in Canadian society and the world in the 1980s, a more challenging and coherent sketch of an alternative development strategy informed by different values, grounded in a much sounder, biblically-based theology centering on solidarity with the oppressed. In my view, these documents represent historic advances in Catholic social teaching.

For our purposes here, though, it is important to note the coherent character of this teaching; the various parts fit together more smoothly than the parts of the earlier documents do, and the whole perspective has a certain clear logic relating the parts, in terms of the analysis of what is wrong, in the projection of a vision of an alternative future, in the strategy for promoting this vision, in the image of God, and in the mission of the church in this process.

In the major features of the perspective reflected in the earlier documents, the broad horizon was of positive change, of progress. Most importantly, there were no fundamental contradictions internal to this process of development. There were ambiguities but not fundamental contradictions. This horizon was defined in terms of private property on the one hand and the perceived communist threat on the other. The vision was of organic social harmony, with different groups finding ways to work together, to collaborate harmoniously. In what could be called a reformed capitalism, there was a major role for unions to play, but the vision also sanctified private property and by implication the rights and power associated with the particular forms of this institution in advanced capitalist society, and it encouraged joint associations for workers and managers to get together to talk about things. It envisioned the state as neutral, equally concerned about the welfare of all in society, its role to be setting the stage for all of that to happen; the image is of a moderately active state, but not one impinging on the rights and prerogatives of private property or intermediary associations.

Strategy in this earlier set of documents had a heavy focus on unions, and the writings encouraged the expansion of unions, within the framework of cross-class collaboration. Unions and employees in general would have to work together. The operating assumption is the assertion was that there were not—indeed could not be—any fundamental conflicts of interest.

The documents promoted some reforms: cooperatives, credit unions and social welfare policies. But these did not play a major role in the agenda elaborated there.

The ethical methodology on the role of the church in these statements centres on the notion that the church has the answers. There really is little coherent methodology, or framework, for advancing social teaching, an issue I will return to below. And the church itself is seen as above the fray, as serving all people equally.

By way of contrast, in the 1980s the church's documents call attention to fundamental contradictions between capital and labour within nations and in the functioning of the world economy as a whole. Now the contradictions are no longer between one more or less self-contained system, which is good, and another, communism, which is bad. Rather, they are within the Canadian system, with capital on the one side, and on the other side the workers and those speaking on behalf of local communities and of the country as a whole, of the poor abroad, and of the earth. Communism has virtually disappeared as a threat.

This recognition leads to a call for profound changes, radical changes centering on broad participation in economic decision-making, through cooperatives and enterprises owned and controlled by workers and the community, and through decentralized forms of production and decision-making. It calls for ecologically sustainable forms of technology, self reliance and global solidarity, all of which will contribute to justice and peace.

The strategy for pursuing these goals, while not elaborated in detail, suggests criteria and guidelines consistent with these goals. It centres on solidarity of and with the poor, which is not an exclusive option, since all are called—the poor themselves, along with middle class people and the rich—as the only real path to justice and peace. And it emphasizes local initiatives and popular movements.

Clearly, these documents define the role of the church in terms of the option for the poor and oppressed, of solidarity with them, in responding to their suffering and in helping their voices to be heard, and in accompanying them in their struggles to have a say in the halls of decision-making power.

The sense of authority has shifted profoundly too, from a church whose leadership speaks already complete, divinely ordained truths which people have only to heed for the solutions to all our problems, to a pilgrim church in which authority is rooted in the capacity to hear the victims, and to speak clearly and prophetically in the spirit of Jesus about our faith and our ethics and the mission of the church in our own confused and conflictual historical context.

On Hearing the Word and Doing the Word

In closing it is important to return to the issue of the relation between official teaching and institutional practice, for I suggest that this issue has itself become crucial in the future development of social teaching.

These major characteristics of Catholic social teaching through the 1950s reflected the historical judgments that this agenda could be best advanced in a capitalist context by such means as appealing broadly to the members of both classes, workers and capitalists; blessing the foundations of this system in the private ownership of the means of production; denying the possibility of class conflict and urging cross class-collaboration; blessing unions and holding out the possibility of modest reforms in the functioning of this system, together with some space for alternative forms of economic organization such as cooperatives; and in the context of what had become a capitalist world system defined and organized in opposition to the alleged worldwide communist threat, condemning the radical opponents of capitalism, and aligning with the supporters of this system in the worldwide crusade in "defense" of it.

There was a certain kind of historical logic to this set of teachings in its context. But the ambiguities among them, which I pointed to above, and the incomplete character of these teachings regarding specific issues in specific contexts, inevitably resulted in great space for a variety of "Catholic" responses.

Moreover, even apart from the character and the substance of the teachings themselves, there was the simple fact that relatively little attention was paid in the church as a whole to the social teaching documents. There are few sermons on these documents in local churches. These teachings played a small part in seminary training. And they played little part in the policy decisions of institutional officials concerning the ongoing business of the institutions they manage.

Also, it is important to note that the conference of bishops, in whose name these documents have been promulgated, has had no power locally in the church. So what the bishops decide in Ottawa does not automatically trickle down to the local diocese. That depends on the interests, commitments and sensibilities of local officials. And in some cases, such as Cardinal Carter's reaction upon the publication of "Ethical Reflections," reactions have included open, public hostility, to "official" teaching, and public denunciation of it.

On the other hand, however, I would like to suggest that the documents of the 1970s and 1980s reflect the emergence of a different kind of social teaching.

In particular, they have reflected the experience of a significant part of the church, and in turn they have had an enormous impact on numerous social action groups across the country. This includes Roman Catholic groups like the Canadian Catholic Organization for Development and Peace, and ecumenical groups like the interchurch social justice projects, and many secular groups, in particular labour unions. These have been the groups in which the sensibilities and values and commitments reflected in these documents have been fostered and nurtured over the years. In other words, these documents reflect a sort of percolating-up phenomenon. This experiential basis of commitment and concern has given the bishops who listen the confidence that as they sit down with these documents, they are not alone and crazy in speaking prophetically.

These documents also have the enormous benefit of validating the work of these groups, legitimating and supporting them, inspiring them and challenging them. So I suggest that this process reflects something like the pastoral circle that the bishops talk about as their methodology; it actually has been visibly operative in the church in these decades. The commitments and concerns symbolized by these documents have made a difference in the lives of many individuals and organizations, in the church, and in Canadian society generally.

In theological terms, it is clear that these documents resonate deeply with the spirit of the Bible as it has been rediscovered by Christians involved in the various liberation movements in Canada and around the world, which is being articulated in Latin American and other Third World liberation theologies, feminist theology, black theology, and others. And as such these documents have been part of the profound theological and pastoral renewal underway in the church in the last twenty-five years, contributing to the emergence of a different kind of church, with a different mission and relation to the world, and a different kind of authority.

But precisely because they have made a difference, there has been a backlash against them. In Canada organizations like the Business Council on National Issues have enabled corporate leaders and their allies to regain the initiative in defining national issues, articulating alternatives for the future, and in choosing among them (cf. Langille 1987, 41-85). We are witnessing corporate and government attacks on the capacity of the government to manage in the interests of the common good. We are hearing calls to cut back on the welfare state and on the capacity to influence the development of the economy, to align Canadian foreign policy ever more closely with U.S. foreign policy, and in general to open Canada to more U.S. cultural, political and economic influence. This agenda is being promoted in direct opposition to the concerns of the progressive groups supported by many church social justice activists and in which church-sponsored organizations have often played a significant part.

This backlash has also exaggerated certain gaps, problems and weaknesses in the work of progressive social justice groups in the last twenty-five years, including church groups. There was a certain optimism about the time-line for change, a tendency to assume that significant change could occur quickly and relatively painlessly. In general, government policy seemed to be the logical target of pressures for change, and there seemed to be room for such changes. But this focus contributed to an emphasis on research, writing briefs and mobilizing public pressure on government around specific issues. This was "successful" in many cases, but detracted attention from questions concerning more basic and long-term changes, and from the task of broad public "education" concerning the nature of the problems and the hopes for change, at the very time when elites were mobilizing their resources to reassert their own version of a comprehensive, long-term agenda.

Moreover, there was a tendency to form groups to address particular specific "issues," like refugee or human rights issues, and to neglect the interrelations among them, in terms of the theoretical frameworks for analyzing issues, of imagining alternatives, and mobilizing wider constituencies in a movement supporting this agenda. There were no centres for the cross-fertilization of the experiences of different groups of oppressed peoples and those in solidarity with them, for identifying the lessons learned in their struggles, for articulating common interests, for nurturing solidarity across class, racial, ethnic, gender and geographical lines which historically have divided people. Indeed, there was often significant competition among different groups, each competing with the others for attention and support.

Particularly in the Catholic church there has been a strange schizophrenia in splitting "women's" issues off from social justice issues, as if women's issues were not social, and as if understanding them were not essential to understanding the character of the overall system and of our hope to transform it (cf. Kappler 1990).

Other major issues, like racism as a general feature of Canadian society and of the world system, and ecology, have so far received too little attention.

With a few happy exceptions there has been too little emphasis on educating and mobilizing people in the pews concerning these issues and the need to respond. There has been a tendency toward institutionalizing social justice activity in the churches in the hands of a few who define the issues, decide on the appropriate response, and generally manage the strategy of the churches in this regard. The result has been a narrow base of informed interest at a time when shrinking budgets and stronger, better equipped and situated opponents are promoting their own drastic transformation of this work. This leaves churches far more vulnerable than they otherwise deserve to be in terms of growing consciousness about the issues and broad support that exists for more critical perspectives and, potentially, more far-reaching transformations.

In this connection, social justice activity within the churches has proceeded with little emphasis on theological reflection. The operating assumption seems to have been that injustice and the struggles to overcome it are not especially significant theological matters, that they do not challenge the church in any way, that social justice is just one more agenda item to be placed alongside many other important items on the very full plate of the churches. There have been virtually no resources, personnel, time, space, funds, devoted to promoting theological reflection on the meaning of these struggles for the victims, for those in solidarity with them, and for the churches. This means, in the context of reinvigorated conservative and born-again voices in theology, that the capacity to ground this agenda in the discourse of the church is seriously weakened.

Of course, there has been growing opposition too within the church, specifically in the Vatican, against feminist and Latin American liberation theologies, and generally against all critics of capitalism and against every form of questioning about hierarchical authority. This shift has cast a harsh light on problems and weaknesses in church social justice groups.

Not surprisingly, then, in this climate increasingly hostile to any criticisms of the fundamental features of life within this now global system, and to hopes for a different future, many bishops and other supporters of church social justice activities of the last twenty years are losing interest. The issues seem in many cases more complex, the alternatives less obvious, the hope for change more distant, the cost of criticizing higher.

Thus, as we enter the last decade of the twentieth century, we seem to be already in the midst of yet another major shift in the social context and in the key factors which shape Canadian Catholic social teaching. In particular, in the growing public consciousness around a variety of issues there is much evidence that the irruptions of the poor and oppressed in the last twenty-five years, and of the organizations in solidarity with them, including the interchurch social justice coalitions, have made a profound impact. In this sense, I am convinced, the stage is set for a new turn in Catholic social teaching and, more importantly, practice. This time, however, the thrust of prophetic teaching must include the church itself, in its internal organization and functioning, if it is to carry any authority.

Many will resist this step, of course. But it resonates deeply with the emphasis on practice in the biblical parables of the Last Judgment and the Good Samaritan, with the teaching of Israelite prophets and of Jesus, and with the spirit of the social practices of many Israelite and early Christian communities. Only such a step offers any hope of renewing our faith and the churches, and of addressing the problems confronting humanity today.

For clearly the social and ecological crises at the close of the twentieth century raise the most basic questions about the future of life on earth for millions of the world's poor, and ultimately for all. These crises call into question easy proclamations of Christian hope for the fullness of life, and faith in the God who loves all.

The challenge, in a conflictual and divided world, is not simply to proclaim such faith, but to witness concretely, individually and as the church, to this faith and hope in promoting effective forms of solidarity among and with oppressed peoples, and with the earth itself. Everything in the heavens and on earth is at stake in our responses to this challenge.

6. The Public Pieties
of Canadian Presbyterians

Brian J. Fraser

In 1869 Robert Burns assured delegates to the General Assembly of the Free Church of Scotland that "the Headship of Christ over the nations" was the primary principle that guided Canadian Presbyterians in their faith and its social application. Burns, by this time retired from the Chair of Church History and Christian Evidences at Knox College in Toronto, went on to tell his Scottish listeners that Presbyterians in Canada were not satisfied to interpret this principle as "a general and vague idea of certain Christian influences to be diffused over the whole masses." Rather, they were quite specific in their insistence that "nations as such, and the rulers of this world in their legislative and executive capacity, are bound to act under the laws of Christ, and to give their influence in helping the cause of Christ" (Burns 1872, 459-60; see also Bridgman 1976, 104-108). Burns acknowledged that within the Canadian church there was considerable latitude of opinion on the way in which this belief was applied in the social and political life of the new dominion, but the principle itself was a foremost tenet of faith.

Robert Burns' remarks provide a useful framework for this brief overview of the public pieties of Canadian Presbyterians. They identify the common thread running through the tapestry of the Presbyterian involvement in and contribution to Canadian political culture—the principle of the Lordship of Christ over the nation.

Further, the latitude of opinion noted by Burns continued throughout the following century as changing cultural contexts called for changing interpretations of the application of the principle.

By piety I mean basic orientation. The definition has been taken from the work of Kenneth Burke. He describes two elements of piety. The first is a yearning to conform to the source of one's being and the second is a sense of what properly goes with what (Burke 1984, 69-79). In relation to the subject at hand, Presbyterians have sought in their public presence to confess that Christ is Lord of all, and that devotion and loyalty to him requires that they conform to his will in all their public activity. The way the church interpreted and attempted to express that confession has altered, however, as the church's understanding of its mission in the world has changed. Three public pieties have dominated the social theology of Canadian Presbyterians.

From the 1820s until the 1890s, Evangelical Conservatism was the basic stance. It focused its attention on God's moral government of the world and the need for nations as well as individuals to conform to God's order. Evangelical Liberalism dominated from the 1890s until the 1920s. It held a more evolutionary and progressive view of God's moral government of history in which states were seen to have their own moral personalities that shaped the character of their citizens and contributed to the moral and social improvement of the world neighbourhood. From the 1920s until the 1960s, the attitudes of Canadian Presbyterians were shaped primarily by Neo-orthodoxy. Western culture had proven untrustworthy as a bearer of God's moral and social purpose, and the church must seek faithfully and courageously to proclaim the unique power of the gospel to a fallen world. These three pieties offer significantly different ways of conforming to Christ's Lordship and of understanding what properly goes with what in the relationships of Christianity and culture.

This paper does not undertake a detailed survey or analysis of the various ways and institutions through which Presbyterians have undertaken their duties as individual and corporate citizens. These is an increasing number of monographs and papers dealing with the practice of public theology among Canadian Presbyterians (Grant 1988; Westfall 1989; Moir 1975; Cook 1985; Fraser 1988). A compilation of current statements and recommendations for actions approved by the Presbyterian Church in Canada is also available (Horst 1988).

Evangelical Conservatism

Central to the evangelical creed that guided Canadian Presbyterians throughout most of the nineteenth century was the doctrine of God's moral government of the world. This belief is often overlooked in discussions of evangelicalism that focus on individual sin, conversion, and sanctification, but it was a foundational element in nineteenth-century Presbyterian evangelical piety (Vaudry 1985, 170; 1989). The individual was always seen as part of a providential order ruled by God. The internal order of the individual's character had its parallel in the external order of God's universe. Both were to be governed by God's righteous purpose revealed plainly in the Scriptures. The piety of Evangelical Conservatism was best articulated by the Free Church Presbyterians in Canada. They formed the largest branch of Presbyterianism and were the dominant influence in the creation of a national denomination in 1875.

Through the 1840s and the 1850s the political and economic debates within British North America focused on the nature of the nation being born and the kind of citizenship needed to ensure progress. Presbyterians were central figures in those discussions. Their public piety supported the development of liberal democratic political institutions and the unfettered expansion of commercial and economic opportunities. In the public realm, the prime representatives of this public piety were the father-and-son team of journalists, Peter and George Brown (Moir 1980, 39-46), and the politician Oliver Mowat (Evans 1980, 47-56). Their collective careers spanned the last sixty years of the nineteenth century.

The Browns began their Canadian careers with the *Banner*, a newspaper that advocated the cause of the Free Church in the early 1840s and was closely tied to Grit and Liberal politics, while Mowat wrote several religious tracts while Liberal Premier of Ontario from 1872 to 1896. The *Banner's* masthead, "Righteousness Exalteth a Nation," expressed the conviction held by these men and their fellow Presbyterians that nations were responsible to God for the conduct of their affairs, that God blessed obedient nations and punished those who were disobedient, and that Christians had a divine right and duty to articulate the grand principles that ought to guide the citizenry.

The Liberal Party was the political party with which most Free Churchmen aligned themselves throughout the nineteenth century.

That party was seen as the best vehicle of the values of liberal bourgeois democracy—freedom, participation, and prosperity. Parallel values were held in relation to ecclesiastical affairs. The ideal was seen to be a free church in a free society. Church and society were separate spheres, but both were subject to the same Lord and therefore the same principies of order and righteousness.

Writing in the *Canadian Christian Monthly* in 1878, J. Cameron described the four principles of the public piety of Evangelical Conservatism: honour all humanity; love all people; fear God; and honour the king. These were the central values of good citizenship and their practice would ensure, in his mind, a "progressive, prosperous, and permanent commonwealth" (Cameron 1878, 1-9).

The first principle was honour for all human beings as creatures of the one God. In Cameron's mind, this attitude lay at the heart of civic life. There must be "a law of social comity, a common agreement to respect natural rights, or else our marketplaces, our municipal councils, our parliaments will be one sad, unceasing scene of fratricidal strife" (Cameron 1878, 3). Cameron saw this law as central to Canada's destiny as a righteous Christian nation:

> The principle of mutual forbearance and good will, which has heretofore guided the inhabitants of this Dominion, has greatly contributed to the general benefit, by securing those rights without which citizenship ceases to be a blessing, and cementing more firmly the bonds of political union within which all are striving to work out their common destiny (Cameron 1878, 4).

The rights of citizens were grounded, not in the consent of the governed, nor in the will of the majority, nor in some social contract, but in the divine law for all of God's creatures.

The second principle was love for all humanity based on their common origin in Adam and in God. This attitude was strengthened by the common tie forged through the newness of life in Christ. Love of family, state, and God were an inseparable whole. As a result:

> The Christian is the highest style of man, and therefore the best patriot; and if there is in our day and on this continent, as we fear there is, a loosening of the ties that bind men unselfishly to the State, it is because there is going on underneath, a silent loosen-

ing of the ties that bind men to Christ and His Church (Cameron 1878, 5).

An evangelical church, argued Cameron, was the nursery of a free state. "In proportion," he wrote, "that church life is deep, real, and intense, in that proportion will public life be lofty, uncorrupt, and patriotic" (Cameron 1878, 5). Cameron reminded his readers that the Huguenots in France, the founders of the Dutch Republic, the Covenanters in Scotland, and the Puritans in England had taught the church "to know, love, maintain, and defend the freedom they have in civil form transmitted to their posterity" (Cameron 1878, 5).

It was this love for all of humanity, unified as sinners and potentially saved in Christ, that led most Presbyterians in Canada to take a strong anti-slavery stance prior to and during the Civil War in the United States. Michael Willis, Principal of Knox College in Toronto from 1857 to 1870, said that, for an evangelical Christian, slavery was a system that "intercepts the light of Heaven's saving truth from a portion of God's rational offspring; and annihilates and dissolves relationships which the law of Christ and of nature has made inviolate" (quoted in Nicholson 1980, 27-28). Willis was the president of the Anti-Slavery Society of Canada, an organization that existed from 1851 until the abolition of slavery in the United States in 1863. George Brown and Oliver Mowat sat on its executive. An extended theological essay on slavery and social Darwinism was written in 1860 by William McLaren, then minister at John Street Presbyterian Church in Belleville and later Professor of Systematic Theology at Knox College.

The third, and chief, principle in Cameron's public piety was fear of God. Such fear, and the respect for the law of God that flowed from it, was at the heart of the English constitution and set Canada clearly apart from the United States, whose constitution was not based on the Bible. Cameron cites American church leaders who lament the fact that their constitution does not specifically assert the claims of God over the nation, leading to the lowering of standards of public morality and the spread of corruption in public office.

Michael Willis, in an address at the close of the session at Knox College in 1860, thanked God that British North America "still holds Scripture as the basis of its laws." As a result, he said:

. . . that the spiritual and secular departments of society are equally under law to Him who is both Head of the church, and King of nations, surely yields the corollary that they should regard themselves as standing on no antagonistic terms; that each, instead of professing neutrality or indifference, should take a positive interest in the objects of the other. . . . The separation of religion from politics is a plausible cry; but a non-recognition of God and His law in the civil framework of any community leaves men to be governed by an uncertain, conventional, it may be tyrannical, will (1873, 376-77).

For nineteenth century Canadian Presbyterians, civic duty was an essential part of their evangelical faith.

The final principle was honour for the office of the king, meaning essentially reverence for law. While the Bible did not commit human beings to any particular form of civil government, it did require obedience to the civil magistrate unless the laws of the country were "manifestly contrary to God's will." Cameron did allow for the possibility of rebellion, but only when all legal and peaceful means of change had proved futile.

The sense of God's providential moral governance and human accountability to it pervaded Presbyterian political thought throughout the nineteenth century. God's moral governance of the world was as essential an element of the evangelical world view as sin, redemption, and conversion. None of these elements were seen solely in terms of the individual. All were considered to have social consequences. It was the public responsibility of the Christian church, therefore, to make known the laws of God and exhort the citizenry to conform to the principles that would guide the nation to righteousness.

The public piety of Evangelical Conservatism found its world view best expressed the philosophical school of Scottish Common Sense Realism (McKillop 1979; Armour and Trott 1981). When read through the eyes of evangelical churchmen, like Thomas Chalmers and William Cunningham in Scotland and Charles and A. A. Hodge in the United States, this philosophical system supported the emphasis on a clear, comprehensible, and compatible ordering of nature, history, personal character, and revelation by the sovereign God and the ability of human reason to understand it through the inductive method of Bacon (Rice 1971, 23-46; Ahlstrom 1955, 57-72; Noll 1983). It formed the basic world view that defined how these various elements of God's ordered creation fit together for the common good (Vaudry 1989, 59-62). Canadian Presbyterians had no hesitation appropriating the foundational work done by their Scottish and American colleagues. Their own task was to reiterate the principles and apply them to the developing Canadian nation.

The period from the 1820s to the 1890s in Canadian social, political, and cultural development was one of significant, yet predictable, change. It was plausible for Presbyterians to see such changes as the establishment of democratic institutions, the expansion of commerce, and the increase in territory and population as divine rewards for faithful conformity to the law of God. The Canadian commonwealth still had many problems, but the agencies through which citizens of good Christian character could solve them—the family, the school, the commercial enterprises, the legislatures, voluntary societies for social benevolence, and the churches—were in place. The nature and pace of change did not appear to threaten the basic world view they held.

Evangelical Liberalism
The events that shaped Canada between the 1890s and the 1920s changed that perception. As Ramsay Cook and Craig Brown argue in their survey of this period, *Canada 1896-1921: A Nation Transformed*, the Canada of the 1920s was not simply a bigger and better version of the Canada of the 1890s. It was new in quality and spirit. The immigration of more than two million people, the economic, social, and political development of Western Canada, industrial and urban growth concentrated in central Canada, and regional, ethnic, religious, and class tensions transformed the country within. Participation in World War I heightened and quickened many of these changes, but also brought Canada into a new relationship with the rest of the world (Cook and Brown 1974, 1-6).

These changes did not follow the pattern expected by the earlier generation of Evangelical Conservatives. They had been confident that the values of religious, political, and personal freedom that were seen to be advancing throughout the nineteenth century in Canada would continue and eventually triumph in the creation of a Christian commonwealth. Their Evangelical Liberal heirs at the turn of the twentieth century retained their confidence in God's governance and Christ's lordship, but argued that a different world view involving a different understanding of how the Christian faith shaped the world was needed to ensure that the values be preserved and propagated in the face of the challenges of rapid cultural change.

Whereas the Evangelical Conservatives saw themselves called to establish and conserve the righteous order God had ordained and revealed, the Evangelical Liberals saw themselves called to be the agents of God's providential progress as God's will unfolded itself in history. For the Evangelical Conservatives, a static revelation set the ideal to which history must conform. For the Evangelical Liberals, a progressive history was the vehicle through which revelation evolved. For both, God's moral governance was paramount, but their respective understandings of God's nature and manner were very different.

In the public realm, politicians such as William Lyon Mackenzie King and newspaper editors such as James A. Macdonald of the Toronto *Globe* represented a collectivist liberal political stance grounded in an Evangelical Liberal theological perspective. Both King and Macdonald found the intellectual rigor and rigidity of the Evangelical Conservatism in which they were raised inadequate as a means of addressing the gospel to contemporary Canadian society. Both were influenced in the formative stages of their higher education by the philosophical world view of British Idealism, with its critique of Baconian rationality and utilitarian individualism. Both were involved intimately in Liberal politics and continued to see that party as the best political institution for accomplishing the progressive moral and social reforms they were convinced would advance civil liberty and moral righteousness in the urban and industrial Canada that was emerging in the early twentieth century.

The social philosophy of British Idealism broke with earlier forms of political liberalism over first principles. Empiricism, utilitarianism, and realism were not considered adequate principles upon which to build a free and united society. Thomas B. Kilpatrick was a leading spokesman for the public piety of Evangelical Liberalism in Canada (Fraser 1988, 23-43). He absorbed his evangelical piety from his father and the crusades of Dwight L. Moody, and his idealist worldview from Edward and John Caird in Glasgow. He brought it to his teaching responsibilities at Manitoba College in Winnipeg and Knox College and Emmanuel College in Toronto from the late 1890s until his death in 1933.

Kilpatrick argued that the political liberalism of the early nineteenth century, grounded as it was in an inductive appeal to reality as it existed, proved a powerful force in dismantling the old social order based on privilege and authoritarianism. It was powerless, however, to construct a new social order that would preserve and extend the central liberal values of freedom and harmony in the collective society emerging at the end of the nineteenth century.

The first principles necessary to motivate humanity to participate in the endeavour of social construction were to be found in Kant and Hegel. Kant restored the primacy of mind over matter and Hegel extended the governing principle of mind organizing matter from nature to history. Every phase of the world's history is seen as a manifestation of one self-conscious intelligence. As an evangelical Christian, Kilpatrick found little trouble in identifying this guiding force with the mind of God revealed in the person of Jesus Christ. Human goodness came through salvation and consisted of becoming aware of the mind of Christ and identifying oneself with it through knowledge and morality.

Awareness and identification with the mind of Christ was a calling not only for individuals, but for nations and the world community as a whole. Each nation had its own collective personality. Its Christian duty was to develop that personality to its highest moral potential. The primary vehicle for this work was the education of the collective conscience. The guiding principle was the conviction that God's Spirit was truly manifest in history and revealed herself to pious souls as the source of life, social morality, and human progress. The purpose of such collective character development was to contribute to the wellbeing of the global neighbourhood.

John Watson, professor of philosophy at Queen's University in Kingston, Ontario, and identified along with Kilpatrick by Edward Caird as one of his best students, summarized this view when he argued that the ideal Christian life was broad enough to embrace all the elements that constituted the complex spirit of the modern world:

> Every advance in science is the preparation for a fuller and clearer conception of God; every improvement in the organization of society is a further development of that community of free beings by which the ideal of the organic unity of humanity is in process of realization; every advance in the artistic interpretation of the world helps to individualise the idea of the organic unity by which all things are bound together.

Watson and Kilpatrick both found in Jesus' teachings a comprehensive ideal of "the full development of the full means by which the full perfection of humanity is realised." Christian culture, for them, included the Greek ideal of clear thought and love of beauty, the Jewish ideal of righteousness, the Roman ideal of law and order, and the Teutonic ideal of freedom, all of them harmonized by the divine spirit of love to God and humanity (Watson 1897, 215-16; Kilpatrick 1899, 7-37). While Watson focused on the philosophical ideas of Jesus, Kilpatrick claimed that the mind of God was displayed most clearly in Christian moral character. The morality presented in the New Testament was "a type absolutely new in the moral history of the race, of unique and commanding excellence." It incorporated and transcended all other forms of virtue. When, Kilpatrick wrote:

> . . . [We] have entered most fully into the grandeur and beauty presented in Greek sage, Roman soldier or statesman, Hebrew psalmist or prophet, we pass to the New Testament with the distinct conviction that here we have a type congruous indeed with the others, and gathering into itself their excellences, yet supreme in its own loveliness, attracting to itself as they never did the admiration and loyalty of heart and intellect, perpetuated as they never were, nor could have been, in the lives and deaths, not of a select few, but of unnumbered multitudes (Kilpatrick 1899, 4).

Kilpatrick and his colleagues in moral and social reform endeavours were convinced that the cutting edge of the progress of this morality that lay at the heart of Christian culture and civilization was to be found in Canada.

Of central importance to the realization of Christian social ideals was the constructive role assigned to the state in their thought. Government constituted the organized form of the nation's moral and social personality. It served an active and ameliorative function in relationship to its citizens. Its primary focus was no longer the protection of rights, for these were seen to be but preliminary conditions for true human progress. Rather, it had the responsibility to provide the conditions, in Kilpatrick's words, under which "a free, intelligent, and moral life can alone be lived" (Kilpatrick 1899, 247).

Freedom was not simply the existence of free institutions, of rights, or of immunity from interference, but rather the full and better life of social harmony into which humanity grew, once these preliminary developments opened the way. As rational and moral beings, humanity had the capacity to transcend its environments and shape them in conformity with the mind of Christ. Collective action by the state, itself the primary expression of the social organism, was an essential means of creating the conditions for the full development of citizenship in a moral community. "In the service of the State," Kilpatrick claimed, "men will be lifted out of themselves, inspired with motives that are not selfish, and taught to find their highest individual advantage in the furtherance of the public weal" (Kilpatrick 1899, 266). True freedom was realized through the principles of self-sacrifice and devotion to the common good.

The church was essential to the realization of these principles. As the social organism through which God worked most intentionally, it had a crucial role to play in public affairs as the moral conscience of the nation. In "The New State and the New Church," an address delivered at the Social Service Congress in Ottawa in 1914, C.W. Gordon offered an Evangelical Liberal critique of the failure of the church in its public responsibility.

> The Church has failed to conceive itself as that by which God is mediated to the world, as the almoner of God's infinite love and mercy to man. The Church has too often devoted its energies to the upbuilding of itself not in love, but in power, in influence, in numbers, in wealth. The Church has too often been more concerned for the correctness of its creed than for the Christliness of its conduct. The Church has too often been possessed of a passion for power rather than by a passion for men, all of which is a misrepresentation of, rather than a witness to, the Father infinite in love and mercy; so that men have gone soul-starving for God and for the love and sympathy of Brotherhood, which is the true mediation of God to man (Gordon 1914, 197; Thompson and Thompson 1972; Fraser 1987).

The church, Kilpatrick stated, is "the crown and consummation of all the organic relations which link men together in moral and spiritual fellowship." Without it, society would be in perpetual danger of falling back into the "anarchy of mere selfishness" (Kilpatrick 1899, 269).

The source of goodness for the Evangelical Liberals was not so much obedience to the law of God as loyalty to the character of Christ. Christ was the source of Christian character as Moral Teacher, as Example and Standard, and as Redeemer. His power lay in the fact that humans experience him, as did the disciples following the resurrection, not as mere memory or doctrine or precept, but as "a living Person, with whom it was possible to have real fellowship" (Kilpatrick 1899, 7). Christian character was inspired by God's deed of love in Christ that produced the answering love of humanity.

A character modelled on Law is painful, laborious, slow. Christian character acts with the precision and freedom of an instinct. . . . Christian character is the harmony of God's universe and its keynote is this, "He loved me and gave Himself for me." Love in man evoked by and answering to Love in God is the inspiration of life for man. Against it there is no law (Kilpatrick 1899, 37).

The Evangelical Liberals saw themselves progressing beyond a faith grounded in a stern God known through a revelation of law and doctrine that demanded obedience. They were convinced that they had reached a higher conception of God's mind and purpose in their understanding of Jesus Christ as the perfect model of God's redeeming love. Christ invited humanity to participate in the evolutionary construction of a harmonious, cooperative world community based on self-sacrifice and service.

The Evangelical Liberals saw their vision of Christian civilization as standing in essential continuity with that of their Evangelical Conservative forerunners. They sought to provide a new apologetic for the old gospel based on a more accurate understanding of what properly goes with what in the world God was creating through human history. An effective apologetic in word and deed was essential if the immigrant populations were to be Christianized, the West was to be properly settled, the cities were to be civilized, and the tensions created by social changes were to be resolved. Evangelical Liberals were confident this would happen if their vision were implemented by the agencies of moral and social uplift and progress that existed in Canada—the family, the school, the government, the press, voluntary societies, and the church.

Neo-orthodoxy

World War I was a crucial watershed in the Presbyterian perception of Canadian culture. On the one hand, Presbyterians offered fervent support to the war effort, though not in as unquestioning a fashion as once thought (Fraser 1989, 125-43).

On the other hand, the collective experience of four years of mud, murder, and mayhem raised a serious question in the minds of many Presbyterians. Could the culture in which both Evangelical Conservatism and Evangelical Liberalism had placed such trust be seen any longer as the faithful bearer of Christian values and ideals? Neo-orthodoxy, as it developed among Canadian-Presbyterians over the next four decades, looked back to the war years as the beginning of a fundamental questioning of both forms of the cultural Christianity of the nineteenth century.

The seeds of the third public piety of Neo-orthodoxy can be seen sprouting from the ground of Evangelical Liberalism in the final years of the war. In 1917 T. B. Kilpatrick wrote a report on *The War and the Christian Church* for the General Assembly's Commission on the War and the Spiritual Life of the Church. He drew on the theology of P. T. Forsyth and James Denney, later seen to be forerunners of Neo-orthodoxy in Great Britain, to reemphasize the need of humanity for a divine redeemer. Much of Kilpatrick's earlier confidence in the power of Christian character to bring about the Christian commonwealth was chastened. He concluded:

> The Cross of our redemption was once reared on Calvary. The Cross of Christian sacrifice spreads its arms over the field of War itself. A Peace, without a Cross, would be a worse Hell than the War itself. God forbid that we should glory save in the Cross of our Lord Jesus Christ, by whom the world is crucified unto, and we unto the world (Gal. 6:14) (Kilpatrick 1917, 15).

Kilpatrick had always seen the Cross as an essential part of his evangelical theology, but during the war the objective atonement achieved through it came more to the fore than the moral example set by it.

In politics and journalism, there were no Presbyterians of the stature of the Browns and Mowat, or of Mackenzie King and Macdonald, from the 1920s to the 1960s. Mackenzie King did continue in politics as prime minister of Canada, but his earlier identification with progressive reform was replaced by a shrewd balancing of competing interests in Canadian politics and isolationism in international affairs.

The Presbyterian Church in Canada could well be described as isolationist during the first half of the period under consideration. The bitter and disruptive fight over church union among the Presbyterians in 1925 resulted in the creation of two branches of Presbyterianism, one within the United Church of Canada and one continuing as the Presbyterian Church in Canada. The leading Evangelical Liberals were the leaders of the movement for organic union among the Canadian churches, and another essay in this volume picks up their story from 1925. The only thing that united those that stayed out of union was their common resistance to a particular model of ecumenicity. Some, rooted in the theological stance of Evangelical Conservatism and influenced by the modernist-fundamentalist controversy in the United States, resisted in order to protect pure doctrine and polity. Others, admittedly a small minority, did not think the Basis of Union of the United Church of Canada sufficiently modern and liberal to provide an effective apologetic for Christianity in the modern scientific age. A significant majority were sympathetic to greater ecumenical cooperation, but not at the price of splitting the church. A fourth identifiable group began to recognize the need to reexamine the church's understanding of itself, its mission, and its work in the world in the light of the crisis in Western culture that followed the war (Farris, 1978, 95-124). From among this younger group of theologians, Walter W. Bryden emerged as the leading spokesman for Neo-orthodoxy (Vissers 1988, 39-103).

In Europe and later in the United States, the driving force behind this movement for theological and ecclesiastical reformation was the fear that a Christianity dominated by the thought-forms of a disintegrating culture could not survive and, even more, that a cultural religion could have no message of hope to a society that despaired of its powers to better the world. The dominant motifs of the movement were the crisis of humanity's natural powers and the discontinuity of the gospel and the cultural life of humanity (Gilkey 1958, 256-61). In Canada, an additional factor was the search for a theological identity among continuing Presbyterians in the aftermath of church union.

Walter Bryden understood the church to be the sole trustworthy institution through which the revelation of God could be known.

Unlike his conservative and liberal predecessors, he did not trust the various agencies of human culture to be faithful bearers of the gospel. In Bryden's theology, as John Vissers has pointed out:

> The church, as a creature of the judging-saving Word and as the fellowship of the Holy Spirit, and having itself known the judgement and mercy of God, lives out of this genuine knowledge of God in the world in its confessions, its unity in the gospel, its ministry of proclamation, and its relation to the social, economic, and political powers (Vissers 1988, 23).

Such knowledge had to be expressed in thought categories drawn from biblical theology rather than from human philosophical systems. The church stood over against culture as a creation of God to be God's agent in challenging the world with the truth of the gospel.

Bryden found both Evangelical Conservatism and Evangelical Liberalism theologically inadequate as expressions of Christianity. They were heretical in that they attempted to reduce the essential paradox and mystery of the gospel to human dimensions—dogma and doctrine in the case of conservatism and experience and ethics in the case of liberalism:

> In Orthodox circles, men have been enabled to obtrude a system of truths "to be believed," between themselves and God who is the Truth in Christ. In the Liberal circles, men have been permitted to find their religious satisfaction in the recognition and appropriation of certain impersonal ideals, of which they themselves are in last analysis the judges. In both cases, something to accept, or to emulate and achieve, has taken the place of the radically personal challenge by, and the personal reliance alone on, the living Saviour (Bryden 1940, 219).

The church confronted the world with its confession of faith that must be born of an eschatological vision of God. The contemporary example to which Bryden frequently referred was the Barmen Declaration of 1934 in which the Confessing Church in Germany made a bold declaration of the Lordship of Christ over the nations (McLelland 1980, 122).

The impact of this perspective among Canadian Presbyterians was seen in the Declaration of Faith Concerning Church and Nation adopted as a subordinate confessional standard by the Presbyterian Church in Canada in 1955. The initial drafting of this statement began in response to an overture from the Presbytery of Paris in 1939 that pointed out that the Bases of Union in 1861 and 1875 gave Presbyterians in Canada liberty of conscience on Chapter 23 of the Westminster Confession of Faith dealing with the relations of church and state. The effect, the sponsors of the overture concluded, was to prevent the church constitutionally from making any statements or taking any stands on matters such as war, poverty, oppression, and totalitarianism.

Arthur C. Cochrane, a student of Walter Bryden and a member of the Canadian Committee on Articles of Faith prior to going to the United States to teach, analyzed the Declaration in a Festschrift for Karl Barth. He saw the confessional statement as an indication of the influence of both Barth and Bryden on Canadian Presbyterians. Their influence was apparent in the christological doctrine of the state and in the insistence that the church was responsible for the purity of her doctrine and for her Confession of Faith.

Cochrane pointed out that the Declaration followed the Westminster divines and Calvin in the view that the origin of the state was of divine ordination and based upon God's providential government of the world. This stood in opposition to all theories that the origin of the state lay in nature, in fate, in history, or in a social contract of some kind, or in the nature of society. The state, therefore, was not the creature of humans or of natural forces. Its nature and justice could not be understood by natural reason, as claimed in the American and French constitutions. In the Canadian Declaration, Cochrane wrote:

> The State is conceived as being within and under the kingdom of the Triune God, that is, under the rule of Jesus Christ by whose incarnation, death, and resurrection "all things have been made subject to Him." God has established His kingdom over all powers in heaven and earth, and therefore over Church and State. . . . Jesus Christ is "both Head of the Church and Head of the Civil State." He has ordained the State "in His grace," that is, in the grace of His atoning death. Consequently the Declaration affirms that "the righteousness of God, which came to decisive triumph in the cross and resurrection of Christ, is the sole foundation of national justice." The State, no less than the

Church, has its origin in the death and resurrection of Christ (Cochrane 1956, 460-61).

The church, then, serves the state by doing the distinctive thing for which she was ordained, namely, confront the nation with Christ's judgment and grace in her preaching, sacraments, and discipline. The church has the responsibility to bear witness to Christ's justice, even to the extent of exhorting citizens to take up arms for the sake of the state.

Immediately following the adoption of the Declaration, the Presbyterian Church in Canada established a new Board of Evangelism and Social Action as the agency through which this theological mandate could be exercised. This body and its successors have often been criticized, both from within and without the denomination, for their focus on statements rather than on endorsing activism of various sorts. The reason, in part, is to be found in the understanding of the church's responsibility for the state expressed in the Declaration. The church is to proclaim to the state the will of God, confident that the state is a creature of divine providence, subject to the law of love, and under the lordship of Christ.

Another major emphasis of those informed by the public piety of Neo-orthodoxy was Christian education. It was seen as the means whereby the church nurtured the discipleship of those who would live in the world under the lordship of Christ. This could be done by no other agency than the church and became an important focus for those attempting to recover the church's sense of her divine call to proclaim the gospel in and for human history. Canadian Presbyterian James D. Smart, another student of Walter Bryden, spent most of his career in the United States developing Christian education materials and teaching Old Testament at Union Seminary in New York. His writings on the evangelical uniqueness of the teaching ministry of the church had a formative influence on Canadian Presbyterians in the 1940s and the 1950s (Smart 1954; see also Glen 1960).

Those who understood the relation of Christianity and culture from a Neo-orthodox perspective were suspicious of the ability of any cultural agencies, be they families, schools, the press, or voluntary societies, to confront humanity with the judging/saving Word that was Jesus Christ. This task belonged uniquely to the church. The focus of their efforts, therefore, was on the internal life of the church in an attempt to render its witness to the world faithful and courageous.

Since the 1960s no single public piety has been as dominant as these three were in their respective periods. All three are still held by wings of the Presbyterian Church in Canada, but they have lost the coherence and appropriateness that characterized them in relation to the cultural contexts in which they were first articulated. The challenge that faces Canadian Presbyterians today is to witness to a new understanding of what properly goes with what as we live as disciples under the lordship of Christ.

That new understanding, however, is not a rejection of the old. As Northrup Frye has written, ". . . originality does not break with convention; it rediscovers it at a deeper level" (Frye 1988, 200). The originality with which the gospel confronts the world is always a rediscovery of the convention of God's covenant love that Jesus Christ sealed with his life, death, and resurrection. It is the originality of that convention that remains the motive and the criterion of our efforts to relate our faith to our culture.

7. The Champions of the Oppressed? Canadian Baptists and Social, Political and Economic Realities

George A. Rawlyk

Canadian Baptists were once widely regarded as being the "champions of the oppressed." Their evangelicalism was a fascinating blend of experiential religion and profound social concern. And this blend would characterize—until at least the third decade of the twentieth century—a wide spectrum of the Baptist belief stretching from liberalism on one extreme to fundamentalism on the other, a spectrum to be found in all regions of Canada. But during the past half century or so this blend has been radically altered at the expense of the so-called Social Gospel.

I

In 1921 the Maritime United Baptist Convention—but not the Baptist Convention of Ontario and Quebec or even the Baptist Union of Western Canada—adopted the following nineteen-plank "progressive" Social Gospel "Platform":

(1) Every child has the right to be well born, well nourished, and well protected.

(2) Every child has the right to play and be a child.

(3) Every child is entitled to such an education as shall fit it for life and usefulness.

(4) Every life is entitled to a sanitary home, pure air, and pure water.

(5) Every life is entitled to such conditions as shall enable it to grow up tall and straight and pure.

(6) Every life is entitled to a place in society, a good opportunity in life and a fair equity in the common heritage.

(7) The resources of the earth being the heritage of the people, they should not be monopolized by the few to the disadvantage of the many.

(8) The stewardship of property requires that all property held be supervised, moralized and spiritualized.

(9) Work should be done under proper conditions with respect to hours, wages, health, management and morals.

(10) Every worker should have one day's rest in seven and reasonable time for recreation and family life.

(11) Women who toil should have equal pay with men for equal work.

(12) Widowed mothers with dependent children should be relieved from the necessity of exhausting toil.

(13) Employers and employees are partners in industry and should be partners in the enterprise.

(14) Suitable provision should be made for old age workers and for those incapacitated by injury and sickness.

(15) Income received and benefits enjoyed should hold a direct relation to service rendered.

(16) The State which punishes vice should remove the causes which make [people] more vicious.

(17) The bond of brotherhood is the final and fundamental fact, and men are called to organize all life, ecclesiastical, civic, social, industrial, on the basis of brotherhood.

(18) The help should be greatest where the need is most.

(19) What the few now are, many may become. (*United Baptist Year Book* 1921, 112)

Sixty-seven years later, in 1988, the major social, political and economic concern of the Atlantic Baptists was the question of the ordination of practising homosexuals or lesbians. In 1987 the major issue in the Convention was that "concerning the ordination of women," with 149 opposed, 570 in favour and seven who abstained (*Atlantic Year Book* 1988, 33). There is a rather pathetic and plaintive quality to the very brief report of the Social Action Commission in 1987, for example, with its emphasis on the fact that "The work of the Social Action Commission is greatly hampered by lack of funds and personnel" (in *Atlantic Year Book* 1988). At one time the Social Concerns Committee of the Convention was on the cutting edge of the Convention, providing Maritime Baptists with a powerful, prophetic voice. Now, it has apparently been pushed off to the dark periphery of the Convention where its irrelevance is only matched by its powerlessness.

In 1920 the *Year Book* of the Baptist Union of Western Canada printed the annual report of the Reverend D. R. Sharpe (*Atlantic Year Book* 1920, 64-67), who was then the Superintendent of the Baptist Convention of Saskatchewan. According to Sharpe, the life of Jesus Christ provided the inspiring example for true social change.

> He had dared to oppose the forces of reaction, the money changers, the ecclesiastical and commercial autocrats. He made His appeal and dedicated His life to the despised, the lowly, the outcast, and the oppressed. He refused to gain the comfort and the security of one who stands by the ruling class. He dared to stand out against the "Rulers in high places." He chose "men of low degree" for His companions and apostles. He was the Founder of a New Kingdom, the Herald of a New Day and the Champion of a New Order—in which justice would supplant greed, brotherhood displace class privilege, and love conquer selfishness.

Having argued the central importance of Christ for any twentieth century program for social reform, Sharpe then directed the following questions at his fellow Western Baptists and other Canadian Christians: "Do they celebrate His victory over the evil of His day? Are they drawing all men unto them—without distinction of class or wealth or worldly power? Are they giving the good news to the poor? Have they stood by the oppressed and the underprivileged?" His answer was, as might have been predicted, embarrassingly frank:

> The answer is an array of appalling facts. A blood-stained world of famine and starvation on the one hand and colossal self-indul-

gence on the other, with God's human family torn and separated
by international suspicion, class hatred, political partisanship and
industrial conflict. Nine-tenths of the wealth of the United
Kingdom is possessed by less than one-tenth of the people, and
nine-tenths of the people possess only one-tenth of the wealth,
a system which cannot be defended for one single moment, and
for the reason that the greatest Founder of Social Institutions the
world has ever seen laid it down two thousand years ago, "Thou
shalt love thy neighbor as thyself."

Sharpe then went on:

All are entitled to a fair share of the goods of life. Human slavery
in every form is unchristian. The civilization that sacrifices personalities to things, or the welfare of the many to the greed of the
few, is unchristian and is not worthy to live. Moreover, human
welfare is achieved not by each individual, each family, each class
and each nation seeking its own welfare, but in all seeking the
welfare of all. The problems of society, national and international, are solved by the Golden Rule intelligently applied. They can
be solved in no other way. The duty of the hour is the acceptance
of the law of love as the principle of action, as individuals,
families, classes, churches, nations. The nation, the class, the
church that seeks aggrandizement of itself rather than human
welfare has missed the path of Jesus, the only path of prosperity.

Sharpe's powerful Social Gospel emphasis is what one might have
expected from the biographer of the great American prophet of the
Social Gospel, Walter Rauschenbusch. Yet Sharpe, it should be
stressed, as J. B. Scott has recently and persuasively argued, was also
in all likelihood reflecting the point of view of the majority in the
Western Baptist Union in 1920 (Scott 1989).
How things have changed during the past 68 years! The Social
Gospel majority has, it seems, become a tiny remnant huddled in a few
very, very empty urban churches. The fundamental ideological shift
in the Convention from left to right may be captured by examining,
among other things, the Assembly proceedings in recent years. It took
the Assembly three years even to discuss a mildly-worded "Resolution
on Nuclear War" (*Atlantic Year Book* 1986-87, 47, 53). At the 1987
Assembly, the Convention stubbornly refused to denounce "Capital

Punishment . . . because the Christian believes in the inherent worth of human personality and in the unceasing availability of God's mercy, forgiveness and redemptive power." Instead, it was "Agreed that the issue of capital punishment be referred to the churches and that it not be brought back to Assembly" (*Atlantic Year Book* 1986-87, 52).

In 1987 the Church and Community Committee in fact did not even present a report to the Assembly—an eloquent statement of its widely perceived increasing irrelevance. In previous years it was content to underscore its concern about social issues in a very general way. "For the last six years," it reported in 1986, "our Committee has, through brochures, tried to increase awareness of the issues the church faces in our individual and corporate communities. Each congregation is encouraged to look at the needs of its people and the community it serves, then strive to fulfill those needs" (*Atlantic Year Book* 1985-86, 86). There was no perceptive societal critique in the Committee's somewhat vague statement. Nor was there any attempt made to articulate a Baptist position vis à vis the crucial questions confronting Canada and the world. Western Baptists were obviously not eager to lead but to follow—and only follow at a very, very safe distance.

The Social Gospel, broadly defined, significantly affected throughout the twentieth century an influential minority in the Baptist Convention of Ontario and Quebec. On April 10, 1913, for example, the Social Service Committee of the Convention unanimously endorsed the following 21 recommendations. The first sixteen were lifted directly from the statement of the Federal Council of American Churches of Christ, while the five latter recommendations were added by the Committee (Meldrum 1973, 59). Realizing that the Convention, at the time, was far more conservative than liberal in its theological orientation, the Committee members felt it very important that they first stress that evangelism was still the primary mission of Ontario and Quebec Baptists. But the readers of the *Canadian Baptist* were also warned that any

> . . . failure on the part of the Church of Christ to furnish a Christian solution to the painful social disabilities of our time . . . does now and will in an increasing ratio as time advances, nullify our evangelistic appeal at Home and abroad (*Canadian Baptist*, April 10, 1913).

The Committee then put forward its 21 plank platform:

1. For equal rights and complete justice for all men in all stations of life.

2. For the protection of the family, by the single standard of purity, proper regulation of marriage and proper housing.

3. For the fullest possible development of every child, especially by the provision of proper education and recreation.

4. For the abolition of child labour.

5. For such regulation of the conditions of toil for women, as shall safeguard the physical health and moral well being of the community.

6. For the abatement and prevention of poverty.

7. For the conservation of health.

8. For the protection of the individual and society from the social, moral, and economic waste of the liquor traffic.

9. For the protection of the worker from dangerous machinery, occupational diseases and mortality.

10. For the right of all men to the opportunity of self-maintenance: for the safe-guarding of the right against encroachments of every kind, and for the protection of workers from the hardships of enforced unemployment.

11. For the suitable provision for the old age of workers; for those incapacitated by injury; and for needy widows.

12. For the right of Employees and Employers to organize for adequate means of conciliation and arbitration in industrial disputes.

13. For a release from employment one day in seven, and whenever possible, on the Christian Sabbath.

14. For the gradual and reasonable reduction of the hours of labour, and for that degree of leisure which is a condition of the highest human life.

15. For a living wage as a minimum in every employment, and for the highest wage that each industry can afford.

16. For new emphasis on the Christian requirement for honest work and a conscientious fulfillment of all contracts.

17. For insistence upon the application of Christian principles, to the acquisition and use of money and property, and for the most equitable division of the products of industry, that can ultimately be devised.

18. For the application of Christian methods to the care of dependent and incapable persons by the most human and scientific means of administration.

19. For the development of a Christian spirit in the attitude of society toward offenders against law and morality, by sympathetic efforts to evangelize and restore juvenile delinquents, unfortunate women and girls, and others guilty of crimes and misdemeanors.

20. For a proper recognition of the needs of wholesome recreation under such provisions as will best safeguard the moral and physical well being of the life of the community.

21. For the abolition of war, and for the adoption of arbitration as the means of settling international disputes (*Canadian Baptist*, April 10, 1913).

The April 10, 1913, platform was indeed a radical statement—perhaps the most radical general socio-economic statement ever put forward by Central Canadian Baptists. It is not surprising that a number of key Central Canadian Baptists were very critical of the Committee's obvious socialistic emphasis. R. E. R. Hooper, for example, bitterly commented that "Far from Jesus being the first socialist, as some Christian Socialists like to maintain, Judas was the only socialist of the twelve" (*Canadian Baptist*, March 27, 1913).

During the post-World War I period, advocates of radical societal reform within the Baptist Convention of Ontario and Quebec found themselves very much on the defensive. The Shields-McMaster controversy and the Brandon College-MacNeill controversy of the 1920s, and the resulting bitter splits in the Central and Western Canadian Baptist Churches meant, among other things, that taking *all* Canadian Baptist groups in Canada in the post-1930 period into account, there was a perceived movement towards the right of the ideological spectrum. And this movement toward the right would gather even more momentum in the post-World War II period as the process of Americanization profoundly reshaped the contours of all aspects of Canadian life—including the evangelical tradition.

Yet despite the shift to the ideological right in central Canadian Baptist circles in the post-1918 period, there has remained in the Convention until the present a small but influential group advocating basic Social Gospel reforms. For example, at the 1983 Convention, the delegates decided to eject the anti-abortion resolution put forward by the Social Concerns Committee because it was insuffiently "moderate and constructive" in tone and content (*Ontario Year Book*, 1982-83, 214). At the same Convention, a resolution urging "the federal government and the governments of each of the provinces to amend the Canadian Constitution so as to guarantee to every resident of Canada the right to acquire, hold, use and dispose of property" was *defeated* by a standing vote (*Ontario Year Book 1982-83, 194*). *It should also be remembered that the Ontario and Quebec Convention has, over the past number of years, opposed capital punishment and favoured a very positive governmental and denominational policy towards refugees as "effective and practical means of witnessing to Jesus Christ's compassioon for the disinherited and dispossessed" (Ontario Year Book* 1983-84, 80).

For Convention Baptists in Canada, therefore, during the twentieth century, there has been in the East and the West a discernable move in the area of "Social Concerns" from the left to the right on the ideological spectrum. In the centre, however, there has been far less of a tilt to the right even though it is clear from the evidence that there has been a substantial movement away from the radical 1913 position. What appears to have occurred in central Canada in the post-World War II period among Convention Baptists is a fascinating ideological compromise. The Convention has moved theologically to the right, but in the political-economic-social realm it still hovers near the centre—on most issues. Other Baptist churches, however, as Jim Beverly has suggested (Beverly 1980, 267-76), have moved to the right in all areas, including theology and social-political-economic issues. In certain respects their position is a Canadian variant of the "Moral Majority."

II

During the past ten years I have been particularly concerned with the Baptist experience in the Maritimes. It is in this region of Canada that the Baptists, since the early nineteenth century, have been numerically significant and have therefore been in a position to shape virtually every aspect of the culture of the region. In 1871, four years after Confederation, there were 244,773 Baptists in Canada—6.86 percent of the total population of 3,579,782. A century later there were 667,245 Baptists—but they were only 3.1 percent of the population of 21,568,310. In the 1981 census the Baptist percentage had dropped to 2.9 percent, even though the actual number of Baptists had risen to 696,850 out of the Canadian population of 24,083,495. This striking decline of Baptist percentages in Canada may be traced to a number of factors, the most important of which, in my view, is the disconcerting undermining—especially in the post-World War I period—of the Baptist position in New Brunswick and Nova Scotia (Rawlyk 1984, 153-72).

It is sometimes not realized that at Confederation one in four New Brunswickers was a Baptist, and one in five Nova Scotians. These numbers are even more striking when it is pointed out that in the late 1860s, in New Brunswick one in three inhabitants was Roman Catholic and in Nova Scotia one in four. In fact, in New Brunswick the Baptist denomination was the largest Protestant denomination, and in Nova Scotia it was second only to the Presbyterians. In Ontario in 1871, on the other hand, only one in twenty inhabitants was Baptist, and in Quebec fewer than one in a hundred. In 1981, however, only 12.8 percent of the New Brunswick population was Baptist and 12 percent of the Nova Scotia population. The corresponding Roman Catholic percentages were 53.5 percent and 37 percent. In Ontario in 1981 the Baptist percentage was 3.4 percent and in Quebec 0.4 percent. The decline of the Maritimes in the general context of Canada, and the Baptist denomination's decline in New Brunswick and Nova Scotia in particular, it may be argued, helps to explain the sorry state of Baptist numbers in contemporary Canada. If all of these trends continue, by the year 2000 the Baptist percentage in Canada will fall to 2.5 percent, and in New Brunswick and Nova Scotia (as a single political entity) to ten percent or lower.

The Maritime Baptist experience and its evangelical tradition were significantly affected by Henry Alline and his disciples—men like Harris Harding, Joseph Dimock, James and Edward Manning, and Theodore Seth Harding—the so-called "Baptist Patriarchs" (Rawlyk 1984, 73-136). These men, together with the remarkable American Methodist itinerant Freeborn Garrettson (Rawlyk 1985, 105-26), had constructed by 1800 the evangelical underpinnings not only of the Baptist position in the Maritimes, but also that of the Methodists. These underpinnings, though largely eroded in the twentieth century, are still to be found, and not only on the periphery of the Convention.

At the core of the Maritime Baptist evangelical tradition was to be found an emphasis upon individual conversion and community regeneration. And this emphasis, it may be argued, substantially impinged upon the total Maritime historical experience in at least three *major* ways.

First, there are the raw denominational numbers. By the late nineteenth century, for example, to repeat my earlier argument, one in four New Brunswickers was a Baptist, and one in five Nova Scotians, but only one in twenty Islanders. In New Brunswick and Nova Scotia combined about one in ten of the population was a Methodist, and on Prince Edward Island one in eight.

Second, there was an important, almost contradictory evangelical impact on the region's political culture, broadly defined. On the one hand, in the revivalistic tradition tremendous stress was placed on individual conversion—upon the individual's special and continuing personal relationship with Christ and with eternal verities rather than with the mundane, here and now largely ephemeral societal problems. Because of this some historians have understandably concluded that Maritime revivalism strengthened considerably the conservative political culture of the region. "The political culture of the region," it has been argued as late as December, 1987, had congealed by the 1850s into something "fundamentally conservative" and traditional, and this process of congealment owed a great deal to the power of Evangelical religion in this region (Rawlyk 1987, 52).

It would be wrong, however, to stop here and to forget "the other hand"—the communitarian side of the evangelical message. Alline, Garrettson and their scores of nineteenth century disciples were also very concerned about transforming society—about making it more Christlike. This was their unique brand of the Social Gospel. Converted individuals, they contended, were under a spiritual obligation to transform society into the "New Jerusalem." Alline and Garrettson were certainly not preoccupied with the imminent and apocalyptic end of the world. In fact, it may be effectively argued that both of these charismatic preachers and most of their followers—well on into the twentieth century—tended to equate true conversion on this earth with an almost immediate entry into heaven and eternal bliss. "Heaven on earth," for Alline and others, was something they "blissfully" experienced. For Alline, in particular, there was no such thing as linear history. Since God lived in what Alline often referred to as the "One Eternal Now," surely, the Nova Scotia preacher argued, the truly redeemed of the Lord "must inhabit the same" at precisely the moment he or she reached out to the Almighty, since "the work of conversion is instantaneous" (Alline 1783b, 65). According to Alline, for all those who had experienced the "New Birth," there was indeed no sense of "Time, and Space, and Successive Periods." "Salvation and Damnation," Alline argued,

> ... originate here at your own Door; for with God there never was any Thing, as before or after, Millions of Ages, before time began, and as many more, after Time is at a Period, being the same very instant; consider neither Time past nor Time to come, but one Eternal Now; consider that with God there is neither Succession nor Progress; but that with Him the Moment He said let us make Man, and the Sound of his last Trumpet, is the very same instant, and your Death as much first as your Birth ... with God all things are NOW ... as the Center of a Ring, which is as near the one side as the other (1783b, 20-21).

Regeneration was thus seen by Alline and many of his Baptist followers as the mystical process which destroyed artificial time and space and astonishingly transformed, for each individual, the mundane—what Alline described as the world of "Turnips, Cabbages and Potatoes"—into the cosmic and heavenly, "the Eternity you once, was, and knew" (1783a, 65).

While on this earth, Alline's followers were urged to labour diligently "for the promotion of religion, the advancing of Christ's kingdom, as far as the influence of your several stations and capacities in life may extend" (Rawlyk 1986, 108). Even though he instructed his followers to abandon "their earthly joys, pleasures, and recreations" and to reject "the carnal world and pleasures of Egypt" (Rawlyk 1986, 49, 60), they were expected to use their Christian zeal not only to witness to others but also to try to transform North American society. This key point must be emphasized. It was Alline's contention that regeneration "will naturally produce a christian deportment externally as fire will produce light" (Rawlyk 1986, 96-97). He therefore urged the leaders of Nova Scotia and New England society—"the capital men" and the "Counsellors"—to "be a Terror to evil doers" (Rawlyk 1986, 97). "O embrace the unspeakable privilege," Henry Alline once declared

> ... and let me intreat you to adorn your station by the grace of God, and live as lights in the world, and for the Lord's sake, your own soul's sake, and the sake of others around you arise up and

witness for God, and let all your deportment espouse the redeemer's cause, and the welfare of souls (Rawlyk 1986, 97).

And the "welfare of souls," for Alline, meant being lovingly concerned about "ye Poor, ye blind, ye sick, ye sore, ye lame, and miserable" (Rawlyk 1986, 145). This is what Alline really meant when he preached about "advancing . . . Christ's kingdom as far as the influence of your several stations and capacities in life may extend."

Charles Finney's post-millennial optimism was apparently shared by most Maritime Baptists and Methodists in the nineteenth and early twentieth centuries (Rawlyk 1988b). In 1846, for example, Finney, the great American evangelist, declared:

> Now the great business of the church is to reform the world—to put away every kind of sin. The church was originally organized to be a body of reformers. The very profession of Christianity implies the profession and virtually an oath to do all that can be done for the reformation of the world. The Christian church was designed to make aggressive movements in every direction—to lift up her voice and put forth her energies in high and low places—to reform individuals, communities and governments, and never rest until the Kingdom and the greatness of the Kingdom under the whole heaven shall be given to the saints of the Most High God—until every form in iniquity shall be driven from the earth (*Oberlin Evangelist*, Jan. 21, 1846; also Smith 1976).

Should one be shocked to discover, therefore, as has been pointed out earlier, that in 1921 the Maritime United Baptist Convention adopted these, among other, radical Social Gospel planks?

(7) The resources of the earth being the heritage of the people, should not be monopolized by the few to the disadvantage of the many.

(11) Women who toil should have equal pay with men for equal work.

(12) Widowed mothers with dependent children should be relieved from the necessity of exhausting toil.

(13) Employers and employees are partners in industry and should be partners in the enterprise.

(14) Suitable provision should be made for old age workers and for those incapacitated by injury and sickness.

(15) Income received and benefits enjoyed should hold a direct relation to service rendered.

(17) The bond of brotherhood is the final and fundamental fact, and men are called to organize all life, ecclesiastical, civic, social, industrial, on the basis of brotherhood.

(18) The help should be greatest where the need is most.

(19) What the few now are, many may become (*United Baptist Year Book* 1921, 112).

As late as 1940, moreover, the Maritime Baptist Convention endorsed the statement "that far reaching changes . . . in the political and economic life of the nation . . . are coming, and in fact have come which are bound to greatly affect the economic system." "We believe," the Social Service Report went on, "that future movements will be inevitably toward greater governmental and centralized control and regulation. We have faith, however, that there will come a larger and a fairer distribution of the national income among all classes" (*United Baptist Year Book* 1940, 154).

Similar strong progressive social gospel declarations were endorsed by the Maritime Conference of the United Church in the late 1920s and 1930s. This evangelical Social Gospel consensus was superbly captured in the Maritime United Baptist Convention declaration of 1936:

> It might be said of our Baptist fathers that they brought religion to the towns, villages and settlements of these provinces, for they went everywhere preaching the word. We trust that it will be said for us and our generation, that we kept religion alive in these places, that we nurtured every wholesome social endeavor and that at all times we have put in the first place, the Kingdom of God and His righteousness (*United Baptist Year Book* 1936, 153)

In the post-World War II period, however, most Maritime Convention Baptists lost much of their enthusiasm for the Social Gospel. Feeling very much on the defensive, because of their declining numerical importance in the region, they tried to abandon their earlier commitment to the oppressed and disadvantaged in the hope of recapturing their former significance and power. But in so doing, they failed to realize that they were indeed abandoning their unique evangelical tradition.

There is a third way in which the Baptist evangelical emphasis also impinged upon the region. The revivalist tradition, it should be observed, had always placed greater emphasis on "promoting a good work" (Archives, 140)—or in other words, bringing about conversions and revivals than on theological or doctrinal purity and conformity. The evangelical mainstream, from the time of Alline and Garrettson, especially at the grassroots level, has been basically open to diversity as well as to the experiential. This was emphatically the religion of an Alline or a Garrettson rather than that of a T. T. Shields—the influential twentieth century Ontario Baptist fundamentalist. And this experiential, and sometimes mystical, open-minded evangelical theology would characterize the Maritime Baptist religious experience until the late 1920s and even beyond. In the post-World War II period, however—and this point merits repetition—as the Maritime region was both increasingly Upper Canadianized and Americanized, this unique religious culture—a crucially significant element in the Maritime identity—would be undermined by the corrosive impact of modernity and so-called progress, as well as by a growing lack of confidence in the region in things uniquely Maritime.

As the twentieth century unfolded, the revivalist tradition in the Maritimes obviously lost much of its power and influence. The so-called "evangelical twentieth century" was replaced by the largely secular twentieth century. Baptist numbers significantly fell—for example, Baptists in the early 1980s make up a little more than ten percent of the total Maritime population. And, moreover, the Social Gospel tradition has been largely abandoned by many Baptists and replaced for many by a largely imported variant of American-fundamentalist neo-conservatism. Furthermore, the Allinite-Garrettsonian emphasis on experiential religion and zeal balanced by order has been pushed to the periphery of the religious culture of the region by an increasingly closed-minded narrow religiosity largely borrowed from the United States and central Canada.

In the twentieth century, however, much of what would be preached by the new prophets of evangelical consumerism and greed would, in fact, be the antithesis of nineteenth century evangelicalism (Rawlyk 1988a, 34-40). And the decline in importance of Canadian and Maritime revivalism may be a significant religious statement. Instead of being attracted to what is seen as the gross hypocrisy of the modern gospel and revolted by the spiritual hubris of much of fundamentalism, tens of thousands of Canadians are satisfied with abandoning Christianity altogether. For the fastest growing religious group in Canada in the 1980s continued to be the "one that professes no religion at all." In the Maritimes, as Reginald Bibby (1987) has recently argued, there has been an almost desperate attempt by many Protestants especially to cling to whatever might remain of the crumbling edifice of the nineteenth century evangelical consensus. They thus slide into the twenty-first century, looking longingly backwards to a nineteenth century past, which even to the sharp Maritime eye is becoming dimmer and dimmer. Or is it? Perhaps they are merely resonating with Jacques Ellul's bitter lament, "Beyond Jesus, beyond him, there is nothing— nothing but lies" (quoted in Frank 1986, 277).

III

On the surface, at least, it seems that during the past half century or so Christianity in general and the Baptists in particular have had very little impact on Canadian political life. Or at least this is the general consensus reached by a myriad of scholars. Canadian voters, when compared to their American neighbours, seem strangely indifferent as to what their political leaders actually believe—in a religious sense. Since the 1930s Canada has had among its prime ministers W. L. MacKenzie King, a Presbyterian spiritualist who was an enthusiastic advocate of the occult and a man who loved to talk to his long dead dog and mother. There were his two Liberal successors, Louis St. Laurent, whose intense Catholicism was carefully hidden from Canadian voters, and Lester B. Pearson, whose lapsed Methodism was something few took seriously. Between St. Laurent and Pearson came John G. Diefenbaker, the Baptist firebrand from Saskatchewan whose Prairie Christianity seemed both pragmatic and contrived. It is noteworthy that in Diefenbaker's three volumes of memoirs the following are the only explicit references to the possible impact of religion on the former Conservative prime minister's politics:

> However trying the circumstances, there was a simple acceptance of the fact that all things worked together for good for those who loved the Lord. This attitude may never be recovered, but some of it would do today's society no harm.... All through the defeats, I had never lost faith. Faith does not deny realities, but it generates hope. Faith carries one on. In achieving the leadership

of my Party, I had a deep sense of thankfulness to Almighty God and appreciation for those who had stood with me through the years (1975, 44, 282).

After L. B. Pearson, in 1967, there was Pierre Eliot Trudeau, whose lifestyle made any private or public religiosity virtually irrelevant. And then came Joe Clark, a Tory from Alberta whose Catholicism, when made public, surprised friend and foe alike. John Turner, who succeeded Trudeau very briefly, was a pious Roman Catholic—one of the most committed Christians to be prime minister of Canada since the time of Alexander MacKenzie, the dour Scots Baptist from Sarnia, Ontario, who served the Canadian nation from 1874 to 1878. There was some truth in John A. Macdonald's jibe that Canadians had shown in 1878 that they preferred John A. drunk to the pious Alexander MacKenzie sober. MacKenzie was indeed a committed evangelical Baptist who prayed daily and read his Bible frequently and regularly. Canada's present prime minister is a Roman Catholic, but the evidence suggests that Brian Mulroney's Catholicism is not of primary importance to him. Moreover, Mulroney has made it very clear to his biographers "that his private religious principles do not carry over into politics" (see Murphy et al. 1984, 32).

No Canadian prime minister in the twentieth century, to my knowledge, has publicly stated that he has experienced the New Birth. And no Canadian leader of any major federal Canadian political party in recent years has attempted to appeal directly and explicitly to any religious constituency. In fact, the evidence suggests that the vast majority of Canadian voters are not at all interested in the religious views of their politicians. It is highly unlikely that this prevailing attitude will quickly change. The fact that the present premier of British Columbia, Bill Van der Zalm, is what he calls a "fundamentalist Catholic" is regarded as further proof that the Pacific province is always the peculiar exception to the Canadian norm. Van der Zalm was elected premier, not because of his religious views but despite them, and because the British Columbia elite desperately wanted to keep the much feared and despised New Democratic Party out of office. Even if the remarkable growth of those Canadians with "No Religion" does not in fact help to transform the federal political landscape into a genuine three-party system, and even though the new Social Gospel may not be channelled into the N.D.P., Canadian politics in the 1980s has followed a somewhat different pattern than in the United States. And this is taking place at the precise moment that the Canadian economy is being fully integrated into that of the United States. Because of the increasing strength of the N.D.P., the Liberals have been compelled to push to the left and the Progressive Conservatives have, in certain respects, followed suit. Politics in Canada, once again, has tilted slightly to the left—or so it seems. It may be that this tilt is occurring largely to counteract the almost inexorable move to free trade. As Canada becomes a northern economic frontier of the United States, there seems to be a growing collective need in Canada to exaggerate those differences that continue to exist between the two countries. There is in this response what Freud once called "the narcissism of small differences." But there is more than this, of course.

According to the influential Canadian thinker Harold Innis, the way in which a particular medium of communication impinges on the eye or the ear delineates the essential bias of the medium. The eye stresses space and distance, and translates this sense of space and distance into a basic survival creed. Canadians, it may be argued, are a people of the eye—a people who have been overwhelmed by a sense of space and distance—and consequently they have created a survival creed or ideology which owes very much to the continuing Canadian concern with the real and imagined threat posed by the United States. They have seen America's "providential hand" and they have, moreover, felt its stinging impact, and they realize how important it is to cultivate an ideology of community permeated by a survival creed which, in fact, may after all be the most coveted and cherished North American ideal. And what George Grant has called this crucially important "thrust of intention into the future" (1965, 12), must ironically have at its core, according to a growing number of Canadian political activists, people usually on the left of the political spectrum, an uncompromising Christian component.

IV

In conclusion, and returning to the Baptist core of this paper, it is both noteworthy and perhaps ironic that the two most influential *Baptist* politicians in Canada during the past half century have been Tommy Douglas and William Aberhart. For most scholars, Douglas and Aberhart were polar opposites, the one a liberal Christian Socialist and the other a fundamentalist neo-Fascist. The truth, however, is far more complex, and those two Baptists may have had far more in common politically than they had separating them.

Despite the powerful forces of secularism which in recent years have shaped Canadian culture in general and the C.C.F. and N.D.P. in particular, there remains an important Social Gospel element in contemporary democratic socialism in Canada. T. C. Douglas, an ordained Baptist minister, the first democratic socialist premier of a Canadian province, and the first leader of the N.D.P., once explained his own commitment to the Social Gospel:

> The religion of tomorrow will be less concerned with dogmas of theology, and more concerned with the social welfare of humanity. When one sees the church spending its energies on the assertion of antiquated dogmas, but dumb as an oyster to the poverty and misery all around, we can't help recognize the need for a new interpretation of Christianity. We have come to see that the Kingdom of God is in our midst if we have the vision to build it. The rising generation will tend to build a heaven on earth rather than live in misery in the hope of gaining some uncertain reward in the distant future (quoted in Thomas 1982, 60-61).

It is noteworthy that in 1935, in Alberta, another Canadian Baptist had become premier of a Canadian province. "Bible Bill" Aberhart, an "ordained apostle" of an independent fundamentalist Baptist church in Calgary, had swept into power as the leader of the Social Credit Party. It has often been argued that Aberhart's political movement was a Canadian prairie variant of European Fascism—something one might expect to be coaxed into existence by a charismatic premillennial fundamentalist. Recent scholarship, however, suggests something quite different: that Social Credit was "in fact leftist" (see Elliott and Miller 1987, 320) and had a great deal in common ideologically—until Aberhart's death in 1943—with the C.C.F. There was a growing Social Gospel bias in Aberhart's thought as the 1930s unfolded. The *Edmonton Bulletin* of May 24, 1943, certainly realized this fact when it declared in its obituary of Aberhart that it was

> ... important to remember that the social legislation [that affecting health care, labour, education, oil and gas conservation, and moratoriums on foreclosures] was the product of a burning sympathy for the aged and the sick and helpless. This will be his

epitaph, whatever one may think of his politics, that he was the champion of the oppressed.

Aberhart and Douglas, very different kinds of Baptists, were indeed "champions of the oppressed." Their religious commitment, throughout their political careers, significantly shaped their political ideology. Canadian Baptists of all religious stripes, if they remain true to their historical heritage, must also, I would contend, be committed "champions of the oppressed."

8. A Lutheran Witness in Canadian Society

David Pfrimmer

Introduction

On October 31st, 1517, an obscure Augustinian priest who was teaching at the University at Wittenberg posted "Ninety-five Theses" on the door of the college chapel. This event has been celebrated as the beginning of the reformation and has been revered by Lutherans, as evidenced by their Reformation Festivals, as the initiation of the Lutheran church.

From these modest beginnings Lutheranism has emerged as a major global church, the largest non-Roman Catholic denomination. Particularly in recent times, historical currents have very much shaped Lutheranism outside of the European context. Even the Reformation itself reflected a convergence of both historical factors and theological insights. As the noted Luther scholar Roland Bainton observed:

> There are those who say that . . . Luther's religious affirmations were in no sense novel and when previously made had no such effect. Luther happened to emerge amid a set of circumstances peculiarly auspicious. Without such a state and without concomitant events both economic and political the Reformation would never have taken hold (Bainton 1972).

The historical context provided fertile soil for the political and economic changes that resulted from Luther's rejection of Rome.

Yet the reformation also provided an important watershed to restore key biblical and theological insights. Luther would be appalled to be perceived primarily as an agent for social change. For Luther, the reformation moment was deeply conditioned by his struggle with fundamental questions of the faith. Luther sought to restore integrity to matters of faith amidst what he perceived to be severe distortions in matters of faith and life. With respect to the "Lutheran disturbance," Luther wrote in 1521:

> I hope that (God) will acknowledge that (the Reformation) has been begun in His name, and if any impure motives have crept in—since I am a sinful man of ordinary flesh and blood—will graciously forgive them and will not deal severely with me in His judgement (Luther [1897], 279ff).

Lutherans believe that the significance of Luther's contribution to the Church was his reaffirmation of the central core of the gospel. The incarnation of God in Christ was the principal unique event in human history. Luther viewed the events of the world around him in terms of the central perspective that a loving God would offer an only son that humanity might be brought into a new relationship with its creator.

In considering how Lutherans have historically participated in shaping their culture, these two currents, the historical context and the theological affirmations, need to be considered. The following is an attempt to look at Luther's theological assertions in the light of historical developments in Canadian Lutheran history. We will begin by briefly developing some of Luther's basic theological assertions: "sola fide," the "theology of the cross," and the "two kingdoms." Then we will consider how those theological insights have affected the three distinct chapters of Canadian Lutheran history—the era of arrival (1753-1850); the era of expansion (1850-1910); the era of convergence (1910-1986). The question is the degree to which Lutherans have developed an integrated theological view of their place and role in the world that are honest to Luther's understandings.

What follows is an attempt to represent a classical Lutheran approach to social ethics. While it may be self-evident to many, it should be stated that there are various Lutheran writers and thinkers who would approach this question from a different starting point.

However for the sake of this analysis a more conventional Lutheran approach may be the most helpful.

Major Lutheran Theological Reference Points

Sola Fide (By Faith Alone)
Luther was by many accounts a troubled young priest. After entering the Augustinian order he rose quickly to the rank of professor. By 1511 he was lecturing at the newly formed University in Wittenberg. In 1513 he was lecturing on the Psalms and in 1515 on Paul's Epistle to the Romans (Bainton 1978, 39ff). What tormented Luther's spirit was his perception of a harsh and avenging God. As Luther said himself:

> Is it not against all natural reason that God out of his mere whim deserts men, hardens them, damns them, as if he delighted in sins and in such torments of the wretched for eternity, he who is said to be of such mercy and goodness? This appears iniquitous, cruel and intolerable in God, by which very many have been offended in all ages. And who would not be? I was myself more than once driven to the very abyss of despair so that I wished I had never been created. Love God? I hated him! (Bainton 1978, 44).

Luther found no comfort in the existing ecclesiastical prescriptions for resolving this inner conflict. The more he struggled to seek God's justice, the more it eluded him. In the spring of 1513, in his tower room study in the Black monastery at Wittenberg, Luther began the study of Paul's Epistle to the Romans (Lilje 1952, 62ff). There he read in Romans 1:16, 17 (Revised Standard Version):

> For I am not ashamed of the Gospel: it is the power of God for salvation to everyone who has faith.... For in it the righteousness of God is revealed through faith for faith; as it is written, "He who through faith is righteous shall live."

This "tower experience" led to Luther's primary theological insight that people are justified (made personally righteous) by faith as a free gift of grace from a loving God. It was this basic principal that not only shaped Luther's understanding of faith but also his view of the role of Christians in the world.

A Theology of the Cross

Based upon his personal experience, Luther recognized the contradictions of the faith. These contradictions confounded those who sought reasoned explanations of the faith. Luther observed that "God hides his power in weakness, his wisdom in folly, his goodness in severity, justice in sins, his mercy in anger" (Bainton 1978, 48). This paradoxical nature of faith was most complete in the death of Christ on the cross.

By 1517-18, in his lectures on the Epistle to the Hebrews, Luther began to speak specifically of a "theology of the cross" (*theologia crucis*). For Luther a theology of the cross meant essentially that God revealed himself in the cross of Christ. The first implication of this insight was, "The love of God toward sinners is only recognizable in the love with which the Son of God took upon himself the punishment for all our sins upon the cross." But there is also a second aspect that affirms, "This love of God which is manifested in the cross is only appropriated by us in so far as we are willing to take up our own cross. Since Christ actually bore our punishment upon his cross, and since his cross is in the last analysis identical with ours, to hate our own cross is at the same time to hate his, and to love his cross is at the same time to love our own" (Prenter 1971, 3-4).

Luther's "theology of the cross" was a theology of paradox that sought to address the contradictions of the human faith experience. In the cross Christ accomplished all, and therefore salvation was not dependent upon personal action to accomplish what God had already accomplished in faith. For Luther the cross becomes the criterion for all Christian thought and life.

Luther's "theology of the cross" has very much shaped the way in which Lutherans view their role in society. As the noted Lutheran theologian Carl Braaten observed:

> From Luther's point of view, a church that wants to be great and glorious in worldly terms, vocal and victorious in political terms, is deeply suspect. There is something wrong with the church when it refuses to accept its suffering condition as essential to its very nature in history (Braaten 1985, 29).

Far from advocating a masochistic view of suffering for the sake of suffering itself, Luther sought to reassert that Christ was a "suffering servant" for the sake of a fallen humanity. As part of the continuing paradox that necessitated the cross, Christians live in two ages, the old age of Adam characterized by human sinfulness, and a new age characterized by God's redemptive action in Christ. Luther summarized the tension of this paradox in his treatise on "The Freedom of a Christian" when he stated that "A Christian is free and independent in every respect, in bondage to no one." At the same time, "A Christian is a dutiful servant in every respect, owing a duty to everyone" (Luther [1957], 327ff).

Emanating from this theological framework, William Lazareth has identified at least three ethical consequences for the work of the church in society. The first, as we have already mentioned, is that "the Christian belongs to both ages at the same time." The Christian does not cease to be sinful even though forgiveness of sins and new life has been realized by Christ on the cross. Secondly, "The law and the gospel have very different functions to perform in the two ages of Adam and Christ." The gospel liberates people to serve their neighbour in response to God's gracious action in Christ, while the law serves to convict people of their sin. Thirdly, "The church is primarily the agency of the gospel in the new age of Christ, while the state is primarily the agency of the law in the old age of Adam" (Lazareth 1965, 4-5). It is the implications of this third ethical consequence, most commonly referred to as Luther's Two-Kingdom theory, that has been important for Lutherans in understanding the relationship between church and state.

The Two-Kingdom Doctrine

The paradoxical nature of the Christian experience of being "in the world but not of the world" is portrayed in Luther's reassertion of Paul's view that Christians live in two ages. This is further elaborated in Luther's articulation of the doctrine of the "two kingdoms." In many ways this doctrine was Luther's attempt to come to terms with the social-political reality of his time. This doctrine, as expressed also in the principal confessional document of all Lutherans, *The Augsburg Confession*, has been the source of much misunderstanding by Lutherans on their appropriate role in society.

Luther perceived that the principal struggle in the world for Christians was between good and evil, God and Satan. Luther sought to understand the appropriate role of the church and of the state. To this end, Luther saw that there were two ways or modes by which God acted within human history. The first was that of the "worldly kingdom" that might be called the "secular realm" in this modern time. It included everything required for human survival such as physical necessities, social institutions like government, and cultural and economic relationships. This "worldly kingdom" is a sinful world governed by princes and kings. The second realm was the "kingdom of Christ." This realm was governed by the Church in its faithful proclamation of God the Redeemer (*kerygma*), nourishing the believers in fellowship through the Holy Spirit (*koinonia*) and motivating Christians to bear fruit in the world of God the Creator (*diakonia*).

Luther described this two-kingdom understanding in his treatise on "Temporal Authority: To What Extent it should be Obeyed" in 1532:

> We must divide all the children of Adam into two classes: the first belong to the kingdom of God, the second to the kingdom of the world. Those belonging in the kingdom of God are all true believers in Christ and are subject to Christ . . . and the gospel of the Kingdom. . . . All who are not Christians belong to the world and are under the law. Since few believe and still fewer live a Christian life, do not resist evil, and themselves do no evil, God has provided for non-Christians a different government outside the Christian estate and God's kingdom, and has subjected them to the sword. . . . For this reason the two kingdoms must be sharply distinguished, and both be permitted to remain; the one to produce piety, and the other to bring about external peace and prevent evil deeds. Neither is sufficient in the world without the other (Luther [1974], 51ff).

Luther here was putting forward a "concept" by which to understand the theocratic nature of his own society. The fundamental unity of the two kingdoms was basic to Luther's understanding. Luther was not trying to divide the world into sacred and secular. As William Lazareth points out (12), Luther's chief objective was "to put the church back under God's gospel."

In distinguishing these two kingdoms, Luther sought to assert the appropriate arena for ethical action and social change. The proper work of God (*opus proprium*) was the redemptive acts of God that called people to repentance and offered forgiveness and salvation in Christ through word and sacrament. This Christian righteousness motivated the faithful to respond to God's gracious actions in love toward one's neighbour. Yet all Christians *lived* in the world (creation) and thereby were called to exercise a "civil righteousness." This "civil righteousness" is expressed in a ". . . social morality of which all God's rational creatures are capable—Christians included—in the form of law-abiding political justice" (Lazareth 1965, 15).

Thus Lutherans reject any notions of "Christianizing" or redeeming social institutions. For example, orthodox Lutherans would have to reject the idea that Canada is a "Christian country." On the other hand, Lutherans have traditionally been able to assert that responsible citizenship is a proper response to the gospel. Luther maintained that Christians ". . . are under obligation to serve and assist the sword by whatever means you can, with body, goods, honour and soul. For it is something which you do not need, but which is very beneficial and essential for the whole world and for your neighbour" (Luther [1974], 51ff). The key to understanding how this citizenship in the "worldly kingdom" is to be exercised is Luther's understanding of "vocation" (*Berufe*). Christians are "called" to serve God through their everyday tasks and occupations. The world becomes the forum for ethical action. As Dr. U. S. Leupold, former Dean of Waterloo Lutheran Seminary, concluded in a study of "Luther's Social Ethics Today,"

> The deeper unity of both orders consists in the truth that both are expressions of God's love and that we can serve God in both (kingdoms). They have different methods but the same goal. They are a part of the same kingdom. There is no peculiarly Christian ethics over or beside secular ethics. Faith leads us not into a separate existence, but into a sharpened and deepened participation in the ethical problems and tasks of mankind (Leupold 1966, 244).

Historical Expression in Canadian Lutheranism
How have these reformation themes been reflected in the Canadian context? Canadian Lutheranism has a rich and varied expression, given the pattern of immigration in this country. This reality is evident in the cultural/ethnic mix summarized in a 1980 study entitled "Profiles of Lutherans." In that study, of the 700 Lutherans surveyed in Canada, 58 percent described themselves as of German ancestry, 19 percent as of Scandinavian ancestry (Danish, Swedish, Norwegian,

etc.) and 20 percent from other European countries (Estonia, Latvia, the Slovak nations, etc.) (Profiles 1980, H3).

The development of this broad cultural panorama that characterizes Canadian Lutheranism can be traced to three historical periods of immigration: the Era of Arrival (1750-), the Era of Expansion (1850-), and the Era of Convergence (1940-). Each of these particular chapters in Canadian Lutheran history can be characterized by a particular ethical imperative for involvement in Canadian society.

The Era of Arrival (1750-)
The first Lutheran worship service was held in Canada in 1619 by Pastor Rasmus Jensen, chaplain to the 65 men of a Danish expedition led by Danish Captain Jens Munck that landed in Port Churchill on Hudson's Bay. But it was not until 1753 with the arrival of 250 German families from the Duchy of Lunenburg in Germany that a more permanent Lutheran presence was established in Lunenburg, Nova Scotia (Cronmiller 1961, 46ff).

During the period immediately following the American Revolution, there were many United Empire Loyalists who were of German ancestry and had fought for the English crown, who emigrated to Upper Canada from the United States. While the United States had made them a generous offer at the conclusion of the conflict, they were attracted to Canada because of the generous offers of land and because of their loyalty to the English crown which helped them escape the conflicts and religious persecution in Europe. Many of these loyalists went to Nova Scotia and were assimilated into the English-speaking community and churches. Others settled in the St. Lawrence River valley and still others went on to settle west of Toronto.

During this era the principal ethical struggle for Lutherans was survival. Their attitude toward the governing authorities was generally supportive. While they may not have shared a common social purpose, their respective self-interests often were compatible. For example, in Nova Scotia in 1750 "foreign Protestants" were brought from Europe as settlers to help undermine the strong Roman Catholic influence among the Acadian communities (Walsh 1956, 90).

During this period many Lutheran communities were absorbed into the Anglican church. For many Lutherans, Anglicanism was the state church of the British crown, which made adoption of Anglicanism a natural step in the process of acculturation. But for other Lutherans the conversion efforts of Anglicanism were a threat to be confronted. There were numerous instances of Lutheran communities losing their pastors to Methodism or Anglicanism. While there was support generally for the governing authorities, among those remaining in the Lutheran church family there was always a healthy suspicion of any efforts to establish a state church. Guaranteeing a source of pastoral leadership became an important strategy for the survival of Lutheranism in Canada. The result was the emergence of two Lutheran seminaries, one in 1911 in Waterloo, Ontario, and one in 1918 in Saskatoon, Saskatchewan, as well as numerous colleges and a continuing concern about educational issues.

An Era of Expansion (1850-)
A second chapter in Canadian Lutheranism began in the 1870s with the opening to settlement of land that formerly belonged to the Hudson's Bay Company in the Canadian northwest. Settlers came from Germany, Russia, Iceland, Denmark, Norway, Sweden and other predominantly Lutheran countries in search of land and opportunity. With this influx the cultural and ethnic plurality was further expanded. The oldest Lutheran congregation in western Canada was organized at Gimli, Manitoba, in 1876 (Threinen 1977, 8ff).

During this era the principal ethical struggle could be characterized as the struggle for legitimacy. Now that a Lutheran presence had been established, the next need was to consolidate it. Many of those leaving Europe were supported in their search for new opportunities by the Lutheran churches in the new land. For Lutherans in Canada this was a way to build stronger Lutheran congregations. This effort was driven to a large degree by a "pietism" that was brought from the free church traditions present in Europe and also in the United States, the gateway for many of the new arrivals to Canada.

One notable development that reflected this approach to the Canadian context was the establishment of the Lutheran Immigration Board of Canada (LIB) in April, 1923 (Threinen 1983, 8). The purpose of the LIB was to help settle European Lutheran refugees in close proximity to Lutheran communities. To accomplish these goals the LIB worked cooperatively with the government of Canada and the Canadian railways. In describing the needs of these refugees, Pastor Traugott O. F. Herzer said that LIB was trying to give new immigrants an opportunity to earn their own living here in Canada since, ". . . because of the great poverty overseas, it is no longer possible there" (Threinen 1983, 36).

With the outbreak of World War II, leaders from seven Lutheran denominations met in Winnipeg in April, 1940, and organized the Canadian Lutheran Commission for War Services (Threinen 1983, 40). The purpose of this commission was to provide services to civilian internees, appoint military chaplains, provide pastoral services to members of the Canadian armed forces, and to minister to Lutheran prisoners of war held in Canada. The principal objective of the commission was ". . . to speak and act for all parts of the Evangelical Lutheran Church in Canada" before the government, government agencies and departments ". . . as the need and opportunity arises" (Threinen 1983, 41).

It was a struggle for Lutherans to achieve legitimacy within Canada during this period of their history. The focus of much of their social ministry was to build their own congregations, and secondarily to address the pressing need of their fellow Lutherans to escape poverty. This experience has led Dr. William Hordern, a Lutheran theologian and former Dean of the Lutheran Seminary in Saskatoon, to write:

> Canadian Lutherans have tended to remain inward looking. Lutheran churches have been constructed to "serve their own," often with worship services in languages other than English or French. They have been slow to take up an outreach into the total community. Taken as a percentage of the population, Lutherans have been under-represented among politicians and elected officials (Hordern 1977, 27).

An Era of Convergence (1945-)
With such diversity, Lutherans in North America began to consolidate their church expressions. The General Synod which included the Canada Synod and the Manitoba Synod eventually became a part of the United Lutheran Church in America in 1918. The Ohio Synod, through a series of consolidations, eventually became a part of the American Lutheran Church which formed in 1961-62. The Missouri Synod continued as a third Lutheran denomination in Canada. Thus the face of Lutheranism in Canada was changing.

More importantly, following World War II there were other substantive changes in the posture of Canadian Lutherans in their society. This period of consolidating many Lutheran denominations into one national expression, known today as the Evangelical Lutheran Church in Canada (ELCIC), was also a time to participate more fully in the broader Canadian society and enter increasingly into ecumenical partnerships for ministry. Thus the ethical struggle in this chapter of Canadian Lutheranism was to participate more fully within the family of churches and in Canadian society. It was an effort to integrate the "two kingdoms" more fully.

There are many examples that could be cited to illustrate this chapter of Canadian Lutheran history. However, two or three may suffice. The first example is the creation of Canadian Lutheran World Relief (CLWR). At the end of the war the Canadian Lutheran Commission for War Services received news from Europe of the desperate situation of people there. Permission was requested of the government to send relief supplies. This was denied, given that a state of war still existed between Germany and Canada. However, the Department of War Services later requested the Canadian Lutheran Commission for War Services to take action. On March 14, 1946, a small advisory group met in Ottawa, and Canadian Lutheran World Relief was established and began a major effort to deliver relief to a devastated Europe and to resettle in Canada those who had been displaced by the war (Hordern 1977, 46). It was an interesting twist that Lutherans would be asked by the government to undertake this work. Since that time CLWR has worked closely with the Canadian government and has established a good reputation for its work in refugee resettlement and delivery of development aid through Lutheran World Service.

The experience of CLWR and its work with refugees increased awareness of the needs of social welfare. Through the Canadian Lutheran Council, a committee was struck to consider what role the Council could play to meet the needs. It was observed that many social welfare needs were being filled ". . . largely by individual pastors who were much concerned but usually cannot give the time and effort necessary for an adequate program" (Hordern 1977, 106). Following a survey of the needs, the report called for congregational welfare committees, annual workshops at the regional level, provincial Lutheran Welfare Councils and a Lutheran Welfare Council of Canada. The latter Council was formed, and Rev. Cliff Monk was appointed as the first executive staff person.

From these experiences, the Lutheran community became more socially and politically engaged. During the 1960s Lutherans participated in the establishment of the many ecumenical coalitions. In addition, a whole body of social teaching was developed that included some thirty-two major social statements in addition to countless resolutions at church conventions and hundreds of letters and exchanges with government on a wide range of issues, many of which have been published as *Horizons for Justice* by the Institute of Christian Ethics at Waterloo Lutheran Seminary, Waterloo, Ontario.

Some qualification is in order at this point. First, the changes described here pertain mostly to the Evangelical Lutheran Church in Canada. Presently the Missouri Synod, or Lutheran Church—Canada, takes a very conservative approach to its involvement with government and society, limiting itself for the most part to acts of charity. Second, one must acknowledge changes that have taken place in all the churches in Canada. The marked differences between "then" and "now" in other churches certainly have influenced changes within Lutheranism.

With these qualifications, there has been a marked difference in the way Lutherans perceive their role in the world. Dr. Roger Nostbakken, a Lutheran theologian and former vice-president of the Evangelical Lutheran Church of Canada, in addressing a Lutheran convention in 1979, stated,

The day is over when the pastor can go about his holy business and not be a functioning part of the community in which s/he lives. The church does not stand over against the world, it is *in* the world, a part of it—as Christians we share the life of communities in which we live. As Christians we are not intrinsically smarter, or better or more righteous than others. We share the same kinds of problems and personal ambiguities as everyone else. The difference is that the Christian faces life with a different perspective and a different set of loyalties. That perspective and those loyalties are bound up in the belief in and commitment to serve Jesus Christ. But this is a view of life and an orientation to be expressed in this world. It is not a style of life to be lived in isolation from others (Nostbakken 1979).

Dr. Nostbakken's observations summarize the hopes of many Lutherans in this most recent chapter of Canadian Lutheranism.

Interestingly, in a 1980 survey of Lutherans, 56.1 percent of the laity and 78.5 percent of the clergy felt the church should be involved in government-related issues (Profiles 1980, H3). Therefore, it is clearly both a commitment and a hope that the new Evangelical Lutheran Church in Canada will participate politically and socially in addressing the crucial questions that will shape the Canadian social agenda.

In Conclusion
While the face of Canadian Lutheranism has changed in Canada in the past two hundred years, Lutherans have very much been shaped by the modern Canadian context. In that evolution Lutherans have sought to be faithful to the confessional principles articulated by Luther. Luther's central insight of *sola fide* led him to perceive the human experience within the framework of a "theology of the cross" as manifested in the "two kingdoms." For Luther faith served to guarantee ethical action.

The context for ethics has changed. Lutherans are not dealing with a theocratic society, for example. Secularism is probably a greater threat to faith than clericalism. Lutherans have sought to reflect an integrated understanding of Luther's "two kingdoms" and the actions that would ensue. Within the practice of Lutheranism there has been an expanding perception of the role of the Lutheran community *in and for* the world. Recognizing this reality, Lutherans will continue to reform their witness to Canadian society. As William Lazareth aptly observed regarding the important opportunities of this changed context, "Luther had to put the Church back under God's gospel; we have to put the state back under God's law" (in Neuhaus 1977, 185).

9. Mennonites in Canada:

Their Relations with and Effect on the Larger Society

William Janzen

Introduction

The questions I wish to address include the following: how have Mennonite churches related to Canadian society historically; how have they understood their mission theologically; what activities have they undertaken, other than missionary and evangelistic activities; what effect have they had on Canadian society; and what might be an appropriate approach for the future.

It is challenging to consider the life and work of Canadian Mennonites in light of these questions. At the present time approximately 150,000 people, including children, attend Mennonite churches in Canada. This represents less than one percent of the Canadian population. Still, Mennonites have been in Canada for two hundred years and during this time they have related to the larger society in certain identifiable ways. Two themes that stand out are "separatism" and "service." Broadly speaking, separatism was the primary characteristic before 1950 and service was emphasized more strongly in subsequent decades. But neither theme was emphasized to the exclusion of the other. There was a significant degree of service before 1950 and a degree of separatism later. Nor are these the only two themes of Canadian Mennonite life. A close examination would reveal a number of other impulses and characteristics. Unfortunately, on this occasion I am able to provide only a broad survey, not a close examination.

Separatism: Developments before 1950

Mennonites in Canada, from late in the 1700s to the 1950s, tended to live in communities unto themselves. In most cases this was not a rigid separation. A number of Mennonites participated significantly in the larger society. And the degree of Mennonite separation was not particularly unusual. Many immigrant groups tended to live in communities by themselves for generations. Nevertheless, Mennonites had certain theologically-based concerns which made them distinctive and which required special accommodating provisions. These provisions included a 1793 Upper Canada law assuring them, as well as Quakers and Tunkers (now Brethren in Christ), of exemption from military duties, and an 1809 law giving them the right to make affirmations instead of oaths. Swearing an oath was incompatible with their interpretation of the biblical teaching in Matthew 5:34. In spite of these distinctives, the early Upper Canada Mennonites were quick to join with others in building roads and operating schools. Indeed, some Mennonites led the way in establishing schools. It appears also that they were charitable in responding to human need and that they had good relations with native Canadians and other settlers. Also, some Mennonites served on County Councils.

Late in the 1800s more Mennonites immigrated to Canada, this time to the west. Some of these had a stronger desire to live in communities by themselves. One group of 7,000, coming from Russia in the 1870s, received an elaborate Order-in-Council from the federal government which reaffirmed Mennonite exemption from military service and gave them freedom to operate their own schools. In addition, the federal government modified the new homestead system so that they could settle in blocks, exclusively by themselves, and live in villages. Some decades later, more Mennonites came but these were less concerned about living in exclusive communities, though they identified with the importance of being exempted from military service.

Soon after World War I some of the more conservative Mennonites in Manitoba and Saskatchewan became involved in a tragic governmental encounter. At issue were the new public schools. These Mennonite groups had 1600 school-age children in the two provinces together, and they sent them to their own German-language schools.

The curriculum was limited but they felt that it adequately prepared their children for life in their communities. They also felt that they could not, without violating their religious principles, turn the education of their children over to governments. The provincial governments, however, had determined that all children were to attend public schools. They also had the necessary constitutional authority, notwithstanding the promise of educational freedom given to the Mennonites by the federal government in 1873. The provincial governments then began to impose fines on the parents of school age children who were not attending public schools. The Mennonites paid these fines, eventually selling land and cattle in order to do so. When all pleading and negotiation failed, about 6,000 of these conservative Mennonites moved to Latin America.

While these conservative Mennonites objected to the public school system, other Mennonites cooperated with it extensively. Indeed, they were pioneers in setting up teacher training institutes—in Manitoba in 1889 and in Saskatchewan in 1905—with which they also served educational needs outside of their own communities. But even these Mennonites reflected a significant separatism. They had little involvement with the large Prohibition and Social Gospel movements of the time. This reflected certain theological perspectives, but it may also have been due to their rural setting and to the serious military exemption difficulties that they experienced in World War I. These exemption controversies gave rise to such a strong public feeling against Mennonites that the federal government, in 1919, passed an Order-in-Council prohibiting further Mennonite immigration. Fortunately, this prohibition was quietly lifted in 1922 with the result that another 21,000 Mennonites from Russia immigrated later in the 1920s. Getting these people properly resettled took up much Mennonite energy for years thereafter.

The World War II experience, while reinforcing a self-understanding of separateness, also encouraged other tendencies. Early on, Mennonite leaders, hoping to avoid the negative public feeling of World War I, proposed an alternative national service program to the government. This was accepted, reluctantly at first, but before the war was over, some 7,500 Mennonite men had participated in it. Another 3,000 participants came from various other denominations. This experience broke down some of the differences among Mennonite groups. It also strengthened Mennonite interest in programs of practical service in the larger society and around the world.

Service: Canadian Mennonites after 1950
The service orientation of Canadian Mennonites became stronger
after 1950, but it had been present earlier already. In addition to
responses to local needs, there were relief efforts directed at India in
the 1890s, at Russia in the 1920s, and at the Middle East in the
inter-war years. During World War I, Ontario Mennonites joined with
other groups in setting up the Non-Resistant Relief Organization.
And in western Canada Mennonites also collected monies for "war
sufferers relief," as the victims of war were then known. After World
War II there were extensive efforts to assist with reconstruction and
refugee needs in Europe and other areas devastated by that war. In
more recent decades Mennonite churches have sent teachers, agricul-
turalists and other resources to the fifty countries where the Mennonite Central Committee (MCC), the relief and development
organization set up in 1920, is active. Clearly, many Mennonite service
efforts have been directed at international needs but the focus of this
paper is on their contributions to Canadian society. I will list the
following.

A More Charitable and Internationalist Spirit
Mennonites have made a modest but significant contribution to the
development of a more charitable and internationalist attitude in
Canadian society. The contribution has been made through a number
of activities.
    1. Mennonite Disaster Service (MDS). MDS was formed in the
1950s when the federal government was promoting a civil defence
program. Mennonites did not want to participate in that program
because of its military aspects. They then set up an organization of
their own to respond to natural disasters, and to do cleanup and
reconstruction work. The MDS response to the tornadoes which
struck Barrie, Ontario, in 1986 and Edmonton, Alberta, in 1987 are
among the recent projects. The "hands-on" work of ordinary men and
women under the MDS umbrella helped many people whose posses-
sions had been destroyed. This work received considerable attention
in the media.
    2. The Relief Sales. In 1967 Mennonites in the Kitchener area
decided that one additional way of raising money for the international
work of MCC would be to organize a sale of various donated items.
This has now become an annual event in many Mennonite areas of

Canada. The atmosphere of the sales is somewhat like that of large country fairs. Thousands of non-Mennonite people attend, and newspapers, such as the *Toronto Star* and the *Winnipeg Free Press*, promote them generously, often with several pages of stories about the international work for which the money will be used. By 1989 annual receipts from these sales exceeded one million dollars.

3. The Canadian Foodgrains Bank (CFB). Mennonite Central Committee Canada (MCCC) began this project in 1976 and opened it to other church groups some years later. As a result Baptists, Lutherans, Alliance, Christian Reformed, Nazarene, Pentecostal, United, and Evangelical church groups have also joined. The core concept is that farmers donate grain which is then banked until it is needed somewhere in the world. The program utilizes the elevator system on the prairies. CIDA matches the donations on a generous basis. The CFB has shipped over several hundred thousand metric tonnes of grain to various parts of the world.

4. Refugee Resettlement. Canadian Mennonites did much to help resettle Mennonite refugees from Europe after the two world wars, and to assist other refugees in other parts of the world. But they were not active in resettling other refugees in Canada until the "boat people" crisis hit the headlines in 1978-79. They then quickly negotiated an agreement with the federal government (this became a model for fifteen other national churches and organizations), and brought over thousands of Southeast Asian refugees. Subsequently Canadian Mennonites have also assisted with the resettlement of Central American refugees. In these ways Canadian Mennonites have helped to make Canadian society more receptive toward refugees.

5. SELFHELP Crafts. This MCC program imports craft items made by people in developing countries, sells them in Canada, and channels the profits back to the producers. With more than fifty SELFHELP stores in Canada, the annual sales in 1990 exceeded three million dollars. In addition to the money that is transferred, the sales also promote a greater awareness about the countries and the conditions in which the crafts are made.

If Canadian Mennonites have contributed to an internationalist attitude in Canada, it should not be surprising. Canadian Mennonites are an international people. Thousands of Canadian Mennonites have close relatives abroad, some in Russia and some in Latin America. Also, they have worship services, in Canada, in at least nine different languages, reflecting the acceptance of people from different cultures. And they have been generous in sending both money and people abroad, for either missionary or MCC service. The several thousand people who have returned from terms of MCC service abroad, which usually last three years, have gone into various occupations and professions and supported internationalist causes in innumerable ways.

Peace and War Considerations

The history of Canadian Mennonites reviewed in the second section of this paper indicates their long-standing concern about the right to refrain from military service. The first Canadian laws which granted this right restricted it to members of certain religious groups. Gradually the right was broadened, and halfway through World War II anyone, without regard to church affiliation, could appear before a board and argue that he had "conscientious objections" to military service. Mennonites probably contributed to the acceptance of this concept, though other factors were at work as well. (It can be noted here that in 1980, when a Parliamentary Committee was studying the then proposed Canadian Charter of Rights and Freedoms, MCCC made a submission which argued, among other things, that "conscientious objection to the taking of human life" should be expressly included so as to cover situations relating to war, police work, and medicine, e.g., abortions.)

Canadian Mennonites have also made a contribution to broader peace and war issues. One part of this contribution relates to Project Ploughshares, the coalition which does extensive research and writing on Canadian military concerns. In 1990 Ploughshares had a budget of approximately $500,000 and a staff of ten people. Ploughshares' history can be traced to the early 1970s when MCCC, prompted by a concern about the use of Canadian military goods in the Vietnam War, initiated a research project on Canada's arms industry. Ernie Regehr was the researcher and his report was published in 1975 as the book, *Making a Killing: Canada's Arms Industry.* Soon thereafter Project Ploughshares was set up with support from the Quakers, the United Church, CUSO, and MCCC, and with the sponsorship of Canadian Council of Churches. Some years later additional groups joined, but the Mennonite connections remain significant. Ploughshares has published several important books. It issues *Ploughshares Monitor* on a quarterly basis. It prepares numerous governmental submissions and is generally quite influential. In the spring of 1988 Ernie Regehr, who has continued to be a leading Ploughshares staff person, addressed the General Assembly of the United Nations.

Victim-Offender Concerns

Another area where Mennonites have made a contribution to Canadian society relates to people in trouble with the law. The contribution has several parts. One involves a prisoner visitation program begun in British Columbia in 1966. Mennonites were soon joined by Christian Reformed people and later also by people from other denominations. The program is called M2/W2 (Man to Man/Woman to Woman) and involves volunteers who regularly visit individual inmates. The intent is to build personal relationships with the inmates in order to encourage them while they are in the institutions, and to help them become established after they are released. In subsequent years, visitation programs have been set up in five more provinces, involving almost 900 "visitors," of whom approximately one-half come from Mennonite churches.

A second part of the contribution involves residences and farms as alternatives to prisons. Mennonites have set up a number of places like this. A brochure says that offenders, by "living in a group, learning work habits and relating with Christian staff people ... learn new ways of dealing with the joys and sorrows of everyday life. The stability of these homes has provided a new beginning for many."

A third type of involvement pursues reconciliation between victims and offenders. This began in 1974 in Elmira, Ontario, where two young men had gone on a vandalism spree, doing $2,200 worth of damage on twenty-two properties. Six days later, before the court session, a Mennonite probation-parole officer proposed that instead of simply sending the young men to prison they should meet with their victims. The judge agreed and two Mennonite workers, Mark Yantzi and Dave Worth, then arranged the meetings with the victims and helped the offenders to propose suitable forms of restitution. The effort proved successful and the idea has spread. Mennonites now operate reconciliation programs in four Canadian cities with a total of 115 volunteers working on numerous cases. Other groups, both religious and secular, have set up similar programs elsewhere in Canada and the United States.

In addition, Mennonites have given considerable energy to public education and advocacy in relation to legislation. Some of this is done through the Church Council on Justice and Corrections, to which

Mennonites are making a significant contribution. One result is that terms such as reconciliation are now found in certain pieces of legislation and government documents.

Native Canadian Concerns

Mennonites have also made a contribution in matters relating to Canada's native people. During World War II some Mennonite conscientious objectors did their alternative service work as teachers in native communities in northern Manitoba. This soon led the church to a broader program of sending out workers. Some of the work was of a "church-planting" nature, but there has always been a strong emphasis on education, health, and other concerns. For many years there have been at least thirty people who, at any one time, are working under Mennonite church auspices with native people in both urban and rural settings across Canada. Many serve on a volunteer basis for two year terms.

One aspect of this service involvement is an effort to promote resource development that encourages self-reliance. This includes summer gardening. The native people, it appears, have largely lost the art of making gardens for their food needs. Accordingly, in 1977 MCCC began to send out summer volunteers to help native communities make ordinary vegetable gardens. No less important are the efforts to encourage a greater reliance on wild rice. MCCC has developed appropriate technology for harvesting wild rice. This technology is now used by native people quite extensively. MCCC has also worked at developing markets for the rice.

Under the leadership of Menno Wiebe, MCCC has also made numerous submissions and appeals to governments, both federal and provincial, sometimes independently and sometimes through interchurch coalitions and other bodies. Among those the following were made: in 1977, in relation to the planned flooding of native lands in northern Manitoba because of the construction of a hydro-electric dam; in the late 1970s, in relation to the planned Mackenzie Valley Pipeline; in 1981, to have native rights recognized in the Charter of Rights; in 1982, to the Treaty Land Entitlement Commission; in 1982, to the Royal Commission on the Northern Environment; in 1983, to the MacDonald, Barber and Kimmelman commissions; in 1983, '84, '85 and '86, to the First Ministers Conferences to define the charter's reference to aboriginal rights; and in 1986, '87, '88 and '89 to federal authorities in relation to low-level military flying in Labrador.

A variety of themes have been addressed in these submissions, including the ownership by the native people of their resources, the right of native people to set up institutions of self-government, and their right to "sit at the table" when decisions affecting their well-being are made.

Health and Disability Concerns
Like many church groups, Mennonites have long provided certain health care services, particularly for their own people with mental handicaps, but also for others. In Canada this effort to serve both Mennonites and non-Mennonites was strengthened during World War II when some Mennonite conscientious objectors were assigned to mental hospitals for their alternative service work. According to Dr. Aldred Neufeldt, this experience has led to a large number of Mennonites entering the mental health field. Neufeldt himself contributed significantly to the formation, early in the 1970s, of the Canadian National Institute on Mental Retardation. For a time Neufeldt served as the director of this institute. Other leading Mennonites who have contributed in this field include Dr. John Elias, long-time Associate Director of Mental Health Services for Saskatchewan, and Dr. John Toews, former head of the Department of Psychiatry at the University of Manitoba and a leader in the Canadian Mental Health Association. Also to be noted is the Eden Mental Health Centre at Winkler, Manitoba, which has been exemplary in this field.

Mennonites have also been active on concerns relating to people with physical disabilities. In the mid-1970s such people began to form organizations of their own. In 1976 they set up the Canadian Coalition of Provincial Organizations of the Handicapped (COPOH). Several Mennonite disabled people were instrumental in this movement. One of them, Henry Enns, was appointed to the MCCC staff in 1980. Though confined to a wheelchair, Enns contributed in a major way to a movement which soon saw much greater accessibility in buildings, washrooms, sidewalks, transportation systems, educational programs and employment opportunities. Enns also promoted Independent Living Centres to enable people with disabilities to live on their own. The first centre, begun in Kitchener in 1982, had to rely significantly on MCCC funding. Later, governmental bodies became more supportive. In 1990 there were ten Independent Living Centres in Canadian cities.

Enns and other people were instrumental also in 1980 and 1981 in starting an organization called Disabled Peoples International. CIDA provided funding through MCCC and Enns became a chairperson of DPI which in 1990 had memberships in more than seventy countries. In 1986 Enns took a ten week trip to Africa and came back with reports which have prompted CIDA, certain UN bodies, as well as non-government organizations such as CUSO, Oxfam, and CCODP, to give more attention to disabled people in their aid and development programs. Enns has frequently been consulted by the Canadian government. He has received awards from both the Canadian government and the United Nations.

Other Contributions
Contributions in other areas could also be noted. In music, Mennonites in Winnipeg, Waterloo, Saskatoon, Calgary, Lethbridge, and in the lower mainland of British Columbia have made significant contributions. In agriculture, Mennonites were the first settlers in Canada to farm on the open prairie away from rivers and trees. They also helped to open up new farming areas like the Peace River valley in northern Alberta. In rural development, their work in the 1940s and 1950s in southern Manitoba communities such as Winkler, Altona, and Lowe Farm attracted national and international attention. Among other things, they started credit unions and consumer and producer cooperatives. In the education and teaching fields, Mennonites are more strongly represented than their proportion of the population would suggest. The first two graduates of the doctoral program in educational administration at the University of Alberta were Mennonites.

On the environment, Mennonite and other conscientious objectors during World War II did extensive reforestation work, planting over twenty million trees in British Columbia. Later they did pioneering work in recycling. In the mid-1970s, Peter Wiebe and Dave Worth organized recycling drives in St. Catharines and Kitchener respectively. Eventually these recycling efforts were taken over and developed further by the city authorities. Late in the 1980s, Dave Hubert and Cornelius Guenter, supported by MCCC, led the way in organizing the Edmonton Recycling Society, which then received a $6.4 million four-year recycling contract from that city. The Society employs a number of people with disabilities and as such illustrates MCCC's recently instituted effort to create useful employment for marginalized people.

In 1954 MCC began to send teachers to outports in Newfoundland where they usually served two year terms on a volunteer basis. Two decades later when more Newfoundland teachers became available MCC's program was cut back, but a significant involvement in Labrador continues. Mennonites are also involved with several programs to assist girls and women who find themselves pregnant and in difficult situations to help them choose options other than abortions. Across Canada approximately 150 MCC volunteers work in various programs to alleviate human need. Many other Mennonites work out of their local congregations, responding to various needs. Some do peace and justice education work in their communities. Others do missionary and evangelistic work. Indeed, Canadian Mennonites have long been active in various forms of missionary and evangelistic work. However, a discussion of the effect of these efforts on Canadian society is beyond the scope of this paper.

Not to be overlooked are the communications to government, to which some references have already been made. It used to be that Mennonite churches spoke to governments only on issues affecting their own people. In the last two decades this has changed. Now the concern is to speak on behalf of others. In recent years there have been over a hundred significant communications to the federal government on matters of policy. These include presentations before Parliamentary Committees, letters to ministers and personal meetings. Approximately one-third of these communications come from MCCC directly, The rest come from the eight organizations in which MCCC has membership, such as Project Ploughshares, the Interchurch Committee for Refugees, the Canadian Council for International Co-operation, or from organizations such as the Evangelical Fellowship of Canada, with which MCCC has a formal connection though not membership. One "rule of thumb" for our governmental communications is that we speak out of our service experience. Hence we will be more ready to speak to governments on those issues which we are also trying to address with our service programs.

Theological Considerations

What is the theological basis for relating to Canadian society in the manner described in the preceding pages? Instead of attempting a comprehensive answer to this question, I will refer only to certain theological considerations, many of which are not distinctly Mennonite.

Often in Mennonite churches the service orientation is supported by references to biblical passages such as: 1) Matthew 25:31-46 where Jesus, in a parable about the last judgment, emphasizes the importance of giving food to the hungry, drink to the thirsty, clothing to the naked, and shelter to the homeless, as well as visiting those in prison; 2) Luke 4:18, where Jesus begins his ministry by announcing that he has been anointed to preach good news to the poor, release to the captives, sight to the blind, and liberty for the oppressed; 3) Mark 12:31, where Jesus says that the second great commandment is that we should love our neighbour as ourselves; 4) Matthew 20:25-28 where Jesus says that he came to serve, not to be served, and that his followers should not lord it over each other but be servants of one another, all of which is illustrated at the Last Supper where Jesus washes the disciples' feet; and 5) Philippians 2:1-6 where Christians are told to adopt the mind of Christ who humbled himself and took on the form of a servant.

The service orientation is also supported by references to sixteenth century Anabaptist leaders. Hans Denck is quoted as saying, "No one can truly know Christ except he follow him in life." And Menno Simons wrote, "All those who are born of God are prepared by love to serve their neighbours, not only with money and goods, but after the example of their Lord, in an evangelical manner, with life and blood. They show mercy as much as they can. They entertain those in distress. They take the stranger into their houses. They comfort the afflicted, assist the needy, clothe the naked, feed the hungry, do not turn their face from the poor." Related to this call to serve is the Mennonite understanding of what it means to be a Christian and what it means to be the church. As suggested above, in the early Anabaptist movement it was held that to become a Christian involved an individual decision to confess, trust, and follow Christ. Such individuals, it was assumed, would covenant with each other and thus form the church. The church, then, was a voluntary body. Not everyone who lived in a given territory automatically belonged to it. Nor did the church have much of a hierarchy, though leaders were chosen and various ordinances, such as baptism and holy communion, were carefully followed.

The idea of the church as a distinctive body has been interpreted in several ways in Mennonite history. In some settings it has been used to support a separateness in dress patterns, technology, and geography, sometimes with appeals to such New Testament passages as Romans 12:2, 2 Corinthians 6:17, and 1 John 2:15. In other settings it has led simply to a considerable self-preoccupation. Either way, it is not too surprising that in some quarters Mennonites have been seen primarily as an ethnic group. But the theology need not be interpreted in that way. It can also be understood as "separated for service," in which case the concern is not first of all with separation but with a particular commitment and orientation which may or may not be distinctive. This second interpretation is relatively strong among contemporary Canadian Mennonites, though other motifs, reflecting both liberalism and fundamentalism, are also present. The "separated for service" orientation is reflected in the thousands of volunteers who work on the relief sales, the SELFHELP and thrift stores, and the MDS projects, and in the support that congregations give to individuals who go into longer and more formal service programs. These people feel themselves to be the church in action.

If there is a theology for service, is there also one for advocacy work, that is, for speaking to government? In my view there is one but it is not formed in precise and elaborate ways. Indeed, it reflects an ambivalence similar to the separatism and service themes noted above. In the early 1500s most Mennonites held that they should not participate in government. According to Menno Simons,

> ... Disciples of Christ ... have no weapons except patience, hope, silence and God's Word. . . . They are weapons with which the spiritual kingdom of the devil is destroyed and the wicked principle in man's soul is broken down. . . . Christ is our fortress; patience our weapon of defence; the Word of God our sword; and our victory a courageous, firm, unfeigned faith in Jesus Christ.

Nevertheless, Menno Simons also made a number of appeals to rulers, saying that they had been given "the sword of righteousness" and that they should use this moderately to punish evildoers and to "do justice between a man and his neighbour, to deliver the oppressed out of the hand of the oppressor." This suggests that governments, including their reliance on certain weapons, are necessary but that Christians should not use those weapons. Hence, Christians should

not participate in government, at least not in those parts of government where they might be called on to use such weapons.

At certain times in Mennonite history all governmental involvement has been discouraged. However, in recent decades, Mennonite
theologians have emphasized the prophetic tradition from the Old
Testament and the teaching that God cares equally for all people,
including those in countries which our governments may have defined
as enemies. Some have referred specifically to Jesus' teaching that we
should love our neighbour as ourselves and that this should lead us to
use certain political channels in order to work for our neighbour's
well-being, whether our neighbour is a Central American refugee or
a homeless person in Toronto. Other Mennonite theologians, of
whom John Howard Yoder may be the best known, say that Jesus was
faced with several political options, including that of quietism,
zealotry, and conservative social responsibility. Yoder argues that
Jesus rejected each of these but was nevertheless politically engaged.
One of Yoder's essays has the suggestive title, "Neither Guerrilla nor
Conquista: The Presence of the Kingdom as Social Ethic." His most
widely read book is entitled *The Politics of Jesus.*

In my view Mennonite theology, as articulated in recent decades,
provides an adequate basis for certain kinds of political involvement.

What of the Future?

I have no particular insight but I will refer to a few trends. First, it is
my understanding that the charitable giving of Canadians is gradually
but steadily decreasing. To date, Mennonite organizations have not
experienced a decline but if that is a general trend, Mennonites will
not remain unaffected. Secondly, Mennonite agencies have emphasized the sending of people to do the serving. It relates to a
theology of the incarnation—putting the Christian message in human
form. But Canada's social and economic structure, into which Mennonites are now integrated, may make it more difficult for people to
leave for short or longer terms of service and to come back and find
a place. There seem to be less and less flexibility and cushion room.

Thirdly, if Canadian Mennonites once came almost entirely from
one ethnic background, that is no longer the case. They are multicultural now. In addition they now have a substantial interaction with
other churches, including those in the "evangelical" stream and those
in the "mainline" tradition, some of which is referred to in the preceding pages. This ethnic diversity and broader theological interaction

can be both challenging and enriching. It also raises certain questions: will Mennonites become absorbed by the larger streams, as many individual Mennonites already have; will a future historian have to write "Mennonites, *both* Guerrillas and Conquistas;" or is there something in this historical orientation which can survive and continue to contribute to Canadian society?

10. The Pentecostal Assemblies of Canada

Wayne Dawes

The word "culture" conjures up in the mind thoughts of music and art and learning—an improvement or refinement of the mind and manners—the intellectual development of a civilization. There is no doubt that the Christian church at large has made and is still making a positive contribution in this area. Says Paul Tillich, "Religion is the substance of culture, culture is the form of religion" (1959, 42). Discussions in this paper, however, will be restricted to the social concerns and action of the Pentecostal Assemblies of Canada (P.A.O.C.),and in particular to the Assemblies' concerted efforts in this area in the last twenty or so years.

History of Social Concerns

Brief History and Statement of Purpose
Social concern in the P.A.O.C. goes back to the very founding of the organization at the turn of the century. The P.A.O.C. is a product of the revival that occurred in the early 1900s when it would seem that on a worldwide scale there was a spontaneous desire and hunger on the part of many for a greater and deeper personal experience with God. Much prayer and seeking led to a multitude of people entering into a new relationship with God that was marked by experiences of divine healing and glossolalia (speaking in tongues). The revival

spread from Topeka, Kansas, where students and staff at a small Bible school through careful study of the Scriptures, concluded that "speaking in tongues" was the initial evidence of being baptized in the Spirit (Acts 2:4, et al.). After much prayer they received the experience. From Kansas to Texas and finally to Los Angeles the Pentecostal message was preached. The Azusa Street Mission in Los Angeles became a focal point of the new movement. People came from all over the world to hear about the renewed emphasis of the Holy Spirit's fullness and to seek this experience. Robert E. McAlister brought the message from Los Angeles back to Canada: to Vancouver, to Kinburn, Ontario, and to Ottawa. The message attracted people from various religious backgrounds, in particular Methodists and Mennonites. A strong holiness influence developed with an emphasis on personal salvation, a holy and separated life-style, divine healing and a free and demonstrative type of worship, along with the major emphasis on the experience of the baptism in the Holy Spirit and glossolalia.

As the revival spread and the movement grew it became evident that some form of organization was necessary. Because of a fear of losing freedom and the unction of the Holy Spirit, there was a reluctance on the part of some towards any form of organization. James Hebden of the Hebden Mission in Toronto was particularly vocal in this regard (1910, 15). After several attempts, a loose form of organization was established and incorporation was granted the P.A.O.C. in 1919. Hebdens' fears were not realized. In spite of being organized, the P.A.O.C. has continued to grow and to be blessed by God.

One of the seven articles of purpose in the original charter was "to carry on charitable and philanthropic work of every kind." The rationale behind the inclusion of this article is the subject of speculation.

At the end of World War I there was a great need for nation rebuilding. Perhaps this was one of the influencing factors. Certainly in those early days of Pentecostalism many of the people who were attracted to the infant organization were from the poor and needy class. It may also simply have been that the P.A.O.C. was born at a time of great social awareness which began in the late nineteenth century and resulted in the founding of numerous societies and the passing of a significant number of laws to meet the needs of an ever increasing industrial society. A good part of this social movement, particularly in the United States, was spearheaded by the church and in particular by prominent theologians such as Niebuhr and Tillich. In 1917 Walter Rauschenbusch, the father of the Social Gospel (a dated, protestant, liberal phenomenon which lasted until the early 1930s), wrote his *Theology for a Social Gospel.* In this work he challenged the church to go beyond individual salvation and to involve itself in the needs of society. While the P.A.O.C., along with many other evangelical organizations, rejected any radical social gospel and threw all of its eggs into the basket of evangelism and missions, one cannot help but wonder whether his challenge might have fallen on some listening ears.

Early Attempts at Social Involvement
Apart from local activity, little in terms of any organized concerted effort was done by the P.A.O.C. until the mid 1970s. There are some significant achievements, however, that stand out. In 1928 Bethel Home for girls was founded to provide care for unwed mothers. In 1960 it became part of the Benevolent Association of Ontario. The ministry expanded to include the development of academic/vocational skills, re-integration into the family, interpersonal relationships and the development of self-esteem, self-control and self-awareness. The work now includes help for non-pregnant girls with family conflicts or behavioral problems.

The Benevolent Association of Ontario, already mentioned, was established in 1958 for the purpose of ". . . maintaining unmarried mothers and their children and such other charitable work as the Association may desire to enter into. . . ." In response to a challenge by a Toronto newspaper man, R. E. McAlister founded the Shepherd Lodge for seniors in 1961. In 1965 it was expanded to 150 beds. Shepherd Manor with its 263 units was completed in 1976. Many Pentecostal churches have become involved in Senior Citizens apartment complexes and minimal care units as well as low income housing. Another organization which falls under the umbrella of the Benevolent Association is Teen Challenge. This ministry developed out of the work of David Wilkerson in New York City in the 1960s. It was established to provide support for those who recognize a need to resolve personal problems and has had wonderful success, particularly in the area of drug and alcohol rehabilitation (DeWolf 1975).

One of the unique ministries of the P.A.O.C. in the northland is the Hay River Hospital. Because of a need in the north for medical services, meetings were held back in 1952 with the result that a nursing station was set up in the following year. Money from the estate of H. H. Williams, administered by the Stone Church, together with funds raised by both protestants and Catholics, contributed to the establishment of a six-bed hospital which was later replaced by a 22-bed hospital in June of 1965 when the former building was wiped out by a flood. In 1976 the ribbon was cut for a 50-bed hospital. Doctors and nurses work here and at nursing stations such as Pine Point, on missionary salaries. The Hay River Hospital is a very modern facility with the highest possible ranking from the accrediting association.

The Last Ten Years
During those early years we were satisfied in the main with the general moral climate of our society. There was still an emphasis and adherence to basic Judeo-Christian ethics. A decline, however, in individual and public morality in Canada during the last twenty years has sparked the P.A.O.C. to a more definite and organized involvement. Resolutions passed at our General Conferences from the years 1976-1988 show an attempt to deal with issues such as euthanasia, abortion, sexual orientation, pornography, Sunday shopping, prostitution, lotteries, etc. In 1983 a full-time Coordinator of Social Concerns and Public Relations was appointed and a Standing Committee on Social Concerns was created. One of the first things accomplished under the leadership of Rev. Hudson Hilsden was the writing of a position paper on abortion. Other such papers have been commissioned by resolution of the General Conference.

In 1985 and again more recently, a Social Concerns Theological and Philosophical Committee met to determine the biblical framework and to draw up guidelines for the Office of Social Concerns (PAOC 1987, 8). From the discussions, as well as a consideration of our past and our theology, one can gain a sense of at least some of the motivating factors affecting our attitude and involvement in social issues.

Factors Affecting Attitude and Involvement in Social Concerns

Doctrine
The P.A.O.C. has a very brief and loose statement of faith, leaving room for a variety of interpretations in a number of areas. The lack of delineation has sometimes been viewed as a strength rather than a weakness and fits in well with the Assemblies' concept of a coopera-

tive fellowship of autonomous churches. There is little doubt that in several areas of theology our doctrine either implicitly or explicitly has influenced our social involvement. I note the following points.

a) The Assemblies has a strong belief in the inspiration and inerrancy of Scripture. Revelation, we believe, is complete within the pages of the Protestant canon. A tendency to an extreme literal approach on the part of some has led to proof texting and the building of arguments from just a few select Scriptures. This weakness in a lack of a consistent and uniform hermeneutic has resulted in a lack of consensus in such areas as capital punishment, Christian schools, and divorce and remarriage. While the General Conference has approved a position on a woman's place in ministry, we are far from an agreement in this area.

b) In our anthropology there is a strong belief in human depravity and therefore a stress on individual salvation along with separation from the world. There is a strong feeling that personal salvation by its very nature corrects moral and social ills (Gal. 5:6), and that such things as sexual impropriety are reduced. Some may argue against this in light of the recent failures of some high profile Christian leaders, as well as the dismal lack of effect that the millions of people in North America who claim to be "born again" have had on the morality of our society. If anything, the stress on individual salvation by evangelicals has resulted in a failure to give enough importance to the communal and social dimensions of human existence.

c) The Assemblies sees the church as a called-out body of believers that will minister the love of God to the whole person. This again is seen as a natural outcome of a life-changing conversion where "self" becomes less important as we seek to become more like Christ. The church is to serve people on the physical and emotional as well as the spiritual plane. Programs in many churches, however, seek to develop mainly the spiritual side of human life and cater on the whole to the believer rather than minister to the general populace. As John Stott remarks, "Fellowship with each other in the church is more congenial than service in an apathetic and even hostile environment outside" (1985, 35). In practice, then, there has often been a stress on such things as church facilities and programs that feed the saints, sometimes at the expense of ministering to the hurting. One example of this is the number of churches that have relocated from downtown core areas to the suburbs. A re-evaluation and change in emphasis in some of these areas has been encouraging.

d) A slowness to get involved in social activities is also, I believe, implicitly a result of a descending rather than an ascending Christology. The emphasis on the Christ, the Son of God, who came down to be our Saviour, healer and baptizer in the Holy Spirit, rather than beginning with the historical Jesus and the way he ministered to the whole person, teaching us by example and by instruction to do the same. It would be important to note that in the passage where Jesus refers to the time of judgment (Matt. 25), the basis for judgment is whether we fed the hungry, clothed the naked and visited those in prison. Contemporary socio-critical and liberation theologies stress an ascending Christology and see the Lord's ministry as both redemptive and social as in Luke 4:18.

e) In the area of eschatology the P.A.O.C. takes a pre-tribulation position with a strong belief in the immanent return of Christ to rapture the church. As John Stott (1985) and Harvey Cox (*Piety and Politics*) suggest, the evangelical church—and in the case of Cox—the Pentecostal Church, has sometimes opted out of social involvement because it would have little effect on a world that was becoming increasingly decadent, and social activity may interfere with the coming of Christ, who is seen as the only hope for the world.

Stress on Evangelism

Perhaps the way that our eschatology has influenced us the most is that it has led to a stress on evangelism. If Jesus is coming back soon for his church, then we must be about our duty to spread the good news of salvation to as many as we can as fast as we can. There is great concern in the Assemblies to keep evangelism a priority.

"The fulfilment of the great commission, in the light of the immanency of Christ's return, must remain the highest priority in the church's relationship with the world" (PAOC 1987, 8). This has been re-emphasized in our mission policy where the statement of purpose reads, "The primary objectives of the P.A.O.C. overseas mission department policy shall be to preach Christ and lead people to receive Him in saving faith and to gather these believers into local congregations." The P.A.O.C. supports over 280 full time missionaries, and many of them are involved in various areas of social concern. Among other things, the Assemblies has a school for the blind in Thailand, a 150 acre agricultural development project in Zambia, community health care centres in India, a veterinary project among the Masai of Kenya, a reforestation project in Ethiopia, and basic adult literacy programs in Liberia and Malawi. Our missionaries are involved in various areas of teaching, medicine and training to improve people's skills. ERDO—Emergency Relief and Development Overseas—which is a division of our missions department, works with governments and other agencies in providing food for the hungry around the world. These things are seen as a Christian obligation and a way of earning for us the right to be heard—a door to the preaching of the gospel.

The relational aspect of social concerns and evangelism is still under discussion. The difficulty of a consensus can be seen in the discussions held in Lausanne at the International Congress on Evangelism, and more recently in meetings at Grand Rapids.

Separation of Secular and Spiritual
One last item which would seem to influence evangelicals and certainly Pentecostals in their social involvement is the separation of the secular and the spiritual. We see ourselves, as the Scriptures say, as being in this world but not of it, as pilgrims passing through and heading for that heavenly city whose builder and maker is God. The secular, material aspects of life are then to be minimized and the stress is on the spiritual. Feeding the poor, vocational training, fighting against pornography, abortion and prostitution are sometimes then seen as merely secular activities that are often done by the non-Christian. The spiritual exercises of preaching and worship, of evangelism and discipleship are seen to be the focus of the Christian life, with a stress on prayer and the power of God to take care of all our needs, both physical and spiritual. There has sometimes then been a lack of appreciation for the medical profession, social work and agencies which seek to cater to our temporal needs.

A Look at the Future—Some Personal Observations
With some exceptions as noted, the emphasis in the area of social concerns in the P.A.O.C. to this point has been mainly in the area of moral issues rather than social action. This is partly due, as mentioned, to a background in the holiness tradition and a theology which calls for a radical spiritual change in depraved mankind whose original creation in the image of God has been marred due to the fall. It is also partly due to a sense of inadequacy. There is a reluctance to speak out on issues such as apartheid, nuclear war, etc., without being informed and able to give a sound rational and biblical response. What the

P.A.O.C. has done it has done well, and it has made a major contribution in those areas of involvement, sometimes also being in the vanguard.

A biblical framework along with guidelines for social action in the future has been developed and will be under review. To have a theological and philosophical undergirding was important to us, and we now need to be open enough and flexible enough to allow that biblical theology to influence and change us and challenge us to further action.

In discussions at various levels we are also concluding that we need to get serious about social concerns if we really desire to be the "salt of the earth" and the "light of the world." We have taken some strong stands in a number of areas and we now need to deal with the consequences of our commitment. This means making finances, personnel and training available in order to give further direction and to offer alternatives. It is encouraging to see more of our churches developing crisis pregnancy centres, adoption agencies, relief centres, and offering support and counselling to those in need. This kind of commitment, of course, necessitates a holistic view of ministry and an anthropology that sees all people as made in the image of God and precious in his sight. We must realize that whatever we do, we do to the glory of God and we must minimize or eliminate completely the gulf between the secular and spiritual. Says Tillich, "The universe is God's sanctuary. Every workday is a day of the Lord, every supper a Lord's Supper, every work the fulfilment of a divine task, every joy a joy in God. In all preliminary concerns, ultimate concern is present, consecrating them. Essentially the religious and the secular are not separated realms" (Tillich 1959, 41). While we could have difficulty with a great deal of his theology, in this area he seems to be in agreement with the words of James 1:27, "Religion that God our father accepts as pure and faultless is this: to look after orphans and widows in their distress and to keep oneself from being polluted from the world."

Ronald Sider chides the evangelical community for abandoning the examples set by such reformers as Charles Finney, William Wilberforce and John Wesley. He points out that they all focused on justice for the poor, the needy and the oppressed. If we are going to be faithful to our roots and our heritage we need to broaden our vision and our concern. This will mean that we must evaluate our lifestyle, our emphasis and our priorities. We will also have to strive for consistency in both our message and our action. Surely the teachings of Jesus challenge us to be pro-life and pro-justice, whether in the gutter of our large cities at home, in the drylands of Ethiopia, the struggles of South Africa or in the unrest of South and Central America. At the same time we need to search continually for balance, to be careful we don't get caught up in the materialism and prosperity emphasis of the new religious right, while at the same time we must be careful to avoid the extremes of the left that border on a Protestant liberation theology.

The basic position of the P.A.O.C. as to social concerns is reflected in this statement: "Social responsibility must never be viewed as an end in itself but as a legitimate means of bringing the love of God to a dying world and enhance our attempts at evangelism and discipleship. It must never become the main reason for our existence as a fellowship" (PAOC 1987). We echo an "Amen" to this statement, and also go on to suggest that there would be very few better reasons for our existence. As Stott says, "Mission is our human response to the divine commission. It is a whole Christian life-style, including both evangelism and social responsibility dominated by the conviction that Christ sends us out into the world as the father sent him into the world, and that into the world we must therefore go—to live and serve, suffer and die for Him" (Stott 1985, 36).

11. The Orthodox Church in Canada

Daniel J. Sahas

At the 1984 Learned Societies Conference held at the University of Guelph some fifty scholars attempted to form a "Society of Orthodox Studies in Canada." All of them were involved in teaching and research on various aspects related, directly or indirectly, to Orthodox Christianity. The history and the fate of that attempt is in itself an interesting piece of information and evidence, relevant to the subject of "Christianity and Canadian Culture," but we will not deal with this topic now.

At our first meeting of this experimental venture, Professor Robert Barringer of St. Michael's College (now president of St. Joseph's University College in Edmonton) circulated a list of statistics on Orthodox Christians in Canada, broken down into such ethnic blocks as the Antiochians, Bulgarians, Greeks, Romanians, Russians, Serbians and Ukrainians. But before we speak of numbers it will be interesting to consider the various churches or jurisdictions mentioned under four of these seven broad ethnic groups.

The *Romanians* in Canada form three groups: The Romanian Orthodox Missionary Archdiocese in America, The Romanian Diocese, and the Independent Parishes. The *Russians* also are under three jurisdictions: the Russian Orthodox Greek Catholic Church in America (the Orthodox Church in America), the Russian Orthodox Church Outside Russia, and the Jurisdiction of the Moscow Patriarchate. The *Serbians* consist of the Serbian Orthodox Church in USA and Canada, and the Free Serbian Orthodox Church. The *Ukrainians* are divided into the Ukrainian Greek-Orthodox Church of Canada, and the Ukrainian Orthodox Church in America. The list does not include other smaller Orthodox groups under the Antiochians and the Bulgarians. Nor does it include the Greeks!

These sobering facts give you an idea of the impossible task that I undertook when I agreed to contribute something about the Orthodox Church and the Canadian society and culture! I will not, of course, be able to deliver on that, except by giving you a series of mini-introductions to a variety of related topics, and these mainly from the experience of the Greek Orthodox Church, the largest component of Orthodoxy in Canada, with an estimated 250,000 faithful belonging to some fifty community parishes.

Coming now to the numbers, Fr. Barringer's sources give 570,000 Orthodox Christians belonging to 201 parishes, served by 225 priests at an average of one priest for 2533 parishioners, and administered by seven bishops. A comparison between the population of an ethnic church and the number of its parishes, priests and bishops shows very different ratios and yields some very interesting insights. Obviously these statistics were already outdated in 1984, and they are more so today. This list does not include a large number of Christians who are originally from countries of Eastern Europe, Middle East, Africa and Asia, and who include the adjective "Orthodox" in their church name, as for example, the Coptic Orthodox Church, the Armenian (Orthodox) Apostolic Church, the Ethiopian Orthodox Church, and others.

Barrett's *World Christian Encyclopedia* gives even more optimistic numbers of an Orthodox population of 688,000 representing 2.8 percent of Canada's 22 million professing Christians (Tkachuk 1988). The comparable figures in the same table show 11.5 million Roman Catholics (52.2 percent), and 9.8 million Protestants (44.5 percent). Statistics Canada's *1981 Census by Religion* published in December 1983 lists only 361,000 Orthodox, for less than 1.7 percent of Canada's Christian population (compared with 11.4 million Roman Catholics (51.8 percent), and 9.9 million Protestants (45 percent) (Tkachuk 1988). The federal census was criticized by certain Orthodox leaders for its understatement. Two examples were cited: the Antiochian Orthodox Christian Archdiocese is listed as having only 1,225 adherents nationwide, whereas each of Montreal's two parishes has more than this number alone. The Ukrainian Orthodox has only 7,200 members, where Barrett estimates them at 140,000! (Tkachuk 1988).

The discrepancy between these two published accounts prompted an unofficial census of the various Canadian chanceries. The Orthodox themselves estimate that in October, 1984, approximately 440,000 communicants (adults and children) belonged to more than 500 parishes, representing two percent of Canadian Christians (Tkachuk 1988). The discrepancy between statistics of religious affiliation taken by the religious communities themselves and statistics derived from a public census speaks of the inadequacy of a census to reveal the true religious image of Canada. It infers also a reluctance, confusion, or shift of priority which citizens demonstrate in dealing with their actual religious or denominational affiliation.

Another lesson that we must learn from the study of such data is that in dealing with the question of religion and culture in Canada we cannot group all *Orthodox* people together, in the same way as we cannot group all Protestants together and reach meaningful conclusions. A more diligent approach would be to deal with each ethnic Orthodox group separately. A perennial problem among non-Orthodox observers or students has been that of not recognizing that Orthodoxy constitutes one spiritual body which consists, however, of a very intricate and diversified family of ethnic ecclesiastical bodies. Only when this is recognized can Orthodoxy be taken as one whole and be compared and contrasted with Catholicism or Protestantism, if either one of these two traditions of Christianity is also taken en bloc.

Both these issues, the matter of statistics and the matter of a consistent and realistic treatment of Orthodoxy, must be taken seriously by the ecumenical community and by each Orthodox jurisdiction in Canada. They must be constantly borne in mind, taken seriously and expounded by any student of Orthodoxy.

Another major consideration to be kept in mind is the historical reality and the character of the Orthodox community in Canada—a more direct consideration to our topic of discussion. Father John Tkachuk of the Orthodox Church in America, an Orthodox ecclesiastical body which is committed to a supra-ethnic Orthodox witness in Canada, reminds us that the Orthodox in Canada are, of course, immigrants, but furthermore, that "in the history of Christian immigration to Canada, the Orthodox are relative newcomers" (Tkachuk 1988). The majority of Greeks and Ukrainians at least seem to have settled in Canada since the latest years of the 1960s and in the early 1970s (Ontario Ministry of Culture and Recreation 1979). The history of Greeks in what is now Canada, however, is believed to have started only about a hundred years after the voyage of Columbus, with Apostolos Valerianos. He was a seaman and pilot for the Spanish government who explored the coast of California and in 1592 sailed through the strait between Vancouver Island and the state of Washington (Canada's Multicultural Directory 1979, 95-98; see also *Ecumenism* 1984).

Thus, most Orthodox in Canada belong to the first generation of immigrants with only a recent Canadian-born generation. This fact accounts, in part, for the paucity of non-parochial institutions, such as seminaries and monasteries, and the relative scarcity of comprehensive studies and analyses of the historical, social, cultural priorities and activities of each ethnic Orthodox group (Constantinides 1983; Ioannou 1983; Stathopoulos 1971; Gavaki 1977; Chimbos 1980; Constantelos 1982; Contos 1981). In short, the impact of the Orthodox community upon the society and the culture of Canada is fluid and still in need of being identified, analysed and measured.

However, there is something essential that must be said as a matter of principle and character of Orthodoxy: Orthodoxy and culture are two interwoven categories, each of which marks and accentuates the other. History shows that Orthodoxy respects language, culture, ethnic identity, and national aspirations; it has even served, at times to its own spiritual detriment, as a preserver and inspirer of such human and societal characteristics and needs (cf. Ramet 1988). Consider here for a moment the history of the conversion of the Slavs in the tenth century and the development of the Cyrillic language by the Greek missionary brothers Cyril and Methodius; or the circumstances of the conversion of the Rus exactly one thousand years ago; or the history of the missionary expansion of Orthodoxy by the Russians in Japan and in Alaska in the eighteenth century (Bensin 1967); or that of the present-day missionary activity of the Greek Orthodox Church in East Africa.

Orthodoxy, therefore, not only does not find itself in tension with, but it even embraces and finds its own expression in culture, as demonstrated by this multi-racial, multi-lingual, and multi-ethnic identification of Orthodoxy in the world, and particularly in North America. And yet, beyond its external and cultural maze, which so often is a cause of confusion for the non-Orthodox and a bone of contention among sensitive Orthodox themselves, Orthodoxy holds to a unity and continuity in history, faith and spiritual tradition which can be traced back to the earliest, even to the first, days of Christianity.

Orthodoxy has maintained a positive attitude towards culture because it finds positive foundations and essential *theological* affirmations in the very fabric of the Christian faith. Here, briefly, are some of such theological foundations:

a) The *cosmos*, or the world as a whole, is a reflection of divine wisdom and beauty; thus, goodness and beauty are to be found everywhere.

b) The "earth is of the Lord," governed and adorned by the divine presence and providence; thus, all peoples and nations have something divine to demonstrate through their existence and life.

c) There are no "chosen" people on earth, as all humans are created in the "image of God" (albeit tainted), and empowered with the gift and the potentiality of attaining the "likeness of God;" thus, human life, history and culture everywhere contain the spark of God that can be set ablaze and reach divine proportions.

d) Authority in life and in faith rests with God-the-Holy-Spirit alone who animates, illuminates and directs mankind towards God; thus, no one nation or people holds an absolute claim to spiritual or cultural superiority—let alone authority—over others.

e) The material creation, too, is a sharer in God's accomplished salvation and therefore it is venerable and a means of sanctification; thus, social concern and cultural expression are neither frivolous nor irrelevant preoccupations of a people.

f) The members of the mystical Body of Christ, that is the church, constitute among themselves a "*communion* of saints." This is their most meaningful distinction, and their most essential identification; thus, the Christian community, in spite of its division into ethnic and cultural communities, has a common source of existence and a common goal.

g) Christian theology, in dealing with the mystery of God, is by definition not a rationalistic but a mystical experience; thus, theology is neither product of, nor subject to an interpretation consistent singly with one particular frame of mind, or cultural idiosyncrasy.

h) "Orthodox" actually means and stands for an upright "balanced" (common sense?) faith and right glory of God, two notions and ideals which are transcultural. Right glory implies the best that a people or culture can integrate in expressing its faith, and offer as worship and glory to God. It is no surprise, therefore, that the Orthodox Church historically has given such a prominence to the liturgical arts (architecture, iconography, music, hymnology), and that all of these have been expressed in the characteristic mode of the local indigenous cultures.

i) There is no tension between earthly life, which is short, temporal and determined by material considerations, and the life to come. Creation and life are seen as expressions of God's love and abundance, and as manifestations of his holiness and beauty, qualities which people have been created to share with and witness to others.

j) The Orthodox Church sees and experiences the church as "a communion of *saints*." Thence, it emphasizes communal spiritual growth and fulfilment, sacramental life, acts of spirituality and sanctification (including monasticism and priesthood), and expressions of love for everyone, especially those in need. The Byzantine tradition shows no signs of an absolute separation between church and state (perhaps an idealistic inception of human society, under the experience of the development of history), precisely because it sees a human being as one whole. Part of that "spiritual" concern of the church was also the care for the needy. The Byzantine Church developed a whole tradition and ethos of philanthropy which it based on a theological and spiritual tradition (Constantelos 1968). Christ is often depicted in icons as *philanthropos* (he who loves humankind). The words *philanthropos* and *philanthropia* (philanthropy) are found in almost every invocation, prayer, and hymn of the Orthodox Church.

All these points are derivatives of its theological and traditional self-understanding, which the Orthodox Church can offer and on which it seeks to make itself manifest in any society. They are, indeed, characteristics and theological considerations in principle although, unfortunately, often expressed in principle and less so in practice. The outlook of the Orthodox Church, as it appears to non-Orthodox, as it is experienced by many Orthodox, and as it is manifested in the context of the Canadian society today, may be another phenomenon altogether. The Orthodox Church appears, at times, fragmented into antagonistic ethnic communities; captive to an immigrant mentality and idiom; introverted and marginalized, perhaps, by its own provincialism; uncommitted to the multicultural richness of the Canadian society; archaic and unimaginative in its theological articulation and social activity. The truth or non-truth of this image would, and should be, of great interest to students of the sociology of Orthodoxy, a field of studies that has been totally neglected by the Orthodox Church in its theological curriculum, and something which in itself must be a point of interest to the participants of this conference. Notwithstanding some historical, cultural, statistical studies about some Orthodox communities in North America, long overdue is a study in depth of the characteristics, the problems, the dynamics and the role of the Orthodox Church in the New World in the example of Will Herberg's *Protestant-Catholic-Jew* ([1950] 1960). Without wishing to pre-empt or to determine conclusions *a priori*, I would suggest that the following broad topics would probably emerge from such a sociological study of Orthodoxy in Canada.

1. In the United States the Catholic Church was, for centuries, both a minority church and a church of newcomers to the country. That made it, at the parish and at the hierarchy level, a church that was always seeking to be, and to be seen, as "American." In Canada, Catholicism (through the French connection) has always been a part of the Canadian cultural and historical landscape.

The Orthodox Church, on the other hand, is a relative newcomer to Canada, with some characteristics of its own. Possibly Ukrainians came first, farmers allowed to migrate and to help settle the prairies. Greeks came later to join the thousands of others who would power industry.

2. Being a faith mainly of newcomers, the Orthodox in Canada share in the patriotic tradition of trying to be "super Canadians" who are not too critical of, or sufficiently involved in Canadian society and culture, staying within the confines of their own ethnic and religious ghettos.

The commitment of the Orthodox to a *Canadian* Orthodoxy needs still to be explored, explained and documented as most official affiliations, especially the ones connected with the Church, have an umbilical cord that has its centre somewhere south of the Canadian border, in New York City, or in Washington. In the case of the Greek Orthodox Church, the Canadian Diocese is part of and receives its orders from the Greek Orthodox Archdiocese of North and South America located in New York City. The men's club AHEPA is an "*American*-Hellenic-Educational and Progressive Association." The Youth Group GOYA stands for "Greek Orthodox Youth of *America*" (in Canada the "A" is ingeniously converted at times to "Association," to conceal the American identification). Encyclicals of the archbishop have admonished the Canadian faithful to show their pride in *America*, and support the fund for the restoration of the Statue of Liberty!

3. Another language, another culture, another world view, all serve to keep people inward-looking, looking inside their immigrant parish and diocesan confines. Since there are many needs to be met among the Orthodox people themselves (the sick, the lonely, the children . . .), the churches do not *yet* look outside of that scope. A look, for example, at the social service efforts of the Greek Orthodox Diocese, funded by the Government, will show a tendency to do "Philoptochos-type" (Parish Ladies Auxiliary) direct services, rather than any pro-active advocacy or preventive work.

4. Both Greek and Ukrainian Church leaders seem interested in exercising political power, but still only in order to enhance their ethno-cultural group, not in order to improve and bring about change in Canadian society. Also, more often than not political divisions of the motherland are transplanted by laymen to Canada, to the detriment of the internal unity of the community, and to Canadian adaptation. Furthermore, among the bishops and the titulars of the church the tendency to rule according to the dictates of the old Ottoman model of *millet*, rather than according to the Orthodox tradition of conciliarity and *sobornost* (a model that combines the best of hierarchy and the best of democracy), slows things down, cultivates an unhealthy authoritarianism, and perpetuates the mentality of an Orthodoxy plagued by phyletism.

A ghetto mentality does not encourage people to recognize their own rightful position and contribution to the life of Canada, and to stimulate the assumption of a role of responsibility and excellence in various sectors of Canadian society. Through the Ukrainians, for example, the Orthodox Church can become an even stronger participant in, and heir to, the frontier pioneer rural tradition of the early settlers of this country, and a pillar of Western Canada's side of Orthodoxy. Through the Greeks the Orthodox Church has the possibility of making an input into such sectors of Canadian life as industry, business, and urban life.

5. Possibly due to the social and economic factors of immigration, the Orthodox people have not been very much prompted to become otherworldly and pay attention to their spiritual tradition as well. They came to Canada with a "this world" mindset. An immigrant sees himself as a survivor, and the idea of "pie in the sky" is not very

attractive to him. He may be conservative, and wish to keep some things as they were back home, but frugality, let alone poverty, is not one of them—that does not appeal to him. The administration of the church has also been deeply affected by this same mentality, to the restriction at times of its freedom to be a beacon of spiritual values, and to the dilution of its prophetic role in the church and in the society at large.

6. The power of the laity, especially on financial and local administrative matters of the church, is a new idea and role for the lay person. The change from a state church to a church financially supported by its members has affected the layman's position as a Christian person in society, and as a member in one's own ethnic community. It has changed the laity's relationship to the clergy, priests and bishops. Mistakenly, however, the administrative or financial support which one offers to one's church, or even to one's ethnic community, is often taken as an indicator or criterion of Orthodoxy!

7. Monastic communities, which in addition to their unique role in cultivating and witnessing to spirituality, affect the establishment and delivery of social services (orphanages, schools, hospitals), have not yet developed, as there is not yet a "surplus" of faithful, nor adequate encouragement and commitment on the part of the administration of the church.

8. Training of the clergy, at least in the Greek Orthodox Church, has been left to other countries. So priests never get a substantive education into the Canadian Orthodoxy, its characteristics, priorities and problematics. The experience of Canadian Orthodoxy takes the form of cursory information, impression or misinformation derived from the priest's own personal experience in the field.

9. The family remains the stronghold and the nucleus of ethnic and religious identity and life. The strength of the family is tested by all the well-known, common challenges to any immigrant, "different" family: linguistic discrepancies and communication problems between the ethnic speaking parents and the English or French speaking children. Difference in style and level of education, clashes over customs and traditions between the generations, and dating practices and marriage expectations and standards are some of the most common challenges of an Orthodox ethnic family. One could say that what seems to have been a universal pattern of development of any other religious and ethnic community in the diaspora applies also to the Orthodox ethnic communities in Canada: the second generation, in

its effort to embrace a Canadian identity, rejects or shies away from the lifestyle, standards, customs, and even the language and the faith of the first generation. It is the third generation, no longer feeling threatened by the immigrant syndrome which will seek to discover its roots and thus to return to some of the ideals of the first generation. The church is one of the first beneficiaries of this re-discovery. But the time of a third generation of Orthodox communities has not yet arrived in Canada in full force.

10. The degree of commitment to Canada is proportionate to the degree of knowledge of this country. For many ethnic groups, Canada is only a country for employment, economic and social development—vacation and retirement plans centre in the homeland. The characteristic immigrant mentality has been depicted in the image of someone who sleeps with his suitcases, most of them still unopened, under his bed! For many Orthodox, Canada with its distinctive makeup, temperament, and history has not yet been seen as a country congenial to Orthodoxy, let alone bring potentially an Orthodox country. Rather it is seen as a country of opportunity for ethnic Orthodox groups to practice their own faith freely and temporarily. The formation of the "Orthodox Church in America" has been based on the claim that such a posture is indeed a myth, if not an aberration of Orthodoxy. Time and the ability of this ecclesiastical body to witness to Orthodoxy within the Canadian context will hopefully show that this claim is realistic, and indeed providential.

So it is still the case, partly as a result of these factors, that commitment to the ecumenical movement in Canada on the part of ethnic Orthodox churches is still lukewarm and erratic. The need for inter-Orthodox dialogue, cultivation, education and co-ordination of activities and witness (a kind of intra-Orthodox ecumenism), is becoming increasingly imperative, if it is not long overdue. In the United States SCOBA (The Standing Conference of Orthodox Bishops in the Americas) is a consultative group of hierarchs formed in 1960 to foster administrative unity among almost a dozen ecclesiastical "jurisdictions" organized largely along ethnic lines. Members of SCOBA are (with some interruptions) in full sacramental and spiritual communion among themselves, and with the universal Orthodox Church worldwide. History has shown that, in spite of its many useful effects, the actual function of the SCOBA has been felt mostly in the field of public relations and on the level of ceremonial events, while in other respects SCOBA has been the stage, if not the cause, of deeper ethnic, jurisdictional and personality conflicts. Orthodoxy in Canada, using the SCOBA experience and capitalizing on the Canadian tradition of multiculturalism, accommodation and co-operation, can and should do much better than that. Persons of Orthodox ecclesiastical and ethnic origin are spread across all levels of the social structure and can be found in various levels of the Canadian public life. While numbers and statistics about persons in public service can conceivably be compiled, the study of their function as Orthodox, the possible impact that their Orthodox tradition has had upon their development, and especially the input that they are making into the Canadian society as Orthodox, may prove to be a much more arduous, if not an impossible, job.

The Orthodox communities in Canada still need to discover and be convinced for themselves of the relevance, richness and power of their own tradition, as well as the attraction that Orthodoxy can exercise upon non-Orthodox Christians and upon Canada as a whole. Many Orthodox people are unaware of such present-day expressions of, and testimonies to, the tradition and culture of Orthodoxy in Canada such as that shown in the exhibition of "Seasons of Celebration," a magnificent portrayal of the celebration and stratification of the person and of time as manifested in the rites and rituals, in the holidays, symbolism, sacred objects, icons, art and sacred music of the Orthodox Church, shown from 1986 to 1989 in all provinces of Canada. Orthodox are even surprised by, albeit proud of, such Canadian Orthodox events as the celebration of the millennium of the Christianization of the Rus, and the edition of four 1988 Christmas stamps featuring Byzantine icons (date of issue, October 27, 1988).

Given the relatively short history of Orthodoxy in Canada, the tremendous growth of the Orthodox population, its rapid acceleration in the economic, social, cultural, educational, professional and political fields, one can safely predict that Orthodoxy is here to stay and will make a lasting imprint upon the life and the culture of this country, as it has made to various degrees in England, France, Switzerland, Australia, and closer to home, in the United States. The advice and the longing that one often hears expressed from non-Orthodox is, "If only the Orthodox would get their own act together!"

My own personal dreams, aspirations and hopes go a bit further: that Orthodoxy in Canada may not be tainted by a "free trade" mentality, but will seek rather to strike and cultivate its own characteristic roots, along with those characteristics of Canada—richer in beauty and colour, richer in spontaneity, richer in a sense of social responsibility, alive to excellence, open to the gifts of pluralism and multiculturalism, less imperial, more irenic, more caring and humane than anywhere else. Such qualities are not only more desirable, they are more authentic—and integral to the ethos and to the essence of Orthodox Christianity itself. The beneficiary of a Canadian Orthodoxy will be the Orthodox people themselves and, indeed, Canada as a whole.

12. The Christian Reformed Tradition in Canada

Harry J. Groenewold

I am quite certain that many Canadians are at a loss to understand why Dutch Calvinist immigrants are eager to participate in Canadian public life, while at the same time they insist on functioning through alternative institutions and structures. Dutch Calvinists seem to be one of the few immigrant communities, along with the marginalized Hutterites and Doukhobors, which refuse to sacrifice their inherited belief system; but at the same time they want to be part of the mainstream of Canadian society.

It may be that this Dutch mentality perplexes and occasionally offends Canadians who encounter it. They may wonder whether Canadian churches, schools, labour unions, political structures and other cultural institutions are not good enough for these Dutch immigrants. What gives these Dutch Calvinists the right—and why are they so adamant about it—to look down their noses on the best that Canada can offer? Why did they come to Canada if our institutions offend their religious sensibilities?

Other Canadians, less hostile and critical, are bemused by these hardworking immigrants who are willing to invest tremendous amounts of money, time and energy not only to establish their own churches but also alternative Christian schools, colleges, labour unions and political structures. They admire the success of these immigrants but are unable to fathom the motivations that drive these Dutch Calvinists.

Such bewilderment is quite understandable. Few Canadians are aware of the influences which have shaped these immigrants. We cannot understand their peculiar ways of doing things unless we explore the nineteenth century roots of modern Dutch Calvinism. This period of Dutch history has profoundly shaped the attitudes, belief system and cultural strategy of the Dutch Calvinist community in Canada, which is mostly found in the membership of the Christian Reformed Church.

I wish to examine the Dutch Calvinist community in Canada, and how it has worked to influence Canadian culture, in three historical periods: the nineteenth century Dutch background, the immigrant phase of 1945 to 1975, and the Canadian phase from 1975 to the present.

The Nineteenth Century Dutch Background

As part of the post-Napoleonic settlement in the Netherlands, the Reformed Church was established as the state church in 1816. The new structure was very hierarchical and gave the monarch the right to appoint the members of the synod and other governing bodies in the church. This enabled the king to ensure that the church would be an obedient creature of the state. The new structure repudiated the presbyterian principles adopted by the Synod of Dordrecht in 1618.

The new elites governing the church were strongly influenced by the rationalist humanism of the eighteenth century, a religious liberalism which came to dominate the church in the early part of the nineteenth century.

Reaction to the decay of Calvinist theology and dominance of the government in the state church built up during the nineteenth century. An early movement to restore Calvinist orthodoxy and presbyterian government was the *Reveil*, a Europe-wide movement originating in Switzerland. The greatest spokesman of the *Reveil* in the Netherlands was Guillaume Groen van Prinsterer (1801-1876). Groen led the attack on the secular character of state and society. He was convinced that the pervasive liberalism of his day was nothing less than revolutionary. Therefore he repeatedly denounced the French Revolutionary heritage. Groen was determined to provide an alternative worldview and philosophy able to interpret politics and society on the basis of Calvinist principles.

The *Reveil* played a crucial role in shaping religious debates in the nineteenth century because many of its members came from the upper classes. Groen himself was secretary to the cabinet of King William I, and in that position saw the impact of the revolutionary tide of 1830 in Belgium. Groen's seminal "Lectures on Unbelief and Revolution" have recently been republished in English by Harry Van Dyke (1989).

Groen's denunciation of the spirit of the age was balanced by a firm conviction that the Christian faith could be a significant and positive influence in Dutch culture. He called Christians to develop a position of systematic antithesis toward all spirits and structures in the world that were not in submission to God's Word. There could be no common ground between God and anti-Christ. History itself reveals an endless conflict between good and evil, between the City of God and the City of Man. Implementing the antithesis required the creation of Christian organizations for all areas—politics, labour, journalism, education, social clubs, economic structures, etc.

Another reaction to the rationalist humanism of the state church came from the lower classes and some of their pastors in the form of a secession in 1834. Many adherents of that secession immigrated to the United States in the nineteenth century, founding the Christian Reformed Church there in 1857.

The introduction of a new education bill into the Dutch legislature in 1857 catalyzed Groen and his movement. The bill proposed to establish a public education system controlled by the government in which education would be treated as religiously neutral. Groen vehemently opposed the bill, recognizing that neutral education would be non-Christian education. Members of the *Reveil* interpreted the bill as an implementation of the revolutionary doctrine that children belong to the state. Groen insisted the parents have a prior right to educate their children in accord with their beliefs.

When the education bill was passed, Dutch Calvinists realized that they could not vanquish the liberal spirit dominating Dutch society and shaping its culture. Rather than accepting defeat, they concentrated on setting up an alternative Christian day school system. This strategy contributed significantly to the development of a Calvinist culture block (Daalder 1969, 200).

The leader in the development of that culture block was Abraham Kuyper (1837-1920), whose philosophy and cultural agenda dominated the Calvinist movement in the Netherlands from 1870 to 1920 (Bratt 1984, 3). He articulated a Calvinist worldview and philosophy by which to conduct all human activity in every sphere of life (Kuyper [1898] 1976). He declared that all fundamental principles were religious and were either in service or in defiance of God's will.

Kuyper used the antithesis as the basis for the idea of structural pluralism in society. The notion of antithesis justified separate yet public Christian organizations and activities in every field of endeavour. After all, there was no room for neutrality, no common ground for members of society committed to fundamentally different religious beliefs to organize or work with one another in cultural associations. Within a short period of twenty years Dutch Calvinists, heeding Kuyper's call, established an educational system from primary grades through university, Christian newspapers, a political party (which elected Kuyper as prime minister), a labour union, Christian social services, social clubs, and other associations. Such intensity and diversity demonstrated that it was possible to become involved in cultural activities without endangering or compromising one's faith.

The key slogan in Kuyper's cultural strategy as it shaped distinct structures was "sphere sovereignty." Kuyper believed that each sphere of life—politics, family, church, education, economy, etc.— had its own integrity, and was not dependent on any other power or structure for its right to exist. Each sphere of life exercised a legitimate power and authority and enjoyed certain duties and rights. Each sphere had clearly defined boundaries, and no one sphere had the right to impinge upon another or to interfere in its unique task. The idea of sphere sovereignty was crucial in defining the limits of the political realm. The task of the state was to ensure that each sphere of life could pursue its own legitimate ends. Thus the state's task is one of service.

The ideas and themes developed in the tradition from Groen van Prinsterer to Kuyper were fully worked out in what is called the philosophy of the Amsterdam school (the Free University of Amsterdam, which Kuyper and the Dutch Calvinists founded in 1880) during the interwar years and in the decades after World War II. A central figure in this philosophical development was Herman Dooyeweerd. With him were Dirk Vollenhoven, Hendrik van Riessen and others. C. T. McIntire has written a recent succinct summary of Dooyeweerd's thought (McIntire 1985, 174-78).

The Immigrant Phase, 1945 to 1975

Dutch immigration to Canada during the postwar years and the development of Dutch Calvinist communities has been carefully analyzed by Van Ginkel (1985). She has shown most convincingly the motives and reasons why nearly 143,000 Dutch people came to Canada from 1946 to 1960. They emigrated for a variety of reasons: economic, political and religious. The Netherlands, like many other European countries, had been devastated by the war, and its postwar prospects looked bleak. There was a severe housing shortage in the postwar years, and agriculture, industry and commerce suffered heavy setbacks. Many Dutch people were convinced that their country would not recover from the effects of war and would face an indefinite future of austerity. Given the many obstacles, the Dutch government and private organizations promoted emigration as the solution to the country's postwar ills.

What made emigration to Canada attractive for Dutch Calvinists was the existence of a Dutch Calvinist denomination in Canada known as the Christian Reformed Church. The Christian Reformed Church became very active during the postwar years in attracting immigrants and helping to place them through the work of local immigration societies.

Large scale Dutch immigration to Canada came at the same time as Canadian postwar economic growth and cultural expansion. Canadians and immigrants alike saw Canada as the land of opportunity and the place of new beginnings. This confidence in Canada was most clearly expressed in such major projects as the Trans-Canada pipeline and the St. Lawrence Seaway. It was also voiced in Diefenbaker's northern vision and his dream of one Canada for all Canadians regardless of origin. During the 1960s Canada celebrated its centennial with uncommon exuberance, which included welcoming the world to Expo '67. The following year the people elected Pierre Trudeau, and Trudeaumania swept the country—a new leader with new ideas for a country invited by destiny to greatness.

Dutch Calvinist immigrants eagerly took part in this exciting nation-building. Many had come as hired farm labourers, but within a few years they took possession of prosperous farms, or migrated to good jobs in urban centres, or set up their own businesses. As they climbed the economic ladder they did not want to hold to an ethnic identity as an end in itself. They quickly learned the English language as a means to get ahead (Van Ginkel 1985, 14; Van Brummelen 1985, 13). In their churches, too, language quickly moved from Dutch to English, with encouragement from clergy, including those who had immigrated themselves (Guillaume and Venema 1957, 13, 37). Learning English quickly was a sign of excellent progress, as the clergy, too, wanted the CRC to be a Canadian church, not an ethnic enclave.

Although the leaders of the CRC spoke of Canada in glowing terms and encouraged a significant degree of behavioural assimilation, they were unhappy with the spiritual direction of Canadian culture. They repeatedly pointed out that Canada, like the rest of western civilization, was guided by the heritage of the Enlightenment and the French Revolution (Van Andel 1965, 9). Canada's claims of religious neutrality in public affairs merely disguised the fact that it was not a Christian country.

This concern about Canada's spiritual direction was most frequently voiced by pastors who came from the Netherlands with a sense of mission—to make Calvinism a major force in Canadian culture as it was back home. The American Dutch-speaking pastors who had come from the United States to help with church planting took a different line, though. They saw the central importance of the church as looking after the spiritual, educational, social and recreational needs of its members, but beyond that they encouraged church members to participate in Canadian institutions as individual witnesses to Christian viewpoints (Van Ginkel 1985, 27).

The Dutch immigrant pastors strongly disagreed with this American view. They insisted that the CRC community must establish alternative, non-ecclesiastical institutional structures that reflected their distinctive Calvinist heritage. They insisted that ". . . instead of taking refuge in comfortable compromise with a community status-quo or in convenient world-flight which would deprecate both their Canadian environment and their Christian calling, they determine to tackle their problems radically by facing the underlying issues of the apparent conflict between their new homeland and their spiritual commitment" (De Jong 1960, vi-vii).

The call to spiritual obedience for these people required that they remember the famous slogan of Groen van Prinsterer, which was translated, "In our isolation lies our strength." Pastors such as Guillaume and Venema emphasized this statement when they observed that "the Christian Reformed Church stands strongly isolated in this North American continent. . . . Isolation by way of pure profession is possible here not only because our Church has its confession on paper, but also because of its mighty efforts to maintain those confessions" (Guillaume and Venema 1957, 9).

But Groen and his spiritual heirs did not mean by isolation a world flight mentality. A better translation of that Dutch slogan would be, "In our independence, our firmness of principle, lies our force" (Daalder 1969, 200). Groen's rallying cry called for distinctiveness and uniqueness in a people set apart yet actively engaged in the world.

As heirs of the tradition of Groen van Prinsterer and Abraham Kuyper, Dutch Calvinists in Canada believed that all areas of life must be claimed for Christ the King. They stressed the urgent need to confront the spirits of the age and to recognize that culture was the arena of conflict between good and evil. The doctrine of the antithesis, used so effectively by Kuyper in the Netherlands, also became the instrument to analyze Canadian culture. The conclusion they reached was inevitable: since Canadian structures were not obedient to God's will, the Dutch Calvinist community is mandated by God to be a distinctive witness in Canadian culture and to establish appropriate structures and organizations that would exhibit the Lordship of Christ. The times were right, they said, because "Canada today is still filled with strong convictions of faith about possibilities in the realm of separate Christian organizations" (Guillaume and Venema 1957, 28).

These convictions led the Dutch Calvinist community to build local churches, form political action groups, a become involved in various journalistic ventures. In the years from 1946 to 1985 the number of CRC churches grew from 14 to 223. They were built with the wholehearted support of the members.

Although a large segment of the community also supported the various non-ecclesiastical activities of the Dutch Calvinists, a significant minority opposed or had strong reservations about the idea of a Christian cultural presence. But given the dominant mood in the CRC community, this minority accepted the cultural direction with reluctant acquiescence.

Christian Schooling

The highest priority next to establishing local churches was building Christian day schools. Like their Dutch forebears, many church leaders expressed deep concern about the state's monopoly in education. Pastor Van Andel stated the rationale forcefully in arguing that ". . . as soon as the government requires that not the parent but the state shall educate the children, it threatens the sovereign right of the family" (Van Andel 1965, 11). The parents' prior right over their children's education was essential to ensure that they would be nurtured in the faith and become "Canadian citizens committed to the kingdom of heaven" (De Jong 1960, vi).

Christian schooling provided education and direction for members of the community "catapulted into a social, political and economic arena which . . . seemed long since to have lost vital contact with God's Word which liveth and abideth forever" (De Jong 1960, vi). Education was seen as a vital instrument in the struggle against the evils of this world, in teaching students to discern the spiritual dynamics of contemporary culture, and in educating future Christian leaders so they would be able to contribute to Canadian society. The CRC community regarded its schools as Canadian schools serving clearly defined religious and educational needs (Van Brummelen 1985, 15). It did not seek cultural isolation from the world or the need to preserve an ethnic heritage.

The early idealism and powerful rhetoric encouraged the supporters of Christian schools as they worked to expand the system from a mere three schools in 1945 to 114 schools by 1985. Not all supporters of the Christian school movement shared the grand vision of radical proposals for distinctive education as a means of transforming culture. Many of them had no desire to usher in a new cultural order, and readily supported Christian school boards which wanted school curricula which closely paralleled the curricula of the public school system (Van Brummelen 1985, 25). They accepted the idea of Christian schooling, but within clearly defined limits.

Even while the CRC community was engaged in establishing local schools, a small group met in the early 1950s to discuss the feasibility of Christian higher education. The founding meeting of what eventually developed into the present Institute for Christian Studies took place in Toronto in 1956. The purpose of such higher education was self-evident to those supporting this early venture. They were "hoping for Calvinistically trained lawyers, historians and sociologists, and economists. We need trained, recognized and capable men to lead the thinking of our people and of our nation in every area of life in a thoroughly Calvinistic fashion" (Guillaume and Venema 1957, 20). During the early years of the 1960s the organization sponsored conferences ". . . to bring together scholars and students in a yearly conference and to deepen and strengthen our awareness of the absolute necessity of Reformed Scientific Studies" (De Jong 1960, ii). These conferences reminded students enrolled in public universities that scholarship must serve Jesus Christ.

This concern for Christian higher education was not limited to the foundational graduate studies at the ICS. During the 1970s planning started in Alberta and Ontario to establish Christian undergraduate colleges. The King's College opened in Edmonton in 1979, and three years later Redeemer College opened in Hamilton. Thus the CRC community had erected an impressive educational structure in the span of some forty years.

Other Institutions of Cultural Engagement

Intense involvement in education did not mean that the CRC community ignored other areas of social concern. Its earliest Christian social action organization was the Christian Labour Association of Canada, established in 1952 (Vanderlaan 1979). It grew slowly at first in inhospitable Canadian soil and did not have its first full-time agent until 1961. It did not receive certification as a labour union until 1963, and then only after a long struggle in the courts. Although it grew slowly, the CLAC was strongly supported by many leaders in the CRC community. It was fired by words like, "We would serve God according to His commandments, also in the labor unions . . . and now, in our difficult legal situation in Canada, also about the labor unions, we would have certain spiritual lines drawn by the Church. . . . We must seek the scriptural solution in respect to the labour union question" (Guillaume and Venema 1957, 21).

These same Canadian spokesmen worried aloud that the Synod of the CRC, headquartered in Grand Rapids, Michigan, allowed membership in religiously neutral unions. Calvin Seerveld, presently at the Institute for Christian Studies, came from Chicago in 1964 to give a moving and inspirational speech at the CLAC National Convention in which he urged the union to remain faithful to God's Word in the field of labour (Seerveld 1964; see also Vandezande 1967). He challenged those Reformed leaders who dared to raise objections to the need for a Christian labour union. Given such enthusiastic support the CLAC gradually expanded during the postwar decades so that today it has offices and full-time agents in Ontario, Alberta and British Columbia, with a membership of over 10,000.

A third area of interest for many members of the CRC community was politics. They knew only too well that the existing political order did not acknowledge the Lordship of Christ (Runner 1962, 135-257; Hart 1967). Supporters of Christian political action explored the possibility of an alternative political party, but nothing came of these discussions. The only other avenue open was to establish action groups such as the Christian Action Foundation (1962) in Edmonton and the Committee for Justice and Liberty (1963) in Toronto. The two organizations merged in 1971 into a national organization which today is called Citizens for Public Justice. One of its most ambitious and successful projects was the presentation to the National Energy Board urging a moratorium on the Mackenzie Valley pipeline (Vanderlaan 1979, 13). In recent years Citizens for Public Justice has been active in Native issues, social services, and environmental matters.

A fourth area of interest for many CRC members showed in the formation of Christian farmers' organizations (Vanderlaan 1979, 9-10). The first Christian Farmers Federation was established in 1954 in Strathroy, Ontario. It grew slowly, appointing its first full-time executive director in 1970. With a membership of more than 500 farm families, the Federation is primarily concerned with such issues as land use, marketing, agribusiness and related matters. A similar organization was established in Alberta in 1974 which, like its Ontario counterpart, is committed to the development of farm policies from a Christian perspective.

A final notable area of cultural involvement was the various journalistic ventures undertaken during the postwar years (Van Ginkel 1985, 21). One of the earliest periodicals was the *Canadian Calvinist*, first published in Edmonton in 1945. Then *Contact* appeared in Hamilton in 1949. They merged in 1952 under the name *Calvinist Contact*, which is now published in St. Catharines, Ontario. Although it is not the church paper of the CRC, *Calvinist Contact* functions as a the major source of news and ideas for church members. Other journals which have served the CRC community are *Church and Nation* from 1956 to 1970, *Vanguard* from 1961 to 1980, and *Credo* from the mid-1960s to the early 1970s. Two relatively new periodicals are *Christian Renewal*, published from St. Catharines, and *Catalyst*, published in Toronto as the voice of Citizens for Public Justice.

Many leaders in the CRC community justified the need for these embodiments of a cultural strategy by appealing to the inspirational teaching of Dr. H. Evan Runner, a professor of philosophy at the denominational college, Calvin College. The American-born Runner had become a convert to the tradition of Van Prinsterer and Kuyper as formulated in the philosophy of Herman Dooyeweerd. His teaching and lecture tours in Canada contributed significantly to focus the concerns, fears and aspirations of the early CRC community in Canada. Runner spoke eloquently of the consequences of indiscriminate cultural assimilation, of the need to bring about a new reformation of faith and culture, of the task of carrying out God's mandate to turn the continent to God, and to overcome the spirits of this secular age.

Runner persuaded a significant number of young Dutch-Canadian students at Calvin College to return to Amsterdam for doctoral studies so they could come back to Canada as new leaders of the much-needed reformation. Runner and the Dooyeweerdian movement, as it came to be called, helped to reinforce the consensus that already existed among CRC members in Canada. It also reinforced the felt need for social unity and a cohesive system of beliefs (Mouw 1985, 12).

This movement, a minority and yet the dominant voice in the 1950s and 1960s, exuded a sense of urgency: the overriding need to challenge and confront contemporary culture to expose the false spirits guiding it (Hart 1968). Runner and his followers believed that any period in history or any given culture was rooted in some belief system which must be judged in terms of its conformity to the Word of God. Not surprisingly the doctrine of antithesis, used so effectively by Groen and Kuyper, dominated and determined the analysis of culture. At the same time it defined the options open to the believer. At a student conference in 1959 Runner stated flatly that "... before us, as before Herakles, two ways lie and we must decide which one we will take, the way of accommodation to the present patterns of our world, i.e. the *Way of Synthesis*, or the *Way of Antithesis*" (Runner 1960, 92).

Dr. Hendrik Van Riessen, a professor from the Netherlands, bluntly stated on a speaking tour in 1962, "Back of the antithesis in human life is the clear and radical antithesis between Christ and Satan" (Van Riessen 1963, 61).

Immigrant leaders such as Henry Van Andel echoed the need to proclaim that this vision was absolute, universal and determinative for all thought and action. It required unconditional and unrestricted obedience; the alternative was to face the consequences of synthesis. He wrote, "So easily a synthesis between two opposite viewpoints is deemed to be acceptable. Many people are inclined to compromise when a true vision of God's revelation grows dim and the scientific fundamentals of unbelievers look useful" (Van Andel 1964, 9).

The cultural critique of these leaders, based on the claims of the antithesis and the Dooyeweerdian vision, made short work of modern civilization. Like their forefathers Groen and Kuyper, the leaders of the movement regarded the French Revolution as *the* watershed of western civilization—the triumph of unbelief. Such conclusions intensified a sense of the antithesis and the need to confront the present cultural evils. The metaphor of war, of mustering the troops, of raising the banner of war, permeated many speeches and lectures. Occasionally strident and accusatory language was aimed at doubters and those who dared to disagree with the proclaimed viewpoint and strategies.

In their grim determination to slay the spirits spawned by the French Revolution, the adherents of Dooyeweerd had little patience with mundane history. Whole centuries, peoples and movements were called before the tribunal of the antithesis and judged to be guilty. Except for one popular work by Maarten Vrieze, *The Community Idea in Canada* (Vrieze 1966), until 1975 no one had bothered to undertake a careful analysis of Canadian history, society, customs and traditions. Canada was most frequently taken to be part of the American way of death (and its horrors), or as a bit player on the stage of western civilization. Thus the Dooyeweerdian movement took upon itself to plot a cultural strategy for the CRC community without being conversant with the Canadian cultural context.

As the Dooyeweerdian movement in the 1960s increasingly emphasized the need to transform society, most members of the CRC worked to build their schools and to support the newly-established Christian organizations. This insistence on transformation coincided with the age of countercultural movements which challenged established authorities in all areas of life. Some key spokesmen of the Dooyeweerdian movement participated in the counterculture iconoclasm by attacking the established structures nurtured by the CRC community, including the church itself (Olthuis et al. 1970).

These attacks, very evident during the early 1970s, exacerbated the growing tensions between the Dooyeweerdian movement and the CRC community. After all, by the early 1970s the behavioural assimilation of the Dutch immigrants was largely completed and many members of the community were well on their way to full integration into the cultural life of Canada. They refused to be guided by the transformationalists; they now wished to preserve and nurture what they had accomplished. The majority of the CRC community, although sympathetic to the vision of obedience to God in all areas of life, rejected the radical claims and actions of the Dooyeweerdian movement (Klooster 1983, 210-12). The conflict peaked by 1974 with the withdrawal of substantial support for the movement. That marked the end of confrontational rhetoric and initiated a reassessment by the various groups of their respective places and roles in Canadian society.

The Canadian phase: 1975 to the present
The conflict of the early 1970s was in many ways symptomatic of a fragmentation of the inherited religious consensus so dominant during the earlier postwar years. No longer was there the felt need for social cohesion as CRC members more and more became Canadianized. Now they were primarily concerned to find their individual places in Canadian culture. They had little patience with the old dreams of social transformation, and they rejected the traditional leadership of the clergy and the intellectual elites. Individually, as voluntary groups or local congregations, they pursued their own interests and priorities (Van Geest 1985). The claims of antithesis and its exclusivistic language had little relevance in their efforts to relate their beliefs to those of other Christians. They no longer wished to maintain the sharp lines of demarcation between the CRC and other faith communities. Those seeking integration insisted that the Dutch Reformed community must not cling to the past or to outmoded strategies. Rather, the community must be creative in its adopted cultural environment. In must at all costs avoid the "greenhouse effect" of a theological ghetto mentality. This attitude and proposed strategy is clearly evident in the desire to establish interdenominational Christian day schools and in the expressed wish to cooperate politically with other Christian groups on important social issues.

Not every one shared this readiness to reach out to the larger faith community and lend a Reformed presence to ecumenical work on social issues. Opponents of such a Christian strategy did agree that the old dreams were no longer relevant. But their solutions ranged from an otherworldly spirituality to a North American style of fundamentalism. The moderates, those still seeking an authentically

Reformed Christian witness, were left in an unenviable place in the growing polarization between the so-called "conservative" and "progressive" or "liberal" groups. This polarization cut across theological, political and social lines and issues within the CRC community.

This polarization within the church did not destroy its structural unity, though a minuscule element left to form the Orthodox Christian Reformed Church. The uneasy unity did give rise to the emergence of congregationalist and individualist responses to issues confronting the faithful. The inherited uniformity of ecclesiastical practices crumbled as individual congregations adopted liturgies, hymns and orders of worship appropriate to their local needs. This expression of self-reliance at the congregational level went hand in hand with a desire to pursue local evangelism, outreach projects, and Bible study programs stripped of Reformed theology and jargon.

Those who feared the implications of "progressivism" and "personalism" included those with legitimate concerns about the direction of the Reformed faith as well as a vocal conservatistic or fundamentalistic element. The voice of the former became increasingly muted as the polarized rhetoric of the latter challenged the faith commitment of all who dared to disagree with them. The fundamentalist/conservative movement saw itself as the defender of Reformed orthodoxy with a clear mandate to eradicate all signs of weakness, of wavering, of raising profound questions about the nature and practice of the Reformed faith. Its members seem to be driven by the irrational fear that any change must perforce lead to the religious liberalism into which the sister churches in the Netherlands moved after the postwar immigration to Canada. They believed, and still do so, that an uncritical adherence to the creedal heritage will guarantee that the inherited orthodoxy will be preserved. In the process these staunch defenders of the faith reduced the rich vitality of the Reformed vision to a deadening theological orthodoxy of creed and doctrine.

Such polarization and diversity of interests, evident since the mid-1970s, has made inter-organizational debates quite irrelevant to most members of the CRC community. The call to Christian obedience is interpreted less and less as a communal and organizational response. Rather, it is seen as a personal, ecumenical or ecclesiastical matter. Consequently the CRC has become less influential in such non-ecclesiastical organizations as the Institute for Christian Studies, the Christian Labour Association, Citizens for Public Justice, and to a lesser extent in Christian day schools. Conversely, these organizations exert less and less influence today within the church. The agenda of the church is chiefly concerned with ecclesiastical issues and the demands for orthodoxy of faith expressed in such issues as women in church office, creationism versus evolutionism, children participating in the Lord's Supper, controversial views of professors at Calvin College and Seminary, and the proper role of the institutional church in society.

Conclusion

It is important to remember that, in spite of the polarization and tension-filled debates, the legacy of the CRC community is impressive: a vigorous denomination in Canada, a Christian school system, and Christian social action organizations. The CRC community has exerted a cultural influence in Canada far beyond its size, especially in education and in social policy. Its present difficulties and internal dissentions are an important part of the process of religious integration into the Canadian setting, and the need to formulate an identity and place alongside other Canadian denominations without sacrificing its legacy or surrendering its understanding of how the Christian relates to the surrounding culture.

13. A Personal Coda

Brian Stiller

A discussion on Christ and culture should not be just theoretical. It is rooted in the realities of life. I come to this subject wanting to better see how my faith relates to this cultural reality we know as Canada. My approach will be autobiographical, and I ask you to think of it in the context of your own life. Let's put flesh into our discussion, our flesh. We are real people led by God to do real work. We don't approach this question of Christ and culture in a vacuum.

My father, the son of a Swedish immigrant, was raised on a farm in southern Manitoba, churched in a Mission Covenant community, and educated in a country schoolhouse. He began his pastoral ministry on the prairies during the depression. In searching for spirituality, he encountered the emerging Pentecostal movement. My father, a thoughtful person, survived the clatter of that early Pentecostal movement and emerged in that group as one of its national leaders. Although not an outstanding preacher or a theologian, he effectively modeled godliness to his children.

As a "bishop," that is, an overseer of his denomination's churches in Saskatchewan, he cared for the young and struggling ministers of a despised and a tattered religious group called Pentecostals. Our home was the scene of ministers who would pour out their struggles. Often my father allowed us to sit and listen while he counselled and encouraged.

I recall one Christmas Eve (remember it was the 1950s in a Pentecostal home in Saskatchewan!) that my father allowed his children, along with some friends, to attend a mass at a Roman Catholic church. Entrenched in 1950s sectarianism, he had a sense of the larger church of Jesus Christ. He opened my mind to see beyond our immediate borders, even though he might have lost his position in the church if the story got out.

I remember the sixties: the charismatic movement gave legitimacy to being a Pentecostal. During that time I studied at one of our Bible colleges, then the University of Saskatchewan and the University Toronto. I was increasingly interested in the phenomenon of religion in culture. Producing films (initially in Haiti) heightened my fascination with the cultural expression of religion.

As a student during the sixties, my worldview was shaped by the radical foment of the counterculture. Landon Jones in *Great Expectations* said that in the sixties we studied sociology to change our world and in the seventies we studied psychology to change ourselves. In the eighties, continued Jones, we studied business management to guarantee our economic future.

But what is a legitimate cultural expression of faith? Is our faith simply a reflection of the surrounding culture?

My current work with the Evangelical Fellowship of Canada has forced me to deal more specifically with the dynamics of faith and culture. I recall one day talking on CBC's "Morningside" that Peter Gzowski couldn't understand the difference between "evangelicals" and "evangelists." We ended up spending most of our time defining the word "evangelical."

The Evangelical Community in the Twentieth Century

My sojourn as an evangelical Christian may be similar to yours. If you were a member of First Baptist in Saskatoon during the fifties, you would have stood on a higher rung of the social ladder than I did as a Pentecostal. However, if you spoke with a Dutch accent, you may have memories similar to mine of being on the edge of the social stream. Each of us has a story to tell, and it's our collective story that makes up the church in Canada.

In using the word "evangelical" I mostly refer to those evangelical groups which emerged out of the fundamentalist/modernist controversy earlier in this century. This is not the complete world of evangelicals, I know. That world is much larger. Many of those I am referring to were earlier called fundamentalists, until that became a nasty word.

As this century began, there was optimism and hope for a better world. I'm sure Shirley MacLaine would have felt very much at home then. It would be the great century, the beginning of a new age, many thought. But it wasn't long before expectations were shattered. The Great War surprised the world. So did world economic collapse, drought and the migrations of millions of refugees. It was during that time that the Social Gospel was defined. North American church leaders, influenced by the scientific theories of evolution and the newly developed social sciences of psychology and sociology, determined that human tragedy in the world isn't so much the result of individual sinfulness as of evil social systems and structures. When leaders such as Walter Rauschenbusch explained the liberal biblical roots of the Social Gospel, evangelicals reacted, withdrew and moved to the other side of the debate, as sociologist David O. Moberg documents in *The Great Reversal.*

Evangelicals rejected the idea of social concerns. The reaction intensified a sectarian view of faith which saw itself as being set apart from the world, preparing for the early return of Christ. The Social Gospel was seen by evangelicals as an idea emerging out of a liberal interpretation of the Bible. This added fuel to their entrenched sectarianism, as evangelicals chose a narrow path and generally refused engagement with the mainstream of Canadian culture.

Then came the sixties. Our society showed signs of shifting away from historic religious assumptions. Secularism became the byword. Religious views were increasingly seen as irrelevant to our national public concerns and social conventions. Thus today there is little religious influence apparent on the traditional moral behaviour of Canadians. Faced with that reality, evangelicals are questioning that withdrawal from the public arena and are seriously asking what our role we should be in Canada today.

Naboth's Vineyard
I want to address that question through the Old Testament story of Naboth and his vineyard, found in 1 Kings 21.

> Naboth had a vineyard in Jezreel, beside the palace of King Ahab in Samaria. Ahab said to Naboth, "Give me your vineyard that I may have it for a vegetable garden because it is close beside my house, and I will give you a better vineyard in its place; or if you like, I will give you the price of it in money."

But Naboth said to Ahab, "The Lord forbid that I should give you
the inheritance of my fathers." So Ahab came into his house
sullen and vexed because of the word which Naboth the Jezreelite had spoken to him; for he said, "I will not give you the
inheritance of my fathers." And he lay down on his bed and
turned away his face and ate no food.

But Jezebel his wife came to him and said to him, "How is it that
your spirit is so sullen that you are not eating food?" So he said
to her, "Because I spoke to Naboth the Jezreelite, and said to
him, 'Give me your vineyard for money; or else, if it pleases you,
I will give you a vineyard in its place.' But he said, 'I will not give
you my vineyard.'"

And Jezebel his wife said to him "Do you now reign over Israel?
Arise, eat bread, and let your heart be joyful; I will give you the
vineyard of Naboth the Jezreelite."

So she wrote letters in Ahab's name and sealed them with his seal,
and sent letters to the elders and to the nobles who were living
with Naboth in his city. Now she wrote in the letters, saying,
"Proclaim a fast, and seat Naboth at the head of the people; and
seat two worthless men before him, and let them testify against
him saying, 'You cursed God and the king.' Then take him out
and stone him to death.'"

Ahab, the infamous king of Israel, lived with the even more
infamous queen Jezebel. During his time Ahab allowed the worship
of Baal to increase and Jezebel ordered the killing of all but a hundred
of God's prophets. Ahab conceded gold and silver and wives and
children to Ben Hadad king of Aram. And at the showdown with Elijah
on Mount Carmel, 850 prophets of Baal and Asheroi were destroyed.

From this ancient world emerges the story of a farmer who refuses
to give up his inheritance by caving into the cultural demands of his
world and stands heroically against one who is anointed as king.

The question now is, what is our inheritance? What is worth dying
for?

Evangelicals are faced with a problem. Because our theology is
conservative, we tend to be conservative in economics, politics and
social analysis. What do conservatives do? Conserve. The difficulty is

that in conserving the past, the bad and irrelevant are preserved along with the good. It's critical that we decide what is helpful out of our inheritance and what is just a vestige of the past or nostalgia for a bygone era.

A Trade-off

Naboth was given two offers. The first was a trade-off. It would have been an easy way out for Naboth. He would have retained his land. It would have only been an exchange.

For the first half of this century, evangelicals managed a trade-off. In reacting to the Social Gospel's concern for poverty, health and unemployment, we focused on personal piety and evangelism, narrowly defined. We traded one responsibility for another. We agreed on a social contract with those of mainstream religion: they provided the leadership for society, including government, education, science, and technology; we were left to our own religious agenda: withdrawal into sectarianism.

And here was our trade-off. In essence we said, "You look after society and manage the world and we will deal with the vital issues of personal salvation, spiritual piety, church growth and missions." We could do this because there was a common, unspoken agreement that biblical or Judeo-Christian morality would be basic to the managing of Canada. We trusted the mainline religious community to manage society because we all held those common religious assumptions.

What were the results? Evangelicals lost a biblical understanding of spirituality by narrowing our understanding of salvation into narrow sectarianism which in turn reinforced the secular notion of keeping religious faith separate from the social order.

We were also trapped into believing that spirituality and the management of God's world were mutually exclusive. We believed that in fact God had little interest in public welfare or social structures. In Naboth's terms, we accepted a trade-off.

What it produced was a "remnant" mentality, the belief that we were the few who were truly called of God. We were the godly, the spiritual ones. Of course when you are economically poor, you can always accuse those who are wealthy as being unspiritual. Or when you have little store-front churches on the other side of the tracks, it's not difficult to accuse the fashionable churches of having caved in to worldliness.

However, during that time—and for this I'm most grateful—a high view of Scripture held its ground among us in the debate over whether or not the Bible was the Word of God. Today my generation is the inheritor of that biblical strength.

The Second Offer

There was also the possibility of a buy-out. Ahab offered Naboth a good price. The king would even go above market value. But for Naboth, that was absolutely unacceptable, as his land, his inheritance, was his life. Consider the West Bank in the Middle East today and you can understand the strategic importance and the personal value of land. Naboth, those many centuries ago, would not sell or be bought out.

In looking at the evangelical community, from the sixties onward, I wonder whether there has been a buy-out. Beginning with the sixties there was remarkable growth among evangelicals. We gradually lost our anti-intellectualism, became wealthier, more self-confident and middle class. *Time* magazine even labelled 1976 as "The Year of the Evangelical." Preoccupation with an immediate rapture lessened. In short, we became more like the culture we had preached against.

What was the result? There has been a buy-in to conservatism. Wealth becomes the proof of God's blessing, and church success is identified by crowd numbers and the size of operation. Power in politics is sought. We have begun to espouse much of the culture we had earlier rejected.

In the seventies I was amazed at how the human potential movement was picked up in evangelical churches. Essentially a pop psychology of optimistic individualism, defined by books such as *I'm O.K.—You're O.K.*, many evangelicals were wooed by groups including Amway and May Kay cosmetics. We not only espoused popular culture but were learning to love it.

Dealing with Culture

There are two ways of dealing with culture. One is to react and the other is to proact. Reaction without proaction leads to legalism, and proaction without reaction leads to assimilation. It's one thing to know what you are against, but unless you both know and act on what you are for, you resort to a code of behaviour and you interpret spirituality within the narrow confines of "dont's." We evangelicals have struggled with the issue of whether to be against culture or to join in leading culture.

It is my hope that we are at the place where proaction is considered a legitimate word in our vocabulary. This issue comes to focus in the prolife movement. Its tendency is to become legalistic and misunderstand transformation. Legalism says that the way to transform is to superimpose a code of laws on people. But that denies grace. Jesus saw it differently. The letter kills but the Spirit gives life. Grace is essential for transformation.

The Ahabs of This Age

There are Ahabs who try to remove us by a buy out or trade-off. The church of Jesus Christ is engaged in a cosmic battle. "For our struggle is not against flesh and blood, but against the rulers, against the powers, against the world forces of this darkness, against the spiritual forces of wickedness in a heavenly places (Ephesians 6:12)." We are not dealing simply with the curious artifacts of culture but with the battle of darkness and light, good and evil. Culture is not confined to a discussion on the relationship of ethnic groups but deals with spirituality and God's agenda for his Kingdom.

The Ahabs don't rob us. Instead they offer a good price or a fair trade. And the offer seems so reasonable. So what seducing offers are being made by Ahab? There are a number of "isms" which are expressed in a variety of ways.

A secularist says, "Look at how the world is ravished by religious wars. Isn't it better to keep religion private?" An oldtime sectarian says, "After all, this world is doomed for destruction. So why concern ourselves with anything except the future world." The anti-super-naturalist counters, "Look at the yahoos who with their three-ring circus make foolish the very notion of the supernatural."

How seductive is the religious individualist, "Christ came for the individual, so don't be too concerned about social issues." The narcissist says, "It's very difficult to verify what is true. After all, religion ultimately is what makes you feel good." The organizationalist intrigues us with, "My church is really the only one which can make a significant impact. Best I focus all my energies here." Finally, the pessimist offers the narcotic, "We are just holding on, knowing that the times will wax worse and worse."

What do all this "isms" have in common? A human-centred worldview called humanism. Humankind becomes the centre. Also,

God is neutered. While believing he has all power, we assume he has no intention to intervene. Believing God can but won't, we replace faith with fatalism.

What is the relationship of the church to its surrounding culture? Culture is not bad or evil in itself. I enjoy various forms of music. While my musical training was in classical piano, my real love is jazz piano.

The Social Gospel, its ideas and experience, have important lessons for us. Listen to the questions many evangelicals are asking today and you will know that they sound very much like what was asked by proponents of the Social Gospel. Those questions centre around Christ's announcement of his Kingdom. My interest in examining this early twentieth century movement is to learn from its advocates.

Political leaders in Canada included J. S. Woodsworth in Winnipeg and Tommy Douglas in Saskatchewan. Their concerns often centred around the public issues of health, poverty and unemployment. While evangelicals today are occupied more with moral/ethical issues of abortion and pornography, for example, they are attempting to address some of the same issues that Walter Rauschenbusch wrote about.

The Social Gospel movement offers two lessons. First, its soteriology was inadequate. Influenced by the new sciences of psychology and sociology, it shifted its analysis of sin from the individual, and viewed sin as a relation to societal issues. Social Gospel proponents preached less about personal regeneration and encouraged social protest, writing legislation and forming political parties.

Secondly, its Christology was weakened, in my view, by liberal theology, which eroded a high view of the divinity of Christ. While Christ was seen as the model for life, his divinity was suspect. Thus when society is in need of something more than good legislation or humanitarian social nets, Jesus Christ's power and glory is not seen as a reality to transform society.

The Gospel is compelling. Jesus said, "I am the way, the truth and the life." He didn't say his doctrine was the way, the truth and the life. Neither did he claim the Westminster Confessions were the final embodiment of truth! Only Christ is truth and life.

What Is Needed

It may be that we are in need of an evangelical monastic movement, not to repeat the mistakes of past movements but to challenge the narcissism of culture with a demonstration of costly love.

The most critical need is for evangelicals to construct a biblical framework in which we build and evaluate culture and make sense of what the Kingdom of God is about. We've been caught speculating on the formula of Christ's early return instead of understanding the need for it.

We also need a greater appreciation for the contributions made by others. While we will each want to define what we mean by "the Body of Christ," it's vital that we affirm Christ's plan to bring his church into fellowship and cooperation.

There is something distinct and valuable about our Canadian heritage. Such an affirmation does not necessarily carry with it extreme nationalism. But God does work through nations. It is important that we both understand and appreciate our Canadian roots instead of denying them. My prayer is that we will be strengthened by our national experience.

The Lessons from Naboth

Land is what the conquest of Palestine is all about, for ancient as well as modern Israel. People are willing to give their lives for land. Naboth knew every olive tree, rocky knoll and grapevine. Every piece of the land was carefully groomed and tilled for maximum effect.

In that region the religion of Baal was pervasive. In Canaan the Baalim were gods of the land, owning and controlling it. Because the increase of crops, fruits and cattle were thought to be under Baal's control, farmers came to believe they were completely under his control. Yet Naboth resisted the incursion of Baal worship. He held firmly onto his faith in Jehovah and refused to compromise his standards.

Naboth also refused to conform to the expectations of his culture. If the king wants your land, why not trade or sell? After all he was anointed to be king. Lesslie Newbigin in *Foolishness to the Greeks* comments on what faced the early Christians in Rome in relation to the pressures and expectations of their surrounding culture. They had two choices: To keep their religion private and receive protection from harassment, or to be public in their faith without protection (Newbigin calls that "cultus privatus"). They chose the latter. For while they wished freedom from harassment, it would be giving up too much if they had to keep their faith private.

Naboth, too, refused to concede to power. What can a small farmer do in the face of the power of the king? Jezebel had killed all but a hundred of the prophets of God. Although he knew how this king handled dissent or opposition, Naboth preferred death to giving in.

He also contested injustice. The property was his. He had received it from his father. He was right to affirm what was just, not only for himself but for others. For when one person caves in, it is only a matter of time until others do too.

Naboth contended for his inheritance. He advocated truth. It's one thing to believe, but something else to press for truth. Because our culture sees itself as pluralistic, it assumes no one idea is more correct than another. But some go further by distorting pluralism to say that religious ideas should be silent. Today, more than ever, it's essential that we contend in the public square.

Naboth continued in faith. He rose the next morning, tilled the soil, pruned the olive trees and checked the vines. His behaviour confirmed his resolve to be faithful. The difficulties and pressures would not stop his determination to continue in his calling.

Conclusion

The Canadian evangelical community is under pressure from its surrounding culture. It is antagonized, assimilated and co-opted, vacillating from reaction to proaction.

Given the increased pressure of a secular-minded culture, the greatest danger we face is not theological liberalism but assimilation into a culture of materialistic individualism. My prayer is that the Christ of creation and history will keep us in the orbit of his truth and our theology will come from his self-declaration, "Do not work for the food which perishes, but for the food which endures to eternal life."

Literature Cited

Ahlstrom, S. 1955. The Scottish Philosophy and American Theology. *Church History* 1:24, September 1955.

Allen, Richard. 1973. *The Social Passion*. Toronto: University of Toronto Press.

Alline, Henry. 1783a. *The Anti-Traditionalist*. Halifax.

Alline, Henry. 1783b. *Two Mites . . . .* Halifax.

Anglican Church of Canada. 1987. *Violence Against Women: Abuse in Society and Church and Proposals for Change*. Toronto: Anglican Book Centre.

Archdiocese of Toronto. 1983. *Canada's Unemployed: The Evil of our Times*. Report of the Hearing Panel on "Ethical Reflections on the Economic Crisis." Toronto: Archdiocese of Toronto.

Archives. Public Archives of Nova Scotia. Records of the Church of Jebogue in Yarmouth.

Armour, L. and E. Trott. 1981. *The Faces of Reason: An Essay on Philosophy and Culture in English Canada, 1850-1950*. Waterloo: Wilfrid Laurier University Press.

Atlantic Year Book. 1988. *United Baptist Convention of the Atlantic Provinces Year Book*.

Bainton, Roland. 1972. Interpretations of the Reformation. *The Reformation: Basic Interpretations*, ed. Lewis W. Spitz. Toronto: D. C. Heath and Company.

Bainton, Roland. 1978. *Here I Stand: A Life of Martin Luther*. Nashville: Abingdon.

Bamford, Trevor. 1988. The Anglican Church and the Japanese Canadians in British Columbia. Unpublished M. Th. paper, Vancouver School of Theology.

Baum, Gregory. 1980. *Catholics and Canadian Socialism*. Toronto: Lorimer, chap. 7.

Beck, Jean Ruth. 1975. Henry Somerville and Social Reform: His Contribution to Canadian Catholic Social Thought. *Study Sessions* 42.

Beck, Jean Ruth. 1977. Henry Somerville and the Development of Catholic Social Thought in Canada: Somerville's role in the Archdiocese of Toronto, 1915-1943. Ph.D. thesis, McMaster University.

Bensin, Basil M. 1967. *Russian Orthodox Greek Catholic Church of North America, Diocese of Alaska 1794-1967*. Sitka, Alaska.

Beverley, J. A. 1980. National Survey of Baptist Ministers. *Baptists in Canada: Search for Identity Amidst Diversity*, J. K. Zeman. Burlington, Ont.: Welch.

Bibby, Reginald W. 1987. *Fragmented Gods*. Toronto: Irwin.

Braaten, Carl E. 1985. *The Apostolic Imperative*. Minneapolis: Augsburg.

Bratt, John D. 1984. *Dutch Calvinism in Modern America*. Grand Rapids: Eerdmans.

Bridgman, H. J. 1976. Burns, Robert. *Dictionary of Canadian Biography*, Vol. IX. Toronto: University of Toronto Press.

Bryden, Walter W. 1940. *The Christian's Knowledge of God*. Toronto: Thorn Press.

Burke, Kenneth. 1984. *Permanence and Change: An Anatomy of Purpose*. Berkeley: University of California Press.

Burns, R. F. 1872. *The Life and Times of the Rev. Robert Burns, D.D. . . . including an unfinished autobiography*. Toronto.

Cameron, J. 1878. The Four Cornerstones of a Prosperous and Permanent Commonwealth. *The Canada Christian Monthly*. January 1878.

Canada's Multiculturalism Directory. 1979. Greeks. *The Canadian Family Tree. Canada's People*. Don Mills, Ontario: Corpus. See also *Ecumenism* 74:1984, 18.

Canadian Catholic Conference of Bishops. 1983. *The Code of Canon Law: In English Translation*. London/Ottawa: Collins Liturgical Publications.

Canadian Catholic Hierarchy 1956. Christian Citizenship in Practice. Reprinted in Sheridan 1987.

Canadian Conference of Catholic Bishops. 1983. Ethical Reflections on the Economic Crisis. Episcopal Commission for Social Affairs. Also in Sheridan 1987. Also in Gregory Baum and Duncan Cameron, *Ethics and Economics: Canada's Catholic Bishops on the Economic Crisis*. Toronto: Lorimer, 1984, 3-18.

Carrington, Philip. 1963. *The Anglican Church in Canada*. Toronto: Collins.

Chimbos, Peter. 1980. *The Canadian Odyssey: The Greek Experience in Canada*. Toronto: McClelland and Stewart.

Clark, S. D. 1948. *Church and Sect in Canada*. Toronto: University of Toronto Press.

Coady, Moses M. 1939. *Masters of Their Own Destiny: The Story of the Antigonish Movement of Adult Education Through Economic Co-operation*. New York: Harper.

Cochrane, Arthur C. 1956. A Declaration of Faith Concerning Church and Nation by the Presbyterian Church in Canada. *Antwort. Karl Barth zum siebzigsten Geburtstag am 10 Mai 1956*. Zollikon-Zurich: Evangelischer Verlag AG.

Constantelos, Demetrios J. 1968. *Byzantine Philanthropy and Social Welfare*. New Brunswick, N. J.: Rutgers University Press.

Constantelos, Demetrios J. 1982. *Understanding the Greek Orthodox Church: Its Faith, History and Practice*; esp. ch. 5 "The Greek Orthodox in America." New York: Seabury Press.

Constantinides, Stephanos. 1983. *Les Grecs du Québec, Analyse historique et sociologique*. Montréal.

Contos, Leonidas C. 1981. *2001: The Church in Crisis*. Brookline, Mass.: Holy Cross Orthodox Press.

Cook, Ramsey. 1985. *The Regenerators: Social Criticism in Late Victorian English Canada*. Toronto: University of Toronto Press.

Cook, R. and R. C. Brown. 1974. *Canada 1896-1921: A Nation Transformed*. Toronto: McClelland and Stewart.

Cormie, Lee. 1990a. Charting the agenda of the church: Vatican social teaching in a changing capitalist world system. *Social Compass* 37:2.

Cormie, Lee. 1990b. Christian responsibility for the world of the free market? Catholicism and the construction of the post-World War II global order. Paper presented at an international conference on "500 Años del Christianismo en America Latina," organized by the Universidad Academia de Humanismo Christiano in Santiago, Chile, July 1990.

Cronmiller, Carl. 1961. *A History of the Lutheran Church in Canada*, vol. I. Toronto: The Evangelical Lutheran Synod of Canada.

Crysdale, Stuart. 1961. *The Industrial Struggle and Protestant Ethics in Canada*. Toronto.

Daalder, H. 1969. The Netherlands: Opposition in a Segmented Society. *Political Oppositions in Western Democracies*, ed. R. A. Dahl. New Haven: Yale University Press.

Danylewycx, Marta. 1987. *Taking the Veil: An Alternative to Marriage, Motherhood, and Spinsterhood in Québec, 1840-1920.* Toronto: McClelland and Stewart.

De Hueck, Catherine. 1975. *Poustinia: Christian Spirituality of the East for Western Man.* Notre Dame: Ave Maria Press.

De Hueck, Catherine. 1977. *Sobornost: Eastern Unity of the Mind and Heart for Western Man.* Notre Dame: Ave Maria Press.

De Hueck, Catherine. 1978. *Strannik: The Call to Pilgrimage for Western Man.* Notre Dame: Ave Maria Press.

De Hueck, Catherine. 1979. *Fragments of My Life.* Notre Dame: Ave Maria Press.

De Jong, Peter Y. 1960. Invitation to the Reader. *Christian Perspectives 1960.* Pella, Iowa: Pella Publishing, Inc.

Despland, Michel. 1978. Nationalism. *Religion and Culture in Canada,* ed. Peter Slater. Waterloo: Wilfrid Laurier University Press.

DeWolf, Harold. 1975. *Crime and Justice in America.* New York: Harper & Row.

Diefenbaker, John G. 1975. *One Canada: The Crusading Years, 1895-1956* vol. I. Toronto: Doubleday.

Economist, The. 1988. 309, 7571, 8 October 1988.

Elliott, D. R. and I. Miller. 1987. *Bible Bill: A Critical Biography of William Aberhart.* Edmonton: Reidmore.

EREC. Ethical Reflections on the Economic Crisis. Pastoral letter. See Canadian Conference of Catholic Bishops 1983. Reprinted in Sheridan 1987.

ERSO. Ethical Reflections on Canada's Socio-Economic Order. Brief of the Canadian Conference of Catholic Bishops to the Macdonald Commission. December 1983. Reprinted in Sheridan 1987.

Evans, M. 1980. Oliver Mowat. *Called to Witness,* ed. W. S. Reid. Vol. 2. Toronto: Committee on History, Presbyterian Church in Canada.

Farris, Allan. 1978. The Fathers of 1925. *The Tide of Time: Historical Essays by the late Allan L. Farris,* ed. J. S. Moir. Toronto: Knox College.

Frank, D. W. 1986. *Less Than Conquerors.* Grand Rapids: Eerdmans.

Fraser, Brian J. 1987. Ralph Connor's Christianity: The Evangelical Liberalism of C. W. Gordon. *Toronto Journal of Theology* 3:2, Fall 1987.

Fraser, Brian J. 1988. *The Social Uplifters: Presbyterian Progressives and the Social Gospel in Canada, 1875-1915*. Waterloo: Wilfrid Laurier University Press.

Fraser, Brian J. 1989. Peacemaking Among Presbyterians in Canada: 1900-1945. *Peace, War and God's Justice*, eds. T. D. Parker and B. J. Fraser. Toronto: United Church Publishing House.

Frye, Northrup. 1988. Language as the Home of Human Life. *On Education*. Toronto: Fitzhenry and Whiteside.

Gavaki, Efrosini. 1977. *The Integration of Greeks in Canada*. San Francisco: R and E. Associates.

Gilkey, Langdon. 1958. Neo-orthodoxy. *A Handbook of Christian Theology*, eds. M. Halverson and A. A. Cohen. New York: Meridian.

Glen, J. S. 1960. *The Recovery of the Teaching Ministry*. Philadelphia: Westminster Press.

Gordon, C. W. 1914. The New State and the New Church. *Social Service Congress, Ottawa, 1914: Report of Addresses and Proceedings*. Toronto: Social Service Council of Canada.

Grant, George. 1965. *Lament For a Nation*. Toronto: McClelland and Stewart.

Grant, George. 1969. *Technology and Empire*. Toronto: Anansi.

Grant, John Webster. 1963. *The Churches and the Canadian Experience*. Toronto: Ryerson Press.

Grant, John Webster. 1972. *The Church in the Canadian Era*. Toronto: University of Toronto Press.

Grant, John Webster. 1978. National Identity. *Religion and Culture in Canada*, ed. Peter Slater. Waterloo: Wilfrid Laurier Press.

Grant, John Webster. 1988. *A Profusion of Spires: Religion in Nineteenth-Century Ontario*. Toronto: University of Toronto Press.

Guillaume, Francois and Henry A. Venema. 1957. *The United States and Canada in the Christian Reformed Church*. Toronto: Pro Rege Publishing Company.

Handy, R. T. 1976. *A History of the Churches in the United States and Canada*. New York: Oxford.

Hart, Hendrik. 1967. *The Democratic Way of Death*. Rexdale, Ontario: C. J. L. Foundation.

Hart, Hendrik. 1968. *The Challenge of Our Age*. Toronto: Institute for Christian Studies.

Hebden, James. 1910. *The Promise*. March, 1910.

Herberg, Will. [1950]1960. *Protestant, Catholic, Jew*. New York: Doubleday.

Herman, Edward. 1981. *Corporate Control, Corporate Power*. New York: Cambridge University Press.

Hogan, Brian. 1986. Salted With Fire: Studies in Catholic Social Thought and Action in Ontario, 1931-1961. Ph.D. thesis, University of Toronto.

Hopkins, Stephen. 1982. The Anglican Fellowship for Social Action. Unpublished M.A. thesis at Saint Michael's College, Toronto.

Hordern, William. 1977. Interrelation and Interaction Between Reformation Principles and the Canadian Context. *In Search of Identity, A Look at Lutheran Identity in Canada*, ed. Norman Threinen. Winnipeg: Lutheran Council in Canada.

Horst, R. (ed.). 1988. *Social Action Handbook*. Toronto: Board of Congregational Life, Presbyterian Church in Canada.

Ioannou, Tina. 1983. *La communauté Grecque du Québec (Institut Québécois de Recherche sur la culture)*.

Kappler, Sheila. 1990. Women and Justice in the Teachings of the Canadian Catholic Bishops: Challenging Categories. Ph. D. dissertation, Toronto School of Theology.

Kilpatrick, T. B. 1899. *Christian Character: A Study in New Testament Morality*. Edinburgh: T. & T. Clark.

Kilpatrick, T. B. 1917. *The War and the Christian Church*. Toronto: Presbyterian Church in Canada.

Klooster, Fred H. 1983. The Kingdom of God in the History of the Christian Reformed Church. *Perspectives on the Christian Reformed Church*, eds. Peter de Klerk and Richard R. De Ridder. Grand Rapids: Baker.

Kuyper, Abraham. 1931. [1898]. *Lectures on Calvinism*. Grand Rapids: Eerdmans.

Langille, David. 1987. The Business Council on National Issues and the Canadian State. *Studies in Political Economy* Vol. 24, Autumn 1987.

Lazareth, William. 1965. *A Theology of Politics*. New York: Lutheran Church in America.

Le Jeune, Père. 1636. *The Jesuit Relations and Allied Documents*, 73 vols., ed. R. G. Thwaites. Vol. IX. Cleveland, Ohio 1896-1901. In John S. Moir 1967, 3-4.

Lemieux, Lucien. Provencher. *Dictionary of Canadian Biography*, Vol. VIII.

Leupold, U. S. 1966. Luther's Social Ethics Today. *Canadian Journal of Theology* XII:4.

Lilje, Hans. 1952. *Luther Now*. Philadelphia: Muhlenberg Press.

Lipset, Seymour Martin. 1989. Quoted in *The Toronto Star*, Oct. 12, 1989, B1.

Lotz, Jim. 1975. The Historical and Social Setting of the Antigonish Movement. *Nova Scotia Historical Quarterly* 5:2.

Luther, Martin. [1957]. The Freedom of a Christian. *Luther's Works*, vol. 31. Philadelphia: Fortress Press.

Luther, Martin. [1974]. On Temporal Authority: To What Extent It Should Be Obeyed. *Luther, Selected Political Writings*, ed. J. M. Porter. Philadelphia: Fortress Press.

Luther, Martin. [1897]. *Luther's Works*. The Weimar Edition, vol. 7.

Macdonald, M. C. 1961a. *From Lakes to Northern Lights*. Toronto: The United Church of Canada.

Macdonald, M. C. 1961b. *Our Heritage and Horizons in Home Mission*. The James Robertson Memorial Lectures (mimeo).

Maione, Romeo. 1980. Interview, Ottawa, 4 September 1980.

Maritain, Jacques. 1936. *Freedom in the Modern World*. New York: Charles Scribner's Sons.

Maritain, Jacques. 1938. *True Humanism*. London: Geoffrey Bles: The Centenary Press.

Marshall, Paul A. 1987a. Anglo-Canadian Perspectives on the United States Constitution. *Liberty and Law: Reflections on the Constitution in American Life and Thought*, eds. R. A. Wells and T. A. Askew, 65-86. Grand Rapids: Eerdmans.

Marshall, Paul A. 1987b. Individualism, Americanization and the Charter of Rights. Paper presented to the conference on "The Meech Lake Accord," U. S.-Canada Law Institute, University of Western Ontario, London, Ontario, Oct. 1987.

Marshall, Paul A. 1989. Liberalism, Pluralism and Christianity: A Reconceptualization. *Fides et Historia* XXI:3.

McIntire, C. T. 1985. Herman Dooyeweerd in North America. *Reformed Theology in America*, ed. David F. Wells. Grand Rapids: Eerdmans.

McKillop, A. B. 1979. *A Disciplined Intelligence: Critical Inquiry and Canadian Thought in the Victorian Era*. Montreal: McGill-Queen's University Press.

McLaren, William. 1860. *The Unity of the Human Race*. Belleville, Ont.: E. Miles.

McLelland, J. C. 1980. Walter Bryden "By Circumstance and God." *Called to Witness*, ed. W. S. Reid, vol. 2. Toronto: Committee on History, Presbyterian Church in Canada.

Meldrum, M. 1973. An Examination of the Emergence of a Social Consciousness Within the Baptist Denomination in Ontario From 1890-1914. Honours History Thesis, York University.

Moir, John S. 1967. Ed. *Church and State in Canada, 1627-1867*. Toronto: McClelland and Stewart.

Moir, John S. 1975. *Enduring Witness*. Toronto: Presbyterian Publications.

Moir, John S. 1980. George Brown. *Called to Witness* ed. W. S. Reid, vol. 2. Toronto: Committee on History, Presbyterian Church in Canada.

Morton, Desmond. 1983. *A Short History of Canada*. Edmonton: Hurtig.

Mouw, Richard J. 1985. Dutch Calvinist Influences in North America. Paper presented at the seminar "Reformational Thought and Action in Society," Amsterdam, August 26-30, 1985.

Murphy, R., R. Chodus, N. Auf der Maur. 1984. *Brian Mulroney: The Boy from Baie-Comeau*. Toronto: Lorimer.

National Board 1987. The National Board of the Canadian Hierarchy. Fundamental Principles and Urgent Problems. Reprinted in Sheridan 1987.

Naylor, R. T. 1972. The Rise and Fall of the Third Commercial Empire of the St. Lawrence. *Capitalism and the National Question in Canada*, ed. Gary Teeple. Toronto: University of Toronto Press.

Neill, Stephen. 1977. *Anglicanism*. Oxford: Mowbray.

Neuhaus, Richard John. 1977. *Christian Faith and Public Policy*. Minneapolis: Augsburg.

Nicholson, D. R. 1980. Michael Willis. *Called to Witness*, ed. W. S. Reid, vol. 2. Toronto: Committee on History, Presbyterian Church in Canada.

Niebuhr, H. Richard. 1951. *Christ and Culture*. New York: Harper and Brothers.

Noll, Mark A. (ed.). 1983. *The Princeton Theology, 1812-1921*. Grand Rapids: Baker.

Nostbakken, Roger. 1979. The Context and Mission of Canadian Lutheranism. Presented to the Ninth Biennial Convention of the Lutheran Church in America—Canadian Section, Vancouver School of Theology, Vancouver, B. C., June 21-24, 1979.

Olthuis, John A., et al. 1970. *Out of Concern for the Church*. Toronto: Wedge Publishing Foundation.

Ontario Ministry of Culture and Recreation. 1979. *Greeks* July 1979; *Ukranians* October 1981.

Ontario Year Book. *Baptist Convention of Ontario and Quebec Year Book*.

Pannekoek, Fritz. 1976. The Anglican Church and the Disintegration of Red River Society, 1818-1870. *The West and the Nation*, eds. Carl Berger and Ramsay Cook. Toronto: McClelland and Stewart.

PAOC. 1987. A Theology and Philosophy for Social Concerns with the P.A.O.C., A Working Paper. Toronto: Pentecostal Assemblies of Canada.

Paterson, Thomas. 1988. *Meeting the Communist Threat: Truman to Reagan*. New York: Oxford University Press.

Peake, F. A. 1983. Anglicanism on the Prairies. *Visions of the New Jerusalem*, ed. B. G. Smillie. Edmonton: NeWest Press.

Pope Paul VI. 1975. *Evangelii nuntiandi* (On Evangelization in the Modern World) 8 December 1975.

Porter, John. 1965. *The Vertical Mosaic*. Toronto: University of Toronto Press.

Prenter, Regin. 1971. *Luther's Theology of the Cross*. Philadelphia: Fortress Press.

Profiles, 1980. Profiles of Lutherans, an unpublished study commissioned by the three then-existing Lutheran denominations in Canada to study their membership. Supported and sponsored by the Lutheran Life Insurance Society of Canada.

Pulker, Edward. 1980. The Social Concern of Canon Scott. *Journal of the Canadian Church Historical Society* XXII, 1-16.

Pulker, Edward. 1986. *We Stand on Their Shoulders*. Toronto: Anglican Book Centre.

Ramet, Pedro, ed. 1988. *Eastern Christianity and Politics in the Twentieth Century*. Durham: Duke University Press.

Rawlyk, G. A. 1984. *Ravished By the Spirit*. Montreal McGill-Queens University Press.

Rawlyk, G. A. 1985. Freeborn Garrettson and Nova Scotia. *Reflections Upon Methodism During the American Bicentennial*, ed. R. P. Heitzenrater. Dallas: Bridwell Library Center for Methodist Studies, Southern Methodist University.

Rawlyk, G. A. 1986. *The Sermons of Henry Alline*. Hantsport: Lancelot.

Rawlyk, G. A. 1987. *Henry Alline: Selected Writings*. Mahwah, N.J.: Paulist Press.

Rawlyk, G. A. 1988a. *Canadian Baptists and Christian Higher Education*. Montreal and Kingston: McGill-Queens University Press.

Rawlyk, G. A. 1988b. Revivalism and the Maritime Religious Experience. The Second W. P. Bell Lecture in Maritime Studies, Mount Allison University, Sackville, New Brunwsick.

Regehr, Ernie. 1975. *Making a Million: Canada's Arms Industry*. Toronto: McClelland and Stewart.

Report of the Social Action Commission 1988. See *Atlantic Year Book*.

Rice, D. F. 1971. Natural Theology and the Scottish Philosophy in the Thought of Thomas Chalmers. *Scottish Journal of Theology* 1:24, February 1971.

Runner, H. Evan. 1960. The Relation of the Bible to Learning. *Christian Perspectives 1960*. Pella, Iowa: Pella Publishing, Inc.

Runner, H. Evan. 1962. Scriptural Religion and Political Task. *Christian Perspectives 1962*. Hamilton, Ontario: Guardian Publishing Company.

Sacouman, R. James. 1979. The Different Origins, Organization and Impact of Maritime and Prairie Co-operative Movements to 1940; also see Underdevelopment and the Structural Origins of Antigonish Movement Co-operatives in Eastern Nova Scotia. *Underdevelopment and Social Movements in Atlantic Canada*, eds. Robert J. Brym and R. James Sacouman. Toronto: New Hogtown Press, 1979.

Scott, J. B. 1989. Responding To Social Crisis: The Baptist Union of Western Canada and Social Christianity, 1908-1922. Unpublished Ph.D. thesis, University of Ottawa.

Seerveld, Calvin G. 1964. *Christian Workers, Unite!* Rexdale, Ontario: Christian Labour Association of Canada.

Sharum, Elizabeth. 1977. A Strange Fire Burning: A History of the Friendship House Movement. Ph.D. thesis, Texas Technical University.

Sheridan, E. F. 1987. *Do Justice: The Social Teaching of the Canadian Catholic Bishops (1945-1986)*. Toronto and Sherbrooke: Jesuit Centre for Social Faith and Justice, and Éditions Paulines.

Smart, James D. 1954. *The Teaching Ministry of the Church*. Philadelphia: Westminster Press.

Smith, T. L. 1976. *Revivalism and Social Reform: American Protestantism on the Eve of the Civil War.* Gloucester, Mass.: Peter Smith.

Social Action Department 1956. Canadian Catholic Conference, Labour Day Message 1956: On Labour Unions, Automation, Housing, Advertising, Consumption, Credit. Reprinted in Sheridan 1987.

Social Action Department 1958. Canadian Catholic Conference, Labour Day Message 1958: Unemployment: Part of Economic Warfare. Reprinted in Sheridan 1987.

Social Action Department 1959. Canadian Catholic Conference, Labour Day Message 1959: For a Greater Collaboration between Management and Labour. Reprinted in Sheridan 1987.

Social Action Department 1961. Canadian Catholic Conference, Labour Day Message 1961: The Social Teaching of the Church. Reprinted in Sheridan 1987.

Somerville, Henry. 1933. *Studies in the Catholic Social Movement.* London, England: Burns, Oates and Washburne Ltd. An article and thesis by Somerville's biographer, Ruth Jean Beck, offer the most comprehensive review of his work available to this point. See Beck 1975 and Beck 1977.

Stathopoulos, Peter. 1971. *The Greek Community of Montréal.* Athens: National Centre of Social Research.

Stott, John. 1985. *Involvement*, vol. 1. Old Tappan, N.J.: Fleming H. Revell.

Thomas, L. H. (ed.). 1982. *The Making of a Socialist: The Recollections of T. C. Douglas.* Edmonton: University of Alberta Press.

Thompson, J. L. and J. H. Thompson. 1972. Ralph Connor and the Canadian Identity. *Queen's Quarterly*, 79:2, Summer 1972.

Threinen, Norman, ed. 1977. The American and European Influences on the Canadian Lutheran Churches. *In Search of Identity, A Look at Lutheran Identity in Canada.* Winnipeg: Lutheran Council in Canada.

Threinen, Norman. 1983. *Fifty Years of Lutheran Convergence: The Canadian Case-Study.* Dubuque, Iowa: Wm. C. Brown.

Tillich, Paul. 1959. *Theology of Culture*, ed. Robert C. Kimball. Oxford: The University Press.

Tkachuk, John. 1988. The Orthodox Church in Canada. Parish bulletin *Sign*, vol.10, no.4.

Van Andel, Henry. 1964. *Vision and Obedience.* Toronto: Institute for Christian Studies.

Van Andel, Henry. 1965. *What is Liberty?* Rexdale, Ontario: C. J. L. Foundation.

Van Brummelen, Harro W. 1985. Christian Schools in the Dutch-Calvinist Tradition. Mimeograph.

Vanderlaan, C. J. 1979. Notes on the Origin and Purpose of a Number of Christian Organizations in Canada Established after World War II. Mimeograph.

Vandezande, Gerald. 1967. *The Freedom to Serve.* Rexdale, Ont.: Christian Labour Association of Canada

Van Dyke, Harry. 1989. *Groen van Prinsterer's Lectures on Unbelief and Revolution.* Jordan Station, Ontario: Wedge Publishing Foundation.

Van Geest, William. 1985. Aspects of Interaction between the Dutch Reformed and Canadian Society, 1950-1985. Paper presented at the seminar on "Reformational Thought and Action in Society," Amsterdam, August 26-30, 1985.

Van Ginkel, Aileen. 1985. Assimilation, Transformation or Opposition? Patterns and Models for the Cultural Integration of the Dutch Calvinist Community in Canada. Paper presented at the seminar on "Reformational Thought and Action in Society," Amsterdam, August 26-30, 1985.

Van Riessen, Hendrik. 1963. The University and its Basis. *Christian Perspectives 1963.* Toronto: Institute for Christian Studies.

Vaudry, R. W. 1985. Peter Brown, the Toronto *Banner,* and the Evangelical Mind in Victorian Canada. *Ontario History* 77:1, March 1985.

Vaudry, R. W. 1989. *The Free Church in Victorian Canada, 1844-1861.* Waterloo: Wilfrid Laurier University Press.

Vernon, C. W. 1929. *The Old Church and the New Dominion.* London: SPCK.

Vissers, John A. 1988. The Conception of Revelation in the Theology of Walter W. Bryden. Th. D. thesis, Knox College, Toronto School of Theology.

Vrieze, Maarten. 1966. *The Community Idea in Canada.* Toronto: Institute for Chistian Studies.

Walsh, H. H. 1956. *The Christian Church in Canada.* Toronto: Ryerson Press.

Watson, John. 1897. *Christianity and Idealism.* New York: Macmillan.

Westfall, William. 1989. *Two Worlds: The Protestant Culture of Nineteenth Century Ontario.* Montreal and Kingston: McGill-Queen's University Press.

Whitehead, R. N. 1985. Christ and Cultural Imperialism. *Justice as Mission*, eds. Terry Brown and Christopher Lind. Burlington, Ont.: Trinity Press.

Willis, Michael. 1873. New Testament Ethics: Questions Solved. *Pulpit Discourses, Expository and Practical, and College Addresses, Etc..* London: James Nisbet.

Wise, S. F. and R. C. Brown, eds. 1967. *Canada Views the United States: Nineteenth Century Political Attitudes.* Seattle: University of Washington Press.

Yoder, John Howard. 1985. Reformed versus Anabaptist Social Strategies: An Inadequate Typology. *Theological Students Fellowship Bulletin* May-June, 1985.

Index